C0-AWF-423

*Bibliography of Industrial Relations
in the Railroad
Industry*

CORNELL INDUSTRIAL AND LABOR RELATIONS

BIBLIOGRAPHY SERIES—NO. 12

IN THIS SERIES

Public Employment Bibliography — II
by Robert V. Pezdek
196 pp., paper, $3.00
paper bound in cloth, $4.75

Personnel Research Abstracts
compiled by Richard A. Shafer
and Mary Ann Coghill
60 pp., paper, $3.00
paper bound in cloth, $4.75

*Education and Training for Effective Manpower Utilization:
An Annotated Bibliography*
by Emil A. Mesics
164 pp., paper, $2.50
paper bound in cloth, $4.25

Bibliography of Industrial Relations in Latin America
by James O. Morris and Efrén Córdova
308 pp., cloth, $10.00

ORDER FROM

Publications Division
New York State School
of Industrial and Labor Relations
Cornell University
Ithaca, New York 14853

Bibliography of Industrial Relations in the Railroad Industry

By JAMES O. MORRIS, *Professor of Industrial and Labor Relations, Cornell University, and Director of the Railroad Industrial Relations Project*

A Bicentennial Publication

Universitas
BIBLIOTHECA
ttaviensis

NEW YORK STATE SCHOOL OF
INDUSTRIAL AND LABOR RELATIONS
CORNELL UNIVERSITY, ITHACA, NEW YORK

004 826

Copyright 1975 by Cornell University
All rights reserved

Library of Congress Catalog Number: 75-8878
ISBN: 0-87546-058-5

Price: $5.00

ORDER FROM

Publications Division
New York State School of
Industrial and Labor Relations
Cornell University
Ithaca, New York 14853

Z
7164
·T7M 67
1975

LIBRARY OF CONGRESS CATALOGING IN PUBLICATION DATA

Morris, James Oliver, 1923–
    Bibliography of industrial relations in the railroad industry.
    (Cornell industrial and labor relations bibliography series; no. 12)

    "Outgrowth of the work of the Labor Management Documentation Center at the New York State School of Industrial and Labor Relations, Cornell University."
    1. Industrial relations — United States — Bibliography. 2. Collective bargaining — Railroads — United States — Bibliography. 3. Railroads — Employees — Bibliography. I. Cornell University. New York State School of Industrial and Labor Relations. Labor Management Documentation Center. II. Title.

Z7164.T7M67 [HD6976.R1] 016.331'041'3850973 75-8878 ISBN 0-87546-058-5

COMPOSITION BY UTICA TYPESETTING COMPANY
UTICA, NEW YORK
PRINTED BY VAIL-BALLOU PRESS, INCORPORATED
BINGHAMTON, NEW YORK

THE United Transportation Union and the New York State School of Industrial and Labor Relations at Cornell launched, in 1969, a joint railway labor history program. A major objective of this program was to collect, deposit at Cornell, and process the historical documents and records of the UTU and its predecessor unions. Having successfully completed this objective, the program was phased out in September 1973. Some of the funds contributed by both the UTU and the ILR School were used to initiate this *Bibliography of Industrial Relations in the Railroad Industry*. The UTU is proud to acknowledge its role in the identification of such a voluminous and useful literature on the human problems of railroading.

We continue to encourage the work at Cornell while looking back upon a fruitful contractual relationship. Our joint venture not only permitted the preservation of valuable historical records but also stimulated the first labor-management alcoholism seminars in the railroad industry and other educational ventures.

AL H. CHESSER, *President*
United Transportation Union

THIS extensive *Bibliography of Industrial Relations in the Railroad Industry* is a most welcome addition to the literature of railroading. Its publication recognizes the increasingly critical and complex nature of railroad industrial relations, and it will be a useful tool for shedding much-needed light on the many problems facing the industry today.

The undersigned railroad unions are particularly pleased that the bibliography's publication coincides with the recent launching of the rail labor education program in the Buffalo, New York, area — a program designed to train hundreds of railroad workers and officers and bring to them greater understanding and expertness in the handling of their responsibilities. This goal should be more easily realized now that so much source material on such a broad range of important issues and developments has been identified.

The New York State School of Industrial and Labor Relations is to be congratulated for the service it has performed on behalf of all those working in and interested in the challenging problems and opportunities of America's railroad industry. We are particularly pleased that the Buffalo Railroad Labor Studies Program of the ILR School has found it possible to provide the printing costs of this volume.

DANIEL W. COLLINS, *Assistant General Secretary and Treasurer* United Transportation Union

DON BANCROFT Brotherhood of Railway, Airline and Steamship Clerks, Freight Handlers, Express and Station Employees

CHARLES BETHGE, *Project Consultant* United Transportation Union

ROBERT M. COE United Transportation Union

JOHN F. COLLINS United Transportation Union

EDWARD P. McENTEE, *Assistant to the President* Railway Employes' Department, AFL-CIO

ROBERT W. GODWIN Brotherhood of Locomotive Engineers

STEPHEN LANZA United Transportation Union

J. T. O'CONNOR United Transportation Union

EDWARD J. SHEEHY United Transportation Union

Contents

Preface

THIS bibliography is an outgrowth of the work of the Labor-Management Documentation Center at the New York State School of Industrial and Labor Relations, Cornell University. Over the last six years the Center has been engaged in an ambitious effort to build the finest collection of railroad industrial relations documents and records anywhere in the country. Two years ago the Center set up the Railroad Industrial Relations Project to give more public exposure to its work in this area and to broaden its contacts among railroad unions and companies and other potential sources of railroad industrial relations material. At the risk of immodesty, but not of overstatement, I think we have already built an excellent collection, although our developmental work will undoubtedly continue for many years to come.

Among the Center's holdings to date are the archives of the United Transportation Union, the Order of Railway Conductors and Brakemen, the Brotherhood of Locomotive Firemen and Enginemen, the Brotherhood of Railroad Trainmen, and the Switchmen's Union of North America; microfilms of the inactive records of the National Railway Labor Conference and the historical labor relations records of the Illinois Central Gulf Railroad and the Chicago and North Western Transportation Company; and several personal collections, including the papers of William J. Doble, general chairman, New York Central Lines West, Brotherhood of Railroad Signalmen, and a series of manuscripts by A. E. Lyon, president emeritus of the Brotherhood of Railroad Signalmen and long-time executive secretary of the Railway Labor Executives' Association. The Center has also taped and transcribed more than a hundred oral history interviews with union officers and rank and file, management representatives, and neutrals. Many additional contacts have been made, and it is our optimistic hope that these contacts will soon result in the further expansion and enrichment of our railroad industrial relations collection. We are appealing to all railroad unions, railroad companies, and individuals to make our collection as comprehensive and of the highest quality as possible.

Many people have participated in the making of this bibliography. Over the last few years the following students have put in long hours combing card catalogs, guides, and other sources of information: Ira L. Blank, Sandra Casaw, James R. Grossman, Marcia J. Kusnitz, Alice R. Miller, N. Harriane Mills, Bernard S. Mintz, Elizabeth D. Moore, Elizabeth G. Pagano, and Frederick W. Telling. Typing of the manuscript was done by Katherine Anderson, Connie Bulkley, Jo Churey, Janet Epstein, Gail Hendrix, Maxine Henry, Diana Jones, Sarah Kimball, Carol Nicoson, Judy Stewart, Mary Turner, Donna Updike, and Nancy Voorheis. All of these men and women deserve and hereby receive my sincere written thanks for their work.

Special credits are seven in number: (1) Robert B. McKersie, dean of the ILR School, made available to the railroad project a research assistantship which was used to initiate this bibliography; (2) C. Herbert Finch, archivist, Labor-Management Documentation Center, and assistant director, Cornell University Libraries, contributed generously to the project in the assignment of both LMDC staff time and budget; (3) Richard Strassberg, associate archivist of the Labor-Management Documentation Center, offered expert counsel, compiled the entries from the railroad collection of the LMDC, supervised the work of several of the student researchers, and encouraged the project in many other ways from beginning to end; (4) Gordon T. Law, assistant librarian, Martin P. Catherwood Library, was regularly called upon by all of the student researchers who needed help in locating materials or sources of information; (5) the staff of the Reference Department in Olin Library, and Marcia Jebb in particular, cut many hours from our labors through expert guidance particularly in that "woolly" area of government documents; (6) Frances Benson, editor, Publications Division of the ILR School, simply did a marvelous job of preparing the manuscript for the printer and improved it very much in the process; and (7) finally, the Buffalo Railroad Labor Studies Program advisory council and John Drotning, ILR School associate dean for extension and public service, and Dick Pivetz, western district extension director of the ILR School, agreed to use part of the Buffalo program's budget to pay the printer. Jeanette Watkins, extension associate with the Buffalo Railroad Labor Studies Program, has also lent enthusiastic support to this project. I appreciate very much their indispensable contributions.

Ithaca, New York
January 30, 1975

JAMES O. MORRIS

Introduction

THE objective of this bibliography has been to identify all quality materials of a nonfictional nature, published or unpublished, relating to industrial relations in the railroad industry. The term "industrial relations" is used very broadly and not as a substitute for narrower language such as "collective bargaining" or "labor-management relations." It is meant to include the entire work environment (for example, employment, unemployment, wages, hours, unions, bargaining, strikes, mediation), external influences upon it (legislation, government, technological change), and also its derivative consequences (such as retirement programs and disability insurance). The term "railroad industry" refers to the intercity and interstate rail transportation network, and excludes strictly urban and commuter rail transportation systems as well as the manufacture of railroad rolling stock and equipment.

While any claim that this bibliography is exhaustive would be pretentious, it is much more inclusive than the term "representative" is normally meant to convey. All of the standard guides and indexes to manuscripts, periodical literature, theses, and government documents that were accessible have been consulted; previously published bibliographies on labor and industrial relations, railroads, and the transportation industry in general have been examined; the bibliographies appended to a large sample of books have been checked; and the card catalogs of the Cornell University Libraries have been thoroughly searched for appropriate titles. With respect to periodical literature, all railroad industrial relations articles appearing in journals available in the Cornell University Libraries have been removed from the shelf and internally analyzed. Only those passing a quality test (that is, including some analysis or new information, and of meaningful length) have found a place in this listing; many hundreds of articles have been discarded for failure to meet the quality test.

The bibliography is organized into six categories of source material: part I, Bibliographies; part II, Manuscripts; part III, Books, Pamphlets, and Theses; part IV, Periodical Literature; part V, Government Documents; and part VI, Government Serial Publications. Parts I and II

(Bibliographies and Manuscripts) are understandably small sections, al-. though the relatively small size of the manuscript listing, in particular, is obviously no guide to the size of holdings, which in some cases are huge. In Cornell's Labor-Management Documentation Center alone, there are more than a thousand cubic feet of railroad industrial relations records. Parts III, IV, and V are very large by comparison, especially the Government Documents section, which appropriately reflects the major role played by government in railroad industrial relations in this country. The distinction made between part V (Government Documents) and part VI (Government Serial Publications) is that the former includes all specific content reports, monographs, hearings' records, bills, resolutions, laws, and so forth, while the latter is a much smaller listing of the titles of continuing publications, particularly statistical and reports series, which have been emitted regularly or irregularly by several government agencies. To illustrate, the published record of the hearings on the Railway Labor Act of 1926 appears in the Government Documents section while the Interstate Commerce Commission's monthly report on wage statistics of Class I railroads is listed under Government Serial Publications. Articles from analytical journals published by government departments and agencies (for example, the *Monthly Labor Review*) are placed in part IV (Periodical Literature).

Entries in the three larger sections of the bibliography (Books, Pamphlets, and Theses; Periodical Literature; and Government Documents) are further organized by topics and chronology. The nine topical headings are as follows:

1. General. Any item whose content is so broad that it could be listed under more than four of the remaining eight topics is listed only once under General. Only books, pamphlets, and theses have such overlapping content. There is no General category in the sections on periodical literature and government documents, which tend naturally to be quite specific in content. Any item whose content overlaps up to and including four of the specific topics is multiple listed.

2. Railroads and Government. Material under this heading deals generally with government regulation of railroads in all but the area of labor relations. The listing is only illustrative and not at all intended as comprehensive. Inclusion of the topic in the bibliography is justified on two grounds, namely that some forms of general regulation (for example, rate fixing) can have an important industrial relations impact and that the literature of government regulation provides useful background for anyone interested in railroad industrial relations. There is no material under this heading in the Government Documents section.

3. Management. Unfortunately the literature to be found on this topic is rather sparse. Generally, it covers biographical and autobiographical studies of railroad managers, owners, and developers; management training and development materials; and assessments of railroad managers as a group or as individuals. A fuller literature would allow greater insight into and understanding of the history, nature, and quality of railroad industrial relations.

4. Labor Force. This topic includes sources on the size of the railroad labor force, recruitment, selection, sex and racial composition, employment and unemployment, occupations, the impact of technological change, surplus labor, training, productivity, and mobility as they concern mainly the blue-collar labor force.

5. Working Conditions. The sources under this heading deal with wages, hours, length of run, sanitary and safety conditions, holidays, and other working conditions.

6. Unions and Workers. Under this topic are found histories of individual railroad unions and the railroad labor movement, biographical and autobiographical materials concerning union leaders and unorganized workers, and studies of union structure. With respect to unions, the bibliography covers the operating and nonoperating brotherhoods, the shop crafts, and all other unions with membership in the railroad industry as defined above.

7. Labor Legislation. This topic includes sources reflecting public policy discussion and debate on aspects of railroad industrial relations, the history of the enactment of railroad labor laws, and administrative and court interpretations of the laws. More specifically, the topic embraces policy discussions, hearings, and statutes dealing with hours, wages, the rights to self-organization and collective bargaining, and dispute settlement.,Retirement and protective programs are dealt with separately in section 9, and the application of the laws in actual organizing and bargaining situations is covered in section 8.

8. Labor Relations. This topic covers all facets of the labor-management relationship whether workers are organized or unorganized. It includes, for example, materials on wage and hour "movements" (as the union's negotiating drive has historically been labeled in the railroad industry), agreements, strikes, mediation, conciliation, fact-finding, arbitration, trends in bargaining, and grievance handling or "claims."

9. Retirement, Protective Programs. This last topic covers the enactment, revision, and application of legislation dealing with retirement, accidents, injury compensation, unemployment benefits, and health and sickness insurance. This section and section 7 (Labor Legislation) are concerned primarily with federal laws and programs, although a few state materials are included.

Materials falling within each of the above topics are presented chronologically in four periods, namely 1850–98, 1898–1926, 1926–46, and 1946–present. The rationale for this breakdown is as follows: the railroad labor force did not become numerically significant until the decade before the Civil War when initial efforts were also made to organize railroad workers nationally; 1898 is the year the Erdman Act was passed, launching a new phase of government regulation of, and participation in, railroad industrial relations; the Railway Labor Act, which with amendments continues to govern organizing, bargaining, and dispute settlement in the railroad industry, was passed in 1926; and, finally, a new period is started with 1946 because of the fundamental changes in the economics and the competitive position of the railroads in the post-World War II years — changes which have, in turn, substantially affected railroad industrial relations.

A fifth chronological category of "general" has been added to part III (Books, Pamphlets, and Theses) in order to accommodate those materials that overlap the period breakdowns. Many books and theses, in particular, have been written from a historical perspective and their content often spans all four of the time periods recognized in this bibliography. Because periodical literature and government documents tend to reflect a much more limited time perspective, a "general" category has not been provided in these sections; the relatively few entries that do overlap time periods are simply repeated as necessary.

A majority of the materials that have been included in this bibliography can be found in the Cornell University Libraries, particularly the Martin P. Catherwood Library of the New York State School of Industrial and Labor Relations. The Labor-Management Documentation Center of the Catherwood Library houses what is undoubtedly the largest railroad industrial relations manuscript and records collection in the United States. (See the Manuscripts section of this bibliography for a listing of current holdings.) Other likely depositories of many of the published materials identified herein are the Library of Congress, the U.S. Department of Labor Library, the AFL-CIO Library, the Library of the Association of American Railroads, and the Library of the Railroad Retirement Board.

A few types of literature that have been deliberately excluded from the bibliography are important sources of information, and attention should be called to their existence. First, a variety of labor union documents, records, and reports such as convention proceedings, convention reports of chief executive officers and executive boards, constitutions, rules of order, and bylaws have been published by the railroad unions throughout their histories. No useful purpose would be served in itemizing such extensive and standardized material, but records of this kind are exceedingly valuable, indeed indispensable, primary sources of information on a wide range of subject matter. The complete set of convention proceedings and constitutions for five railroad unions have been microfilmed and are currently available from the Microfilming Corporation of America. The five unions are the United Transportation Union, the Order of Railway Conductors and Brakemen, the Brotherhood of Locomotive Firemen and Enginemen, the Brotherhood of Railroad Trainmen, and the Switchmen's Union of North America. Similar records for ten additional railroad unions will soon be microfilmed and made available for sale. Second, collective agreements and company wage-schedule and shop-rule books have been excluded from this bibliography, though a great many of these are on deposit in the Catherwood Library and in the Library of the Association of American Railroads. Third, railroad company house organs and promotional literature have not been included.

Some explanation of the technical aspects of form followed in this bibliography may be helpful to many of those who use it. In general, the University of Chicago Press *Manual of Style* (12th ed.) has been the guide. With regard to periodical literature, the volume number of a journal is always in arabic for consistency's sake, even though it may appear as a roman numeral in the journal itself, and stands alone, without the abbreviation for "volume," immediately following the journal title. Inclusive page numbers for articles are given at the end of each citation and are preceded by a colon. When the place or date of publication of a title has not been found in the source itself, this information, if available elsewhere, has been supplied and set off in brackets. If the supplied information is not known to a certainty, this is indicated by a question mark. If the place or date of publication is not available at all, the usual symbols have been used to communicate this lack ("n.p." for "no place" and "n.d." for "no date"). Although the bibliography is a simple listing and not an annotated work, some explanatory or clarifying comments have been made within the citation itself or after it. Comments within the citation are set off with brackets. Not all bracketed material has been introduced by this author, however; it has sometimes been part of the original entry as copied from a catalog card or some other source. Total pages have been provided whenever possible, and only in a few instances has the effort to do so failed. A short form has been adopted for the identification of publishers which omits all language such as "Company," "Publishers," and "Press."

The hope of any bibliographer is that others will find his work useful. Railroad industrial relations are an exceedingly important part of the general industrial relations history of the United States. More recent developments in transportation present immense challenges to leadership on both sides of the railroad bargaining table, as well as to government leaders, to improve efficiency of service, increase productivity, and preserve the railroads as an integral part of our transportation system. Despite the pioneering and challenging aspects of railroad industrial relations, scholars have tended to neglect the area. Perhaps the renewed interest, which may now be developing, will find additional encouragement in this publication. It is hoped also that union leaders and management representatives, government officials, adult educators, and other practitioners and professionals who consult this work will find it of value.

PART I

BIBLIOGRAPHIES

ASSOCIATION OF AMERICAN RAILROADS. *List of References on the Railroad Brotherhoods.* Washington, D.C.: Bureau of Railway Economics, Library of Congress, 1938. 18 pp.

————. *Railroad Histories and Sources of Historical Information about Railroads.* Washington, D.C.: Bureau of Railway Economics, 1940. 11 pp.

————. Bureau of Railway Economics Library. *Featherbed Rules: List of References in BRE Library, December 2, 1960.* Washington, D.C.: The Association, 1960. 9 pp.

————. Bureau of Railway Economics Library. *Featherbed Rules: A List of References in BRE Library, October 5, 1962.* Washington, D.C.: The Association, 1962. 6 pp.

BORTZ, N. M. "Organizations of Railroad Labor and Management." *Labor Information Bulletin* 6, no. 7 (July 1939): 8–11.

BUREAU OF INFORMATION OF THE SOUTHEASTERN RAILWAYS. *Index-Digest of Decisions of United States Railroad Labor Board to May 1, 1922 (Decisions Numbers 1 to 949, inclusive).* Washington, D.C.: Railway Accounting Officers Association, 1922. 327 pp.

BUREAU OF RAILROAD ECONOMICS. *United States Railroad Administration Publications: A Bibliography.* Washington, D.C.: The Bureau, 1952. 212 pp.

BUREAU OF RAILWAY ECONOMICS. *Collective Catalogue of Books on Railway Economics.* Chicago: University of Chicago Press, 1912.

BUREAU OF RAILWAY ECONOMICS LIBRARY. *Some References to Material on Arbitration of Disputes between Railroad Companies and Employees by Government Boards of Arbitration.* Washington, D.C.: 1920. 21 pp.

BUSBEY, T. ADDISON, ed. *The Biographical Directory of the Railway Officials of America.* Chicago: Railway Age, 1906. 694 pp.

CHAMBERLIN, ELLEN FAY. *Railways in the United States: A Bibliographic List.* Washington, D.C.: Library of Congress, 1942.

CULLEN, ELIZABETH O. *Suggestions for Books and Other Material on Railroads in the U.S. for Students of Current Transportation.* Washington, D.C.: Association of American Railroads, 1957. 44 pp.

List of Associations of Railway Officials and Employees. Washington, D.C.: Library of Congress, 1914. 52 pp.

"List of References to Books and Articles on the Adamson Law of September, 1916." Mimeographed. Washington, D.C.: Bureau of Railway Economics, 1917. 19 pp.

MAROT, HELEN. *A Handbook of Labor Literature.* Philadelphia: Free Library of Economics and Political Science, 1899. 96 pp.

Railway Economics: A Collective Catalogue of Books in Fourteen American Libraries. Chicago: University of Chicago Press, for the Bureau of Railway Economics, Washington, D.C., 1912. 446 pp.

BIBLIOGRAPHIES

RICHARDSON, HELEN R. *United States Railroad Administration Publications: A Bibliography*. Washington, D.C.: Bureau of Railway Economics, 1952. 212 pp.

TEGGART, FREDERICK, comp. *Catalogue of the Hopkins Railway Library*. Palo Alto, Calif.: Stanford University, 1895. 231 pp.

THOMSON, THOMAS RICHARD. *Checklist of Publications on American Railroads before 1841: A Union List*. New York: New York Public Library, 1942. 250 pp.
Includes state and federal documents.

U.S. DEPARTMENT OF LABOR. *Featherbedding, Work Rules, Restriction of Output: Selected References*. Washington, D.C.: GPO, 1963. 13 pp.

U.S. LIBRARY OF CONGRESS. "Brief List of References on Railroad Shopmen's Strike, 1922." Typewritten. Washington, D.C., 1922. 6 pp.

U.S. NATIONAL ARCHIVES. "Preliminary Inventory of the Records of the Senate Committee on Interstate Commerce: Subcommittee to Investigate Railroads." Compiled by Albert U. Blair and John W. Porter. Mimeographed. National Archives Publication 55–6. Washington, D.C., 1954.

U.S. NATIONAL RAILROAD ADJUSTMENT BOARD. *General Index* [to awards 1–2000]. 1st Division. Washington, D.C.: GPO, 1938. 580 leaves.

PART II

MANUSCRIPTS

1. Guides to Manuscript Collections

CROUTCH, ALBERT, and EDITH FOX. *Brief Description of Railway Material in Cornell University Library.* Ithaca, N.Y., 1949.

FREILICHER, MIRIAM S. *A Preliminary Listing of Oral History Interviews for the Joint Labor History Project at Cornell.* Ithaca, N.Y., 1971. 9 pp.

JACKSON, ELIZABETH COLEMAN. *Guide to the Burlington Archives in Newberry Library, 1857–1901.* Chicago, 1949. 374 pp.

MANN, ANN, comp. *Finding Guide to the Switchmen's Union of North America Records, 1894–1971.* Ithaca, N.Y., 1971. 311 pp.

2. Manuscript Collections

ARIZONA PIONEERS' HISTORICAL SOCIETY COLLECTIONS, Tucson. Organization Collections, 1880–1961. ca. 8,000 items.

Correspondence, minutes, annual reports, news releases, dues records, checkbooks, printed material, and other records of hundreds of local and national organizations working in Arizona including the Brotherhood of Locomotive Engineers and its women's auxiliary.

CENTRAL MICHIGAN UNIVERSITY, Clarke Historical Library, Mount Pleasant. Papers of Theodore M. Joslyn, 1886–1920. 741 items and 6 vols.

Lawyer of Adrian, Michigan family. Correspondence; two diaries and two political canvasser books relating to Joslyn's activities as railway mail employee, teacher, and lawyer; and materials dealing with his efforts in behalf of the Republican party in Lenawee County, Michigan, during the 1896 gubernatorial campaign of Hazen S. Pingree.

CHICAGO HISTORICAL SOCIETY LIBRARY. Papers of Donald Randall Richberg, 1907–57. 7 ft.

Lawyer and author. Includes correspondence, legal papers, speeches, articles, newsclippings, and other papers relating to the Railway Labor Executives' Association for which Richberg was general counsel, the effect of the economic depression on railway employees, proposed unemployment relief programs, local and national politics, and the Progressive party.

—————. Records of the Brotherhood of Sleeping Car Porters, Chicago Division, 1925–69. 12 ft.

Correspondence, minutes of meetings, membership and financial records, agenda, speeches, tape recordings, investigative and findings reports, memoranda, scrapbooks of newsclippings and other papers, divided into three lots. The first group relates to the division offices. The second group relates to Milton P. Webster's service (1941–46) on the President's Committee on Fair Employment. The third group consists of records of the Brotherhood's International Ladies Auxiliary.

CORNELL UNIVERSITY LIBRARY, Department of Manuscripts and University Archives, Ithaca, N.Y. Business Records of the Hammond Family, 1835–1916. 16 ft.
Includes payroll records and board bills for company railroad employees.

————. Papers of Leo P. Noonan, 1940–60. ca. 3 ft.
New York State Assemblyman for Cattaraugus County. Correspondence with constituents, colleagues, and members of state administrative departments, mainly concerning pending legislation on education, railroad, and other labor issues.

————. Papers of the Pittsburg, Shawmut and Northern Railroad Company, 1872–1960. Charles Francis Hitchcock Allen, collector. 3 ft.
Includes Allen's history of the Pittsburg, Shawmut and Northern Railroad Company and predecessor and affiliated lines (3 vols.); letters (1942–60) received by Allen from officials and former employees of the PS&N, fellow railroad historians, mechanical engineers, and others; correspondence of employees concerning maintenance and operation, reports of derailments and other accidents, steam shovel operations, and boiler inspections; train orders; right-of-way agreements; payroll drafts, receipts, seniority rosters, and other employee data.

————. Records of the New York, Ontario and Western Railway Company, 1866–1960. ca. 383 ft.
Includes labor, payroll, and accident records.

————. Records of the New York and Pennsylvania Railroad, 1892–1936. 104 ft.
Includes payroll records.

CORNELL UNIVERSITY LIBRARY, Labor-Management Documentation Center, Ithaca, N.Y. J. F. Miller. "Report of J. F. Miller, General Superintendent, Pennsylvania Lines West of Pittsburgh, Southwest System, to Joseph Wood, General Manager, on the 1894 Strike of the American Railroad Union, June 27 to August 6th." 1 reel microfilm.

————. Minutes of the Ladies Auxiliary of the United Transportation Union, Iowa Joint Board, 1913–72. 1 vol.
Largely minutes of the former Iowa State meeting of the Ladies Auxiliary to the Brotherhood of Railroad Trainmen, which was superseded by the present organization in 1970. 5196.

————. Papers of Frank Columbus, 1901–58. 6 boxes.
Office file of Columbus, legislative representative of the New York State Brotherhood of Locomotive Firemen and Enginemen and trustee of Cornell University as a representative of the railroad brotherhoods in New York State.

————. Papers of William J. Doble, 1930–63. 21 ft.
Largely papers dealing with Doble's work as general chairman, New York Central Lines West, for the Brotherhood of Railroad Signalmen. Files include series on work jurisdiction, political legislation, labor relations, claims and disputes, the union shop,

and other matters relating to collective bargaining and technical innovations of interest to union members in Doble's jurisdiction. Unpublished guide available. 5182.

——————. Papers of Vernon Hortin Jensen, 1961–62. 5 ft.

Includes working papers, carriers exhibits, proceedings, and drafts and final report of the Railroad Marine Workers Commission appointed by the president of the United States, Executive Order 10929 of March 24, 1961 (1961–62). B 34a

——————. Predecessor Records of the National Railway Labor Conference, 1907–55. 63 reels microfilm.

Selected microfilmed records accumulated by the Western, Eastern, and Southeastern Carriers Conference Committees, which served as the collective bargaining units for the member railroads in their jurisdictions prior to the establishment of the National Railway Labor Conference. Filmed records include correspondence, minutes, reports, transcripts, exhibits, and arbitration awards relating to the carrier conference committees, the operating and nonoperating craft unions with whom they negotiated, and the various government agencies that regulate the railroad industry. Unpublished guide available. 5205mf

——————. Railroad Industrial Relations Project Oral History Interviews.

Discussions with various railroad labor and management leaders on questions relating to their personal development as executives in railroad industrial relations and to their interpretation of events in contemporary rail labor history. Includes interviews with William H. Dempsey, chairman, National Railway Labor Conference (restricted), 30 pp.; H. E. Gilbert, retired president of the Brotherhood of Locomotive Firemen and Enginemen, 65 pp.; Daniel P. Loomis, retired president of the Association of American Railroads, 55 pp.; James Paddock, retired president of the Order of Railway Conductors and Brakemen, 74 pp., 90 pp.; and Maynard E. Parks, vice-chairman, National Railway Labor Conference, 41 pp.

——————. Records of Ad Hoc Arbitration Boards, 1913–58. 15 boxes.

Transactions of hearings, reports, minutes of meetings and conferences, arbitration awards, data on employees, wages, cost of living, fringe benefits, cost of union demands, and comparative statistics on wages, hours, and working conditions. Railroad organizations represented include Amalgamated Association of Street, Electric Railway and Motor Coach Employes of America; Conductors Benevolent Association; Connecticut Railways Lighting Company; Independent American Transport Union; International Railway Company; Motormen's Benevolent Association; New York City Transit Authority; The Short Line, Incorporated; Signal Electricians' Benevolent Association; Union St. Railway Company.

——————. Records of the Brotherhood of Locomotive Firemen and Enginemen, 1874–1968. 270 ft.

Includes constitutions and bylaws, 1875–1966; *Proceedings* of the union's convention, 1874–1968; *Report of the Grand Lodge Officers to the Convention*, 1902–68; *Report of the International Officers*, 1910–22; *Report of the Board of Directors to the Regular Semi-Annual Meeting*, 1916–58; minutes of the general policy committee, 1932–58, with gaps; scattered records of the general grievance committee, 1917–56; international president's papers, including fragmented subject and correspondence files, circulars, and bulletins, 1888–1968; and *Monthly Bulletins from the Office of the President*, 1920–65. Also vice-president's files including extensive documentation of the merger of this union with three other operating crafts to form the United

Transportation Union in 1969; the insurance and magazine department's files; the records of the California, Pennsylvania, and New York legislative boards, as well as extensive memorabilia and photographs. 5141

————. Records of the Brotherhood of Maintenance of Way Employees, Cadosia, New York, Lodge No. 1179, 1903–4, 1919–21. 4 in.

Includes minute book, 1919–21; dues book, 1903–4; and ledger, 1919. 5448

————. Records of the Brotherhood of Railroad Trainmen. 1883–1968. 120 ft.

Includes constitutions and bylaws, 1883–1964; convention proceedings, 1884–1968, with gaps; *Reports of the General Secretary-Treasurer*, 1946–64; Reports of the president, 1946–64; Board of Appeals, *Reports*, 1925–68; fragmentary international officers' files including presidential *Circulars of Instruction*, 1897–1956; extensive files on the Canadian wage-rules movement, 1950–68; files on the Trainmen's Political Education League and on state legislative boards as well as scattered local union records; memorabilia and photographs. Unpublished guide available. 5149

————. Records of the Brotherhood of Sleeping Car Porters, Chicago Division, 1925–38. 3 reels microfilm.

Largely intraunion correspondence with A. Philip Randolph and other national officers regarding local organizing efforts, grievances, rival unionism, and other matters of interest to the division. Originals in the Chicago Historical Society. 5462 mf

————. Records of the Ladies Auxiliary to the Brotherhood of Railroad Trainmen, Sunshine Lodge No. 595, Albuquerque, New Mexico, 1917–36. 5 vols.

Minute and roll books. 5207

————. Records of the Order of Railway Conductors and Brakemen, 1881–1969. 30 ft.

Includes constitutions and bylaws, 1881–1968; *Proceedings of the Grand Division*, 1916–66; grand lodge executive committee minutes, 1951–67, with gaps; collective bargaining agreements with various railroads, 1893–1964; scattered grand lodge officers' files which subsume the extensive correspondence of the general secretary-treasurers with the union's numerous general chairmen, 1907–69; also miscellaneous financial documents, publications, memorabilia, and photographs. Unpublished guide available. 5148

————. Records of the Switchmen's Union of North America, 1900–68. 120 ft.

Includes constitutions and bylaws, 1900–67; board of directors' *Minutes*, 1920–68; officers reports, 1913–67; intraunion correspondence of international officers, 1901–68; and separate files series on work rules, 1934–63; strikes, 1921–60; wages, 1909–67; negotiations with carriers, 1901–68; and insurance and benefits, 1902–68. Also correspondence with locals of the union, memorabilia, and photographs. Unpublished guide available. 5034

————. Records of State Fact-Finding Boards, 1899–1952. 9 boxes.

Correspondence, transcripts of hearings, reports, newspaper clippings, and other records of cases before various boards in Massachusetts, New Jersey, and New York. The cases relate to disputes over wages, pensions, hours, union activities, security regulations, strikes, and working conditions. Organizations represented from the railroad industry include Amalgamated Association of Street, Electric Railway and Motor Coach Employes of America; Eastern Massachusetts Street Railway Company; and Yonkers Railroad Company.

————. Records of U.S. Emergency Fact-Finding Boards under the Railway Labor Act, 1950–58. 20 boxes.

Correspondence, transcripts of hearings, reports, charts, tables, and other papers relating to disputes between various unions and carriers that were mediated by emergency boards appointed by the president. Railroad organizations represented include Akron, Canton and Youngstown Railroad Company; Brotherhood of Locomotive Firemen and Enginemen; Brotherhood of Railroad Trainmen; Order of Railway Conductors and Brakemen.

―――――. Records of the U.S. National Mediation Board, 1954–57. 5 boxes.

Transcripts of hearings of cases before the board. Railroad organizations represented include Brotherhood Railway Carmen; Brotherhood of Locomotive Engineers; Brotherhood of Railway and Steamship Clerks, Freight Handlers, Express and Station Employes; Chesapeake and Ohio Railway; Chicago and North Western Railway; Milwaukee, St. Paul and Pacific Railroad; Chicago Union Station Company; Denver and Rio Grande Western Railroad; Illinois Central Railroad; Kansas City Southern Railway; Louisville and Nashville Railway; New York Central Railroad Company; Norfolk and Western Railway; Order of Railroad Telegraphers; Railway Express Agency; Rock Island Frisco Terminal Railway; St. Louis and San Francisco Railroad Telegraphers Organization; Transport Workers Union of America; and the Union Pacific Railroad.

―――――. Report and Supporting Documentation of the United States Presidential Railroad Commission, 1962. 31.6 ft.

Includes transcripts of proceedings; railway labor organizations' exhibits; carrier exhibits; staff documents and the final report of the commission, which held substantial hearings on the fireman manning issue, the basis of pay and assignment, and employment security. Unpublished guide available. 5003

―――――. Selected Correspondence of Alben William Barkley on Railroad Legislation. 1 reel microfilm.

U.S. senator. Includes correspondence relative to the Transportation Act of 1920 (Esch-Cummins Act) and the Barkley-Howell Bill of 1924. Originals at the University of Kentucky. 5160mf

―――――. Selected Documents of the Grand Lodge Ladies Society of the Brotherhood of Locomotive Firemen and Enginemen. 8 in.

Includes constitutions and bylaws, 1910–60; register of the lodges organized, 1884–1971 (2 vols.); and photographs and miscellaneous publications. 5176

―――――. Selected Documents of the United Transportation Union. 1968– . 8 ft.

Formed by the merger of the Order of Railway Conductors and Brakemen, the Brotherhood of Locomotive Firemen and Enginemen, the Brotherhood of Railroad Trainmen, and the Switchmen's Union of North America in 1969. Records include proceedings of the Unification and Constitutional Convention of 1968; circular letters of wages and rules (1969–); Board of Appeals cases (1969–) on awards made by special or Public Law Boards and on health and welfare (1969–). Also agreements and fact-finding decisions relative to the union's bus department (1970–); newsletters of selected locals; miscellaneous publications; memorabilia and photographs. 5139

―――――. Selected Personnel Department Records of the Illinois Central Gulf Railroad, Industrial Relations Department, 1879–1967. 22 ft.

Includes selected personnel department files, largely relating to the nonoperating craft unions, and dealing with a wide range of subjects including railroad legislation, grievances, arbitration, wage-and-hour disputes, vacations, unionization efforts on the road, discipline, and alleged discrimination against and harassment of black workers, 1901–64. Also wage and rule documents for the operating and nonoperating departments of the railroad, 1879–1969. 5295

————. United Transportation Union Merger Documentation Oral History Project. 106 transcripts.

Includes 106 oral interviews with the leadership and selected rank-and-file members of the Order of Railway Conductors and Brakemen, the Brotherhood of Locomotive Firemen and Enginemen, the Brotherhood of Railroad Trainmen, and the Switchmen's Union of North America on questions relating to the possible effects of the merger of these unions to form the United Transportation Union.

————. Unpublished Manuscripts of A. E. Lyon. 3 ms. vols., 3 reels microfilm.

President emeritus of the Brotherhood of Railroad Signalmen. Includes unpublished volume entitled "American Railroad Labor and International Labor Activities" with the following completed chapters: "American Teamsters and the International Transport Workers Federation," 28 pp. (restricted); "Wage Reductions or Deductions: The Willard Agreement of January 31, 1932," 113 pp.; and "International Personalities," (restricted). Also the following unpublished essays: "The Brief and Unfortunate Career of Colonel Raymond J. Kelly as Chairman of the U.S. Railroad Retirement Board," 60 pp. (restricted); "Government Regulation of Labor Relations since 1920," 79+ pp.; "The Healy Years," 23+ pp. (restricted); "The Signal Inspection Act," 129 pp.; "Review of My Brotherhood Career and Events in History of the Brotherhood," 2 vols.; "The Best Secretary of Labor," 36 pp. (restricted). 5450, 5450m, 5450mf

DARTMOUTH COLLEGE, Baker Library, Hanover, New Hampshire. Records of the Connecticut and Passumpsic Rivers Railroad Company, 1848–80. 3 boxes.

Includes claims for injuries, insurance and personnel matters.

DENVER PUBLIC LIBRARY, Western History Department. Papers of Joel Frederick Vaile, 1887–1904. 10 vols.

Lawyer of Colorado and general counsel for the Denver and Rio Grande Railroad. Includes correspondence relating to labor problems, the election of 1904, the Chicago railroad strike, and antitrust law.

DUKE UNIVERSITY LIBRARY, Durham, North Carolina. Papers of John Frederick Neff, 1847–84. 735 items.

Business correspondence and papers reflecting business conditions in the United States, credit policies, and the effect of the panic of 1873. Includes papers (before 1865) of Michael Neff, a Chicago railroad worker.

————. Papers of James Burchell Richardson, 1803–1910. 4,110 items.

Includes letters and papers relating to the use of slave labor on the railroads.

ELEUTHERIAN MILLS HISTORICAL LIBRARY, Greenville, Delaware. Business Letters of George Clinton Gardner, 1875–80. 1 vol.

General superintendent of the Pennsylvania Railroad. Letters concerned with personnel problems as well as shipments and general operations.

————. Records of the Mine Hill and Schuylkill Haven Railroad Company, 1829–69. 5 vols.

Includes payroll account books (1829–1930) of a railroad near Pottsville, Pennsylvania.

LIBRARY OF CONGRESS, Manuscript Division, Washington, D.C. Papers of Otto Sternoff Beyer, 1915–48.

Consulting engineer both to unions and to management in industrial concerns and in railway systems such as the Baltimore and Ohio and the Canadian National Railways. Papers bulk largest for the period 1929–41. Includes a speech and article file containing manuscripts and typed drafts, subject files (separate files have been made for the TVA, the Bonneville Power Authority, and the above-mentioned railways, the latter including minutes of labor-management cooperative meetings), scrapbooks, and correspondence.

————. Papers of John McAllister Schofield, 1837–1906. 38 ft., 30,000 items.

Army officer and public official. Includes material on labor strikes and unrest in Chicago and on the western railroads in the post-Civil War period.

————. Records of the Brotherhood of Sleeping Car Porters, 1939–68. 41 ft., ca. 31,000 items.

General correspondence, railroad agreements, legal and financial papers, printed matter, and miscellaneous material, chiefly 1950–68.

LOUISIANA STATE UNIVERSITY, Department of Archives and Manuscripts, Baton Rouge. Papers of Edwin Lewis Stephens, 1883–1940. 6,656 items and 6 vols.

Includes material relating to personal affairs, political matters, Stephens' employment as a railroad worker in Iowa in 1899.

MARYLAND HISTORICAL SOCIETY LIBRARY, Baltimore. Papers of the Abell Family, 1877, 1930–33. 1 box and 1 package.

Telegrams (1877) sent by George William Abell (1842–94) to A. S. Abell giving news of the railroad strike of 1877 in Baltimore. The Abell family published the *Baltimore Sun*.

————. Papers of William Farquhar Barry, 1877. ca. 70 items.

Army officer. Telegrams sent to Barry while commanding federal troops at Fort McHenry, Maryland, during the Baltimore and Ohio Railroad strike and riots of July–September 1877.

————. Records of the Baltimore and Ohio Railroad Company, 1827–82. ca. 75,000 items.

Includes papers relating to labor problems.

MICHIGAN STATE UNIVERSITY, Historical Collections and Archives, East Lansing. Papers of Edna Z. Emley, 1836–1941. 8 folders.

Resident of Mason, Ingham County, Michigan. Correspondence and miscellaneous papers. Includes letters (1836–57) to Bernhard Stohlman, of Allen, Hillsdale County, Michigan, and letters (1940–41) dealing with a labor dispute over seniority rights of employees of the New York Central.

MINNESOTA HISTORICAL SOCIETY, St. Paul. Archives of the Great Northern Railway Company, 1856–1970. 15,000 linear ft.

Includes personnel records as well as other corporate records and correspondence files of Great Northern officials.

————. Papers of Howard Strickland Abbott, 1859–1948. 500 items.

9

Lawyer of Minneapolis, Minnesota. Includes correspondence, legal papers, and other papers relating to the 1894 railway strike.

————. Papers of William Blake Dean, 1851–1920. ca. 1 ft.

Correspondence, newspaper clippings, and other papers containing information about the building of the Minnesota capitol, the railroad strike of 1894–95, etc.

————. Papers of James Albertus Tawney, 1876–1919. 4 vols. and 15 boxes.

U.S. representative from Minnesota. Includes letters to political leaders and newspaper people on arbitration of disputes between railroad companies and their employees.

Nebraska State Historical Society, Lincoln. Papers of George Ward Holdrege, 1878–1934. ca. 1,910 items.

Employee of the Chicago, Burlington and Quincy Railroad Company in Omaha, Nebraska. Correspondence relating to railroad construction and other matters.

————. Papers of Val Kuska, 1886–1957. ca. 58,000 items.

Employee of the Chicago, Burlington and Quincy Railroad Company.

New York Public Library. Papers of John Huston Finley, 1900–1940. 92 ft.

Editor, educator, author, and civil leader. Papers include his service as a member of a board of arbitration in the eastern railway controversy of 1913–14.

————. Shomburg Collection. Records of the Negro Labor Committee, 1925–69. 15 ft.

Includes some railroad union materials concerning particularly the Brotherhood of Sleeping Car Porters.

Ohio Historical Society, Columbus. Records of the Brotherhood of Railroad Trainmen, Nickel Plate Lodge No. 54, Bellevue, Ohio, 1907–32. ca. 500 items.

Correspondence relating to grievances, working conditions, mutual insurance-benefit system, membership applications and transfers, death claims, benefit certificates, and financial reports.

Oregon Historical Society Library, Portland. Papers of Ola Delight (Lloyd) Cook, 1900–1958. 1 vol. and 6 boxes.

Portland telegrapher and labor leader. Includes correspondence, diaries, constitutions, financial reports, minutes, appointment books, and other papers relating to railroad unions.

————. Records of the Brotherhood of Railroad Trainmen, Sunset Lodge No. 130, Portland, 1901–35. 10 vols.

Ledger books (1901–30) and attendance register (1924–35).

Pennsylvania State University Library, University Park. Records of the Order of Railway Conductors and Brakemen, Wyoming Valley–Wilkes-Barre, Pennsylvania Division, Local 160, 1829–1928. 6 ft.

Correspondence, minutes, financial records, circulars, and reports between Local 160, other locals, and the International Office, Order of Railway Conductors and Brakemen.

State Historical Society of Wisconsin, Madison. Diaries of the Bliss Family, 1867–88. 10 vols.

Diaries kept by Mrs. N. N. Bliss, her husband, and their daughter Ida, residents of Janesville and Baraboo, Wisconsin. Mr. Bliss recorded his daily runs as a railroad engineer.

————. Papers of Roy A. Empey, 1919–54. 2 boxes.

Locomotive engineer, labor leader, and public official. Mainly correspondence relat-

MANUSCRIPT COLLECTIONS

ing to Empey's career, his support of the LaFollettes, his work as campaign manager for Wisconsin State Attorney General John M. Reynolds, 1928–32, cooperation between trade unions and the Progressive party, Empey's participation in John Hickey Lodge No. 266 of the Brotherhood of Locomotive Firemen and Enginemen at Green Bay, his activities as a lobbyist for the Brotherhood at Madison, his career with the Chicago and Northwestern Railroad, and technical aspects of railroading. Correspondence concerning union grievances is scattered throughout the collection. Correspondents include Joseph D. Beck, John J. Blaine, William Evjue, R. Floyd Green, Daniel W. Hoan, Philip F. LaFollette, Robert M. LaFollette, Jr., Solomon Levitan, Orland S. Loomis, Andrew R. McDonald, John M. Reynolds, and D. B. Robertson.

————. Papers of Roy L. Martin, 1901–54. 1 vol. and 3 boxes.

Railroad hobbyist. Papers include correspondence with old employees of the Wisconsin Central reminiscing about their experiences.

————. Records of the Brotherhood of Railroad Trainmen, 1885–1938. 8 vols.

Minutes (1885–89) of Local 177, Baraboo, Wisconsin; minutes (1897–1909, 1917–38) and membership register (1908–11) of Local 410, Chippewa Falls, Wisconsin.

SYRACUSE UNIVERSITY LIBRARY, New York. Records of the Delaware, Lackawanna and Western Railroad Company, 1828–1960. 2,000 ft.

Records of the board of managers, the president, the vice-president, and of the coal, land, tax, law, operating, and treasury departments; labor records; U.S. Interstate Commerce Commission valuation studies (1854–1932); correspondence, minute books, stock certificate and stock transfer books, journals, ledgers, and other records of subsidiary, predecessor, and leased companies; and glass negatives of railroad scenes.

UNIVERSITY OF ARKANSAS LIBRARY, Fayetteville. Papers of Charles Hillman Brough, 1895–1935. 8 ft. and 6 reels microfilm.

Lawyer, educator, lecturer, author, and governor of Arkansas. Contains some material relative to his appointment to the Railway Mediation Board.

UNIVERSITY OF CALIFORNIA, Bancroft Library, Berkeley. Papers of Chester Harvey Rowell, 1887–1946. 27 boxes and 10 cartons.

Journalist and publisher. Includes correspondence, other writings, and pamphlets relating to the Railroad Commission and the railroad strike (1929).

————. Records of the Southern Pacific Company, 1907–40. 14 cartons.

Includes clippings relating to railroad labor disputes.

UNIVERSITY OF ILLINOIS, Chicago Circle Campus Library. Papers of Edgar A. Jones, 1909–59. ca. 8 ft.

Lawyer and U.S. representative from Chicago. Includes various bills relating to taxation, financial affairs, railroad retirement, and diversion of the Chicago river water.

UNIVERSITY OF MICHIGAN, Michigan Historical Collections, Ann Arbor. Business Records of Railroad Companies, 1843–1904. 122 items and 13 vols.

Includes payroll books.

————. Papers of the Michigan United Railroads Company, 1907–11.

Business correspondence relating to the operations of this interurban and city railroad, timetables, payrolls, inventories, annual reports, contracts, and financial statements.

11

MANUSCRIPTS

UNIVERSITY OF OREGON LIBRARY, Eugene. Papers of Daniel Pittinger Loomis, 1943–67. 1 ft.

Lawyer and American Railroad Association officer. Papers include speeches, statements before congressional committees, and memoranda and other material relating to the President's Special Emergency Board on Wage Claims of Non-operating Railway Employees (1943–44) and the President's Commission on Railroad Work Rules (1960).

UNIVERSITY OF TENNESSEE LIBRARY. Papers of Ben W. Hooper, 1911–26.

Correspondence, scrapbooks, clippings, minutes, and other papers concerning Tennessee politics and the work of the Railroad Labor Board.

UNIVERSITY OF TEXAS AT ARLINGTON, Texas Labor Archives. Records of the Brotherhood of Locomotive Firemen and Enginemen, Midland Lodge No. 147, Temple, Texas, 1883–99. 1 ft.

Minutes, attendance records, and financial records.

————. Records of the Brotherhood of Maintenance of Way Employees, Local 2754, Harlingen, Texas, 1948–57. 300 items.

————. Records of the General Committee of Adjustment of the Texas and Pacific Railway, 1886–1909. 100 items.

Minutes of a general grievance and bargaining committee representing the five local divisions of the Brotherhood of Locomotive Engineers that were organized on the Texas and Pacific system.

UNIVERSITY OF TEXAS LIBRARY, Texas Archives, Austin. Papers of Eugene Victor Debs, 1884–1941. 174 items.

Labor leader and socialist. Correspondence, speeches, certificates, pamphlets, broadsides, clippings, books, programs, and other material relating to affairs of the Brotherhood of Locomotive Firemen (1885–92) and the American Railway Union.

————. Papers of Walter Flavius McCaleb, 1900–62. ca. 2 ft.

Banker and author. Correspondence; manuscripts of books, articles, and speeches; newspaper clippings; and scrapbooks concerning McCaleb's work in labor. Includes material on his association with the Brotherhood of Railroad Trainmen and the Brotherhood of Locomotive Engineers.

UNIVERSITY OF VIRGINIA LIBRARY, Charlottesville. Papers of William Jett Lauck, 1915–49. 125 ft.

Lawyer and economist. Correspondence, diarylike accounts, speeches, labor reports and studies, drafts of congressional bills, legal briefs, scrapbooks, personal papers, and other papers concerning labor problems and legislation, immigration, banking, railroads, the coal industry, unemployment, codes of the Taft-Walsh National War Labor Board, the Railway Labor Act of 1926, collective bargaining under the New Deal acts, government competition with private business, the American Association for Economic Freedom, and the New York Power Authority.

WAYNE STATE UNIVERSITY, Archives of Labor History and Urban Affairs, Detroit. Papers of Carl E. Person, 1910–20. 5 ft.

Strike organizer. Includes correspondence, hearing proceedings, strike bulletins and notes relating to the Illinois Central and Harriman lines strike (1911–15); proceedings of Person's trial for the murder of a strikebreaker; ms. of his book *The Lizard's Trail* (1918); and correspondence with the International Association of Machinists, of which Person was a member.

MANUSCRIPT COLLECTIONS

WEST VIRGINIA UNIVERSITY LIBRARY, Morgantown. Records of the Hansford, West Virginia, Sheltering Arms Hospital, 1902–40. 17 vols. and 1 folder.

Minute book (1906–23), medical case records (1902–22), and miscellaneous papers of a hospital designed to serve the medical and surgical needs of miners and railroad workers and their families.

PART III

BOOKS, PAMPHLETS, AND THESES

1. General

General

ABDILL, GEORGE B. *This Was Railroading*. Seattle: Superior, 1958. 192 pp.

ANDREWS, CYRIL BRUYN. *The Railway Age*. New York: Macmillan, 1938. 145 pp.

BUCHANAN, LAMONT. *Steel Trails and Iron Horses: A Pageant of American Railroading*. New York: Putnam, 1955. 159 pp.

CHANDLER, ALFRED DUPONT, ed. *The Railroads, the Nation's First Big Business: Sources and Readings*. New York: Harcourt, Brace, 1965. 213 pp.

DANIELS, WINTHROP MORE. *American Railroads: Four Phases of Their History*. Princeton, N.J.: Princeton University Press, 1932. 120 pp.

DAUGHEN, JOSEPH R., and PETER BINZEN. *The Wreck of the Penn Central*. Boston: Little, Brown, 1971. 336 pp.

DODGE, GRENVILLE MELLEN. *How We Built the Union Pacific Railway, and Other Railway Papers and Addresses*. Denver: Sage Books, 1965. 171 pp.

GATES, PAUL W. *The Illinois Central Railroad and Its Colonization Work*. Cambridge, Mass.: Harvard University Press, 1934. 374 pp.

HOLBROOK, STEWART HALL. *The Story of American Railroads*. New York: Crown, 1947. 468 pp.

HULTGREN, THOR. *American Transportation in Prosperity and Depression*. New York: National Bureau of Economic Research, 1948. 397 pp.

HUNGERFORD, EDWARD. *From Covered Wagon to Streamlines*. New York: Greystone, 1941. 64 pp.

————. *Men and Iron: The History of New York Central*. New York: Thomas Y. Crowell, 1938. 424 pp.

LONG, BRYANT ALDEN. *Mail by Rail: The Story of the Postal Transportation Service*. New York: Simmons-Boardman, 1951. 414 pp.

OVERTON, RICHARD C. *Burlington Route: A History of the Burlington Lines*. New York: Knopf, 1965. 623 pp.

————. *Burlington West: A Colonization History of the Burlington Railroad*. Cambridge, Mass.: Harvard University Press, 1941. 583 pp.

RAILWAY AGE. *Railway Age Centennial 1856–1956: A Look Back, a Look Ahead.* Orange, Conn.: Simmons-Boardman, 1956. 392 pp.

SAYLOR, ROGER BEHM. *The Railroads of Pennsylvania.* University Park, Pa.: Bureau of Business Research, College of Business Administration, Pennsylvania State University, 1964. 332 pp.

SHARFMAN, ISAIAH L. *The Interstate Commerce Commission: A Study in Administrative Law and Procedure.* 4 vols. New York: Commonwealth Fund, 1931–37. 2967 pp.

STOVER, JOHN F. *American Railroads.* Chicago: University of Chicago Press, 1961. 302 pp.

————. *The Life and Decline of the American Railroad.* New York: Oxford University Press, 1970. 324 pp.

TAYLOR, GEORGE ROGERS. *The Transportation Revolution, 1815–1960.* New York: Rinehart, 1951. 490 pp.

THOMPSON, SLASON. *A Short History of American Railways, Covering Ten Decades.* 1925. Reprint. Freeport, N.Y.: Books for Libraries Press, 1971. 473 pp.

1850–98

ABDILL, GEORGE B. *Pacific Slope Railroads from 1854 to 1900.* New York: Bonanza Books, 1959. 182 pp.

ADAMS, CHARLES FRANCIS. *Railroads: Their Origin and Problems.* New York: Putnam, 1878. 230 pp.

ARMSTRONG, GEORGE BUCHANAN. *The Beginnings of Mail Service and the Work of George B. Armstrong in Founding It.* Chicago: Lakeside, 1908, 84 pp.

ATKINSON, EDWARD. *The Distribution of Products; Or, The Mechanism and the Metaphysics of Exchange.* 5th ed. New York: Putnam, 1892. 365 pp.

BENSON, LEE. *Merchants, Farmers, and Railroads: Railroad Regulation and New York Politics, 1850–1887.* Cambridge, Mass.: Harvard University Press, 1955. 310 pp.

BERGE, GEORGE W. *The Free Pass Bribery System.* Lincoln, Neb.: Independent, 1905. 313 pp.

CAMPBELL, EDWARD GROSS. *The Reorganization of the American Railroad System, 1893–1900.* New York: Columbia University Press, 1938. 366 pp.

CARR, CLARK EZRA. *The Railway Mail Service: Its Origin and Development.* Chicago: A. C. McClurg, 1909. 48 pp.

CLARKE, THOMAS CURTIS, *et al. The American Railway: Its Construction, Development, Management, and Appliances.* New York: Scribner, 1889. 456 pp.

DELAWARE AND HUDSON COMPANY. *A Century of Progress: History of the Delaware and Hudson Company, 1823–1923.* Albany: J. B. Lyon, 1925. 755 pp.

DENNIS, WILLIAM JEFFERSON. *The Traveling Post Office: History and Incidents of the Railway Mail Service.* Des Moines: Homestead, 1916. 128 pp.

HANEY, LEWIS HENRY. *A Congressional History of Railways in the United States.* 1908–10. Reprint. New York: A. M. Kelley, 1968. 608 pp.

HEDGES, JAMES BLAINE. *Henry Villard and the Railways of the Northwest.* New Haven, Conn.: Yale University Press, 1930. 224 pp.

History of the Illinois Central Railroad Company and Representative Employees. Chicago: Railroad Historical Company, 1900.

15

JOHNSON, EMORY RICHARD. *American Railway Transportation.* 2nd ed. New York: D. Appleton, 1909. 434 pp.

KIRKLAND, EDWARD C. "Railroads: Building and Finance," chap. 3, pp. 43–74; "Railroad Pricing Policy," chap. 4, pp. 75–96; "Railroad Reform," pp. 97–115; "Railroad Commissions: Breakthrough or Stalemate?," pp. 116–36. *Industry Comes of Age: Business, Labor, and Public Policy.* New York: Holt, Rinehart, 1961.

NORTHERN PACIFIC RAILROAD COMPANY. *The Northern Pacific Railroad: Its Route, Resources, Progress and Business; The New Northwest and Its Great Thoroughfare.* Philadelphia: J. Cooke, 1871. 46 pp.

PRATT, EDWIN A. *American Railways.* New York: Macmillan, 1903. 309 pp.

RIEGEL, ROBERT E. *The Story of Western Railroads.* New York: Macmillan, 1926. 345 pp.

RIPLEY, WILLIAM Z. *Railroads: Finance and Organization.* New York: Longmans, Green, 1915. 638 pp.

SHURZ, C. *Corporations, Their Employes and the Public.* New York, 1884. 19 pp.

STEVENS, FRANK WALTER. *The Beginnings of the New York Central Railroad: A History.* New York: Putnam, 1926. 408 pp.

STIMSON, ALEXANDER LOVETT. *History of the Express Companies and the Origin of American Railroads.* 2nd ed. New York, 1858. 287 pp.

TAYLOR, GEORGE ROGERS, and IRENE D. NEU. *The American Railroad Network, 1861–1890.* Cambridge, Mass.: Harvard University Press, 1956. 113 pp.

TRYON, ROLLA MILTON, J. JAMES, and CARL RUSSEL FISH, eds. *Transportation: Early Railroad Period, 1840–1880.* Indianapolis: G. F. Cram, 1957.

1898–1926

ARMSTRONG, GEORGE BUCHANAN. *The Beginnings of Mail Service and the Work of George B. Armstrong in Founding It.* Chicago: Lakeside, 1908. 84 pp.

BERGE, GEORGE W. *The Free Pass Bribery System.* Lincoln, Neb.: Independent, 1905. 313 pp.

CAMPBELL, EDWARD GROSS. *The Reorganization of the American Railroad System, 1893–1900.* New York: Columbia University Press, 1938. 366 pp.

CARR, CLARK EZRA. *The Railway Mail Service: Its Origin and Development.* Chicago: A. C. McClurg, 1909. 48 pp.

CLEVELAND, FREDERICK A., and FRED WILBUR POWELL. *Railroad Promotion and Capitalization in the United States.* New York: Longmans, Green, 1909. 368 pp.

DAGGETT, STUART. *Railroad Reorganization.* Cambridge, Mass.: Harvard University Press, 1908. 402 pp.

DELAWARE AND HUDSON COMPANY. *A Century of Progress: History of the Delaware and Hudson Company, 1823–1923.* Albany: J. B. Lyon, 1925. 755 pp.

DENNIS, WILLIAM JEFFERSON. *The Traveling Post Office: History and Incidents of the Railway Mail Service.* Des Moines: Homestead, 1916. 128 pp.

DEWSNUP, ERNEST R., ed. *Railway Organization and Working.* Chicago: University of Chicago Press, 1906. 498 pp.

DIXON, FRANK HAIGH, and JULIUS H. PARMELEE. *War Administration of the Railways in the United States and Great Britain.* Preliminary Economic Studies of the War, edited by David Kinley. Vol. 3. 2nd ed. New York: Oxford University Press, 1919. 203 pp.

FLEMING, R. D. *Railroad and Street Transportation.* Cleveland: Cleveland Foundation, 1916. 76 pp.

HEDGES, JAMES BLAINE. *Henry Villard and the Railways of the Northwest.* New Haven, Conn.: Yale University Press, 1930. 224 pp.

HUNGERFORD, EDWARD. *The Railroad Problem.* Chicago: A. C. McClurg, 1917. 265 pp.

JOHNSON, EMORY RICHARD. *American Railway Transportation.* 2nd ed. New York: D. Appleton, 1909. 434 pp.

KING, EVERETT EDGAR. *Railway Signaling.* New York: McGraw-Hill, 1921. 371 pp.

PRATT, EDWIN A. *American Railways.* New York: Macmillan, 1903. 309 pp.

RIEGEL, ROBERT E. *The Story of Western Railroads.* New York: Macmillan, 1926. 345 pp.

RIPLEY, WILLIAM Z. *Railroads: Finance and Organization.* New York: Longmans, Green, 1915. 638 pp.

STEVENS, FRANK WALTER. *The Beginnings of the New York Central Railroad: A History.* New York: Putnam, 1926. 408 pp.

1926–46

BABCOCK, V. B. *A Cooperative Course in Railroad Operation.* Cambridge: Massachusetts Institute of Technology, Department of Civil Engineering, 1930.

HEALY, KENT TENNEY. *The Economics of Transportation in America: The Dynamic Forces in Development, Organization, Functioning and Regulation.* New York: Ronald, 1940. 575 pp.

SCHMIDT, EMERSON P. "The Development of the Street Railway Industry: Technological, Financial, Regulatory and Labor Aspects." Ph.D. dissertation, University of Wisconsin, 1935.

1946–Present

ASSOCIATION OF AMERICAN RAILROADS. Engineering Division. Signal Section. *American Railway Signaling, Principles and Practices.* Chicago: The Association, 1954.

BEHLING, BURTON. *A Review of Railroad Operations in 1966.* Washington, D.C.: Bureau of Railway Economics, 1967. 64 pp.

CORLISS, CARLTON JONATHAN. *The Human Side of Railroading.* Washington, D.C.: Association of American Railroads, [194?]. 81 pp.

GENERAL ELECTRIC COMPANY. *Profiles of American Railroading.* Schenectady, N.Y.: General Electric, 1965. 48 pp.

LEWIS, ROBERT. *The Handbook of American Railroads.* 2nd ed. New York: Simmons-Boardman, 1956. 251 pp.

2. Railroads and Government

General

ADAMS, CHARLES F. *Railroads and the Railroad Question.* New York: Putnam, n.d.

1850–98

BALDWIN, SIMEON EBEN. *American Railroad Law.* Boston: Little, Brown, 1904. 770 pp.

BONHAM, JOHN MILTON. *Railway Secrecy and Trusts.* New York: Putnam, 1890. 138 pp.

DABNEY, W. D. *The Public Regulation of Railways.* New York: Putnam, 1889. 281 pp.

GOODRICH, CARTER. *Government Promotion of American Canals and Railroads, 1800–1890.* New York: Columbia University Press, 1960. 382 pp.

HOLLANDER, JACOB H. *The Cincinnati Southern Railway: A Study in Municipal Activity.* Baltimore: Johns Hopkins Press, 1894. 96 pp.

HUDSON, JAMES F. *Railways and the Republic.* New York: Harper, 1886. 489 pp.

KIRKLAND, EDWARD C. *Men, Cities and Transportation: A Study in New England History, 1820–1900.* 2 vols. Cambridge, Mass.: Harvard University Press, 1948. 1005 pp.

————. "Railroads: Building and Finance," chap. 3, pp. 43–74; "Railroad Pricing Policy," chap 4, pp. 75–96; "Railroad Reform," pp. 97–115; "Railroad Commissions; Breakthrough or Stalemate?," pp. 116–36. *Industry Comes of Age: Business, Labor, and Public Policy.* New York: Holt, Rinehart, 1961.

KOLKO, GABRIEL. *Railroads and Regulation, 1877–1916.* Princeton, N.J.: Princeton University Press, 1965. 273 pp.

LARRABEE, WILLIAM M. *The Railroad Question: A Historical and Practical Treatise on Railroads, and Remedies for Their Abuses.* 11th ed. Chicago: Schulte, 1906. 488 pp.

MILLER, GEORGE H. *Railroads and the Granger Laws.* Madison: University of Wisconsin Press, 1971. 296 pp.

POTTER, DAVID MORRIS. *The Railroads.* New York: Holt, Rinehart, 1960. 66 pp.

1898–1926

BALDWIN, SIMEON EBEN. *American Railroad Law.* Boston: Little, Brown, 1904. 770 pp.

JONES, ELIOT, ed. *Railroads: Cases and Selections.* New York: Macmillan, 1925. 882 pp.

KATHEL, AUSTIN KERR. "American Railroad Politics, 1914–1920." Ph.D. dissertation, University of Pittsburgh, 1965.

KOLKO, GABRIEL. *Railroads and Regulation, 1877–1916.* Princeton, N.J.: Princeton University Press, 1965. 273 pp.

NATIONAL TRANSPORTATION CONFERENCE. *Program of Railroad Legislation.* Washington, D.C., 1919. 185 pp.

RAILROAD ATTORNEYS' CONFERENCE. *Proceedings of the Railroad Attorneys' Conference at Hotel Wentworth, Portsmouth, N.H., August 2–6, 1910.* Louisville, Ky.: Westerfield-Bonte, 1910. 544 pp.

Conference held to consider and discuss questions arising under the Mann-Elkins bill, approved June 18, 1910.

RIPLEY, WILLIAM Z. *Railroads: Rates and Regulation.* New York: Longmans, Green, 1912. 659 pp.

SISSON, F. H. *Russianizing the Railroads: The Real Issue Raised in the Brotherhoods' Plan for Class Control of Transportation.* New York: Guaranty Trust, 1919. 15 pp.

1926–46

LABOR RESEARCH ASSOCIATION. *Railways in Crisis: A Program for Re-Employment, Rehabilitation and Government Ownership.* New York: International, 1939. 48 pp.

1946–Present

RAILWAY LABOR EXECUTIVES' ASSOCIATION. *The Move toward Railroad Mergers, A Great National Problem.* Washington, D.C.: The Association, 1962. 102 pp.

WREN, HAROLD GWYN. "The American Law of Railroad Organization." Ph.D. dissertation, Yale University, 1957.

3. Management

General

ALLEN, FREDERICK LEWIS. *The Great Pierpont Morgan.* New York: Harper, 1949. 306 pp.

MARSHALL, ROSS S. *Working on the Railroad.* Cleveland: Gates Legal, 1956. 179 pp.

MIDDLETON, PHILIP HARVEY. *A Half Century of Teamwork.* Chicago: Railway Progress Institute, 1958. 78 pp.

PENROSE, CHARLES. *L. F. Loree, 1858–1940, Patriarch of the Rails.* New York: Newcomen Society in North America, 1955. 36 pp.

1850–98

CHANDLER, ALFRED DUPONT. *Henry Varnum Poor: Business Editor, Analyst, and Reformer.* Cambridge, Mass.: Harvard University Press, 1956. 362 pp.

COCHRAN, THOMAS C. *Railroad Leaders, 1845–1890: The Business Mind in Action.* Cambridge, Mass.: Harvard University Press, 1953. 564 pp.

GRODINSKY, JULIUS. *Jay Gould, His Business Career, 1867–1892.* Philadelphia: University of Pennsylvania Press, 1957. 627 pp.

HEDGES, JAMES BLAINE. *Henry Villard and the Railways of the Northwest.* New Haven, Conn.: Yale University Press, 1930. 224 pp.

HINE, CHARLES DE LANO. *Letters from an Old Railway Official to His Son, a Division Superintendent.* Chicago: Railway Age, 1904. 179 pp.

JONES, PETER D'ALROY. *The Robber Barons Revisited.* Boston: D. C. Heath, 1968. 128 pp.

19

JOSEPHSON, MATTHEW. *The Robber Barons: The Great American Capitalists, 1861–1901.* New York: Harcourt, Brace, 1962. 474 pp.

KIRKLAND, EDWARD C. *Men, Cities and Transportation: A Study in New England History, 1820–1900.* 2 vols. Cambridge, Mass.: Harvard University Press, 1948. 1005 pp.

————. "Railroads: Building and Finance," chap. 3, pp. 43–74; "Railroad Pricing Policy," chap. 4, pp. 75–96; "Railroad Reform," pp. 97–115; "Railroad Commissions: Breakthrough or Stalemate?," pp. 116–36. *Industry Comes of Age: Business, Labor, and Public Policy.* New York: Holt, Rinehart, 1961.

MARSHALL, ROSS S. *Working on the Railroad.* Cleveland: Gates Legal, 1956. 179 pp.

MOODY, JOHN. *The Railroad Builders: A Chronicle of the Welding of the States.* New Haven, Conn.: Yale University Press, 1919. 257 pp.

NESBIT, ROBERT CARRINGTON. *He Built Seattle: A Biography of Judge Thomas Burke.* Seattle: University of Washington Press, 1961. 455 pp.

PEARSON, HENRY GREENLEAF. *An American Railroad Builder, John Murray Forbes.* Boston: Houghton Mifflin, 1911. 196 pp.

PENROSE, CHARLES. *L. F. Loree, 1958–1940, Patriarch of the Rails.* New York: Newcomen Society in North America, 1955. 36 pp.

POOR, LAURA ELIZABETH, ed. *The First International Railway and the Colonization of New England: Life and Writings of John Alfred Poor.* New York: Putnam, 1892.

PORTER, HENRY H. *H. H. Porter: A Short Autobiography Written for His Children and Grandchildren.* Chicago: R. R. Donnelley, 1915. 40 pp.

SCHLEGEL, MARVIN W. *Ruler of the Reading: The Life of Franklin B. Gowen, 1836–1889.* Harrisburg, Pa.: Archives, 1947. 308 pp.

TODD, CHARLES BURR. *Confessions of a Railroadman.* New York: S.R.I. Community, 1904. 159 pp.

1898–1926

ADAM, B. B., JR. *The Superintendent, the Conductor, and the Engineman.* New York: Interstate Commerce Commission, 1902. 22 pp.

AMERICAN RAILWAY ASSOCIATION. *Historical Statement: Present Activities, August 15, 1921.* New York: The Association, 1921. 134 pp.

HEDGES, JAMES BLAINE. *Henry Villard and the Railways of the Northwest.* New Haven, Conn.: Yale University Press, 1930. 224 pp.

HINE, CHARLES DE LANO. *Letters from an Old Railway Official to His Son, a Division Superintendent.* Chicago: Railway Age, 1904. 179 pp.

HOOPER, BEN W. *The Unwanted Boy: The Autobiography of Governor Ben W. Hooper.* Edited by Everett Robert Boyce. Knoxville: University of Tennessee Press, 1963. 258 pp.

KERR, K. AUSTIN. *American Railroad Politics, 1914–1920: Rates, Wages, and Efficiency.* Pittsburgh: University of Pittsburgh Press, 1968. 250 pp.

MARSHALL, ROSS S. *Working on the Railroad.* Cleveland: Gates Legal, 1956. 179 pp.

MIDDLETON, PHILIP HARVEY. *A Half Century of Teamwork.* Chicago: Railway Progress Institute, 1958. 78 pp.

MOODY, JOHN. *The Railroad Builders: A Chronicle of the Welding of the States.* New Haven, Conn.: Yale University Press, 1919. 257 pp.

MANAGEMENT

NADWORNY, MILTON J. *Scientific Management and the Unions, 1900–1932: A Historical Analysis.* Cambridge, Mass.: Harvard University Press, 1955. 187 pp.

NESBIT, ROBERT CARRINGTON. *He Built Seattle: A Biography of Judge Thomas Burke.* Seattle: University of Washington Press, 1961. 455 pp.

PEARSON, HENRY GREENLEAF. *An American Railroad Builder, John Murray Forbes.* Boston: Houghton Mifflin, 1911. 196 pp.

PENROSE, CHARLES. *L. F. Loree, 1858–1940, Patriarch of the Rails.* New York: Newcomen Society in North America, 1955. 36 pp.

PORTER, HENRY H. *H. H. Porter: A Short Autobiography Written for His Children and Grandchildren.* Chicago: R. R. Donnelley, 1915. 40 pp.

TODD, CHARLES BURR. *Confessions of a Railroadman.* New York: S.R.I. Community, 1904. 159 pp.

1926–46

AMERICAN TECHNICAL SOCIETY. *The Railway Foreman and His Job.* Chicago: The Society, 1943. 138 pp.

CHRISTIE, HUGH K., and JAMES MCKINNEY. *The Railway Foreman and His Job.* Chicago: American Technical Society, 1947. 285 pp.

DUNN, PAUL C. *The Selection and Training of Railroad Supervisors.* Cambridge: Massachusetts Institute of Technology, 1942.

JOSEPHSON, MATTHEW. "The Railroad King from Texas [Robert Young]," chap. 8, pp. 188–246. *The Money Lords: The Great Finance Capitalists.* New York: Weybright & Talley, 1972.

MARSHALL, ROSS S. *Working on the Railroad.* Cleveland: Gates Legal, 1956. 179 pp.

MIDDLETON, PHILIP HARVEY. *A Half Century of Teamwork.* Chicago: Railway Progress Institute, 1958. 78 pp.

PENROSE, CHARLES. *L. F. Loree, 1858–1940, Patriarch of the Rails.* New York: Newcomen Society in North America, 1955. 36 pp.

1946–Present

JOSEPHSON, MATTHEW. "The Railroad King from Texas [Robert Young]," chap. 8, pp. 188–246. *The Money Lords: The Great Finance Capitalists.* New York: Weybright & Talley, 1972.

KATZ, DANIEL, et al. *Productivity, Supervision and Morale among Railroad Workers.* Ann Arbor: Survey Research Center, Institute for Social Research, University of Michigan, 1951. 61 pp.

MARSHALL, ROSS S. *Working on the Railroad.* Cleveland: Gates Legal, 1956. 179 pp.

MIDDLETON, PHILIP HARVEY. *A Half Century of Teamwork.* Chicago: Railway Progress Institute, 1958. 78 pp.

RAILWAY SYSTEMS AND MANAGEMENT ASSOCIATION. *The Man in Railroad Management.* Chicago: The Association, 1964. 75 pp.

————. *Railroad Career Development.* Chicago: The Association, 1965. 94 pp.

SATTARI-TEHRANI, HASSAN. "A Study of Management Methods and Problems of the Atchison, Topeka and Santa Fe Railway with Reference to the Administration of Iranian State Railways." Ph.D. dissertation, University of Southern California, 1961.

4. Labor Force

General

LEVINSON, HAROLD M., et al. Collective Bargaining and Technological Change in American Transportation. Evanston, Ill.: Transportation Center, Northwestern University, 1971. 723 pp.

See especially Part 2, "Collective Bargaining and Technological Change on American Railroads," by Charles M. Rehmus, pp. 85–242.

RISHER, HOWARD W., JR., and MARJORIE C. DENISON. The Negro in the Railroad Industry. Philadelphia: Industrial Research Unit, Department of Industry, Wharton School of Finance and Commerce, University of Pennsylvania, 1971. 202 pp.

1850–98

BARNARD, W. T. Service Report on Technical Education, with Special Reference to the Baltimore and Ohio Railroad Service. Baltimore, 1887. 238 pp.

KELLEY, WILLIAM DARRAH. Remarks of Hon. William D. Kelley, of Pennsylvania, in Opposition to the Employment of Slaves in Navy-Yards, Arsenals, Dock-yards, etc., and in Favor of the Pacific Railroad. Washington, D.C.: Scammell, 1862. 8 pp.

LEVINSON, HAROLD M., et al. Collective Bargaining and Technological Change in American Transportation. Evanston, Ill.: Transportation Center, Northwestern University, 1971. 723 pp.

See especially Part 2, "Collective Bargaining and Technological Change on American Railroads," by Charles M. Rehmus, pp. 85–242.

RISHER, HOWARD W., JR., and MARJORIE C. DENISON. The Negro in the Railroad Industry. Philadelphia: Industrial Research Unit, Department of Industry, Wharton School of Finance and Commerce, University of Pennsylvania, 1971. 202 pp.

1898–1926

ADAMS, B. B., JR. The Superintendent, the Conductor, and the Engineman. New York: Interstate Commerce Commission, 1902. 22 pp.

BERRY, R. E. An Analysis of Clerical Positions for Juniors in Railway Transportation. Berkeley, Calif.: University Division of Vocational Education, Research and Service Center for Part-time Schools, University of California, 1921. 104 pp.

BUREAU OF RAILWAY ECONOMICS. Effect of Recent Wage Advances upon Railway Employees' Compensation during the Year Ending June 30, 1911; Variations in the Number of Railway Employees, 1909–1910–1911; Relation of the Number of Employees and Their Compensation to Traffic and Revenue, 1909–1910–1911. Bulletin 28. Washington, D.C.: The Bureau, 1912. 47 pp.

CHRISTIE, HUGH K. The Carman's Helper. Chicago: Trade Educational Bureau of the Brotherhood Railway Carmen of America, 1920. 202 pp.

HOGAN, EDMOND K. The Work of the Railway Carman. Kansas City, Mo.: Brotherhood Railway Carmen of America, 1921. 201 pp.

KERR, K. AUSTIN. *American Railroad Politics, 1914–1920: Rates, Wages, and Efficiency.* Pittsburgh: University of Pittsburgh Press, 1968. 250 pp.

KING, EVERETT EDGAR. *Railway Signaling.* New York: McGraw-Hill, 1921. 371 pp.

LEVINSON, HAROLD M., et al. *Collective Bargaining and Technological Change in American Transportation.* Evanston, Ill.: Transportation Center, Northwestern University, 1971. 723 pp.
See especially Part 2, "Collective Bargaining and Technological Change on American Railroads," by Charles M. Rehmus, pp. 85–242.

NATIONAL INDUSTRIAL CONFERENCE BOARD. *Wages, Hours, and Employment of Railroad Workers.* Research Report 70. New York, 1924. 80 pp.

PARMELEE, JULIUS HALL. "Stability of Railway Operations." *President's Conference on Unemployment: Business Cycles and Unemployment.* Washington, D.C., 1923. 405 pp.

RISHER, HOWARD W., JR., and MARJORIE C. DENISON. *The Negro in the Railroad Industry.* Philadelphia: Industrial Research Unit, Department of Industry, Wharton School of Finance and Commerce, University of Pennsylvania, 1971. 202 pp.

VAUCLAIN, S. M. "The System of Apprenticeship at the Baldwin Locomotive Works." In *Trade Unionism and Labor Problems,* edited by John R. Commons, chap. 13, pp. 304–15. 1st series. New York: A. M. Kelley, 1967.

1926–46

AMERICAN TECHNICAL SOCIETY. *The Railway Foreman and His Job.* Chicago: The Society, 1943. 138 pp.

ASSOCIATION OF RAILWAY EXECUTIVES. *Stabilization of Employment on the Railroads, Report of the Committee on Stabilization of Employment to the Executive Committee.* Atlantic City, N.J.: The Association, 1927. 9 pp.

BROTHERHOOD OF RAILROAD TRAINMEN. *Enemy Hours: The Waste of Manpower on American Railroads Occasioned by Managerial Mispractices in Utilization of Personnel.* Cleveland: The Brotherhood, 1945. 264 pp.

BROWN, B. M. *Apprentice-Training Service. Postwar Apprentices of American Railroads: Vital Importance of Apprentice Training to Meet the Demand for Craftsmen by American Railroads.* Washington, D.C.: U.S. War Manpower Commission, Bureau of Training, 1945. 6 pp.

BROWN, JAMES DOUGLAS. *Railway Labor Survey.* New York: Social Science Research Council, 1933. 153 pp.

CHRISTIE, HUGH K., and JAMES MCKINNEY. *The Railway Foreman and His Job.* Chicago: American Technical Society, 1947. 285 pp.

HOEHN, W. E. "Selection and Training Procedures in Use by Pittsburgh Railways Co." *Proceedings of the American Transit Association.* n.p., 1942. 5 pp.

LEVINSON, HAROLD M., et al. *Collective Bargaining and Technological Change in American Transportation.* Evanston, Ill.: Transportation Center, Northwestern University, 1971. 723 pp.
See especially Part 2, "Collective Bargaining and Technological Change on American Railroads," by Charles M. Rehmus, pp. 85–242.

RISHER, HOWARD W., JR., and MARJORIE C. DENISON. *The Negro in the Railroad Industry.* Philadelphia: Industrial Research Unit, Department of Industry, Wharton School of

Finance and Commerce, University of Pennsylvania, 1971. 202 pp.

SCIENCE RESEARCH ASSOCIATES. *Railroad Workers*. Occupational Briefs of War and Postwar Job Fields No. 22. n.p., 1943. 4 pp.

STEWART, LOTYS BENNING. *The Railroad Industry*. Indianapolis: National Youth Administration for Indiana, 1940. 119 pp.

1946–Present

ASSOCIATION OF AMERICAN RAILROADS. *Facts about Featherbedding in the Railway Industry*. Washington, D.C.: The Association, 1960. 43 pp.

————. Engineering Division. Signal Section. *American Railway Signaling, Principles and Practices*. Chicago: The Association, 1954.

————. Railroad Committee for the Study of Transportation. Subcommittee on Labor and Personnel. *Railroad Personnel Practices: A Report*. Washington, D.C.: The Association, 1946. 93 pp.

BACKMAN, JULES. *Economics of New York State Full-Crew Laws*. New York: New York State Association of Railroads, 1964. 52 pp.

————. *Featherbedding, the Economics of Waste*. Richmond, Calif.: Lynmar, 1961. 7 pp.

CIVIL SERVICE PUBLISHING CORPORATION. *How to Pass Railroad Clerk: Questions and Answers*. Brooklyn, N.Y.: The Corporation, 1965.

COATES, NORMAN. "The Discontinuance of the Use of Firemen on Diesel Locomotives in Freight and Yard Service on the Canadian Pacific Railway Company." M.S. thesis, Cornell University, 1959. 191 pp.

COTTRELL, FRED. *Technological Change and Labor in the Railroad Industry: A Comparative Study*. Lexington, Mass.: Heath, 1970. 159 pp.

HABER, WILLIAM. *Maintenance of Way Employment on U.S. Railroads: An Analysis of the Sources of Instability and Remedial Measures*. Detroit: Brotherhood of Maintenance of Way Employes, 1957. 237 pp.

HOROWITZ, MORRIS A. *Manpower Utilization in the Railroad Industry: An Analysis of Working Rules and Practices*. Boston: Bureau of Business and Economic Research, Northeastern University, 1960. 68 pp.

JAKUBAUSKAS, EDWARD BENEDICT. "The Impact of Technological Change on Railroad Employment, 1947–1958." Ph.D. dissertation, University of Wisconsin, 1960. 248 pp.

KAMIEN, MORTON ISAAC. "An Econometric Study of Structural Changes in the Composition of the Labor Force, with Special Reference to the Railroads." Ph.D. dissertation, Purdue University, 1964. 160 pp.

KATZ, DANIEL, et al. *Productivity, Supervision and Morale among Railroad Workers*. Ann Arbor: Survey Research Center, Institute for Social Research, University of Michigan, 1951. 61 pp.

KENNEDY, W. P. *Automation in the Railroad Industry: The Twentieth Century Challenge to Management and Labor*. Washington, D.C.: Public Affairs Institute, n.d. 29 pp.

KROLICK, REUBEN HARRISON. "A Study of the Changing Economic Status of Skilled Occupations: Railroad Engineers and Airline Pilots." Ph.D. dissertation, Stanford University, 1966. 356 pp.

LABOR-MANAGEMENT COMMITTEE [of the Railroad Industry]. Task Force on Terminals. St. Louis Terminal Project. "Evaluation of Changes in Terminal Operations: A Progress Report to Task Force on Terminals." Multicopied report. May 15, 1974.

————. "Program of Experiments Involving Changes in Terminal Operations: 1974 Progress Report."

LEVINSON, HAROLD M., et al. Collective Bargaining and Technological Change in American Transportation. Evanston, Ill.: Transportation Center, Northwestern University, 1971. 723 pp.

See especially Part 2, "Collective Bargaining and Technological Change on American Railroads," by Charles M. Rehmus, pp. 85–242.

LIEB, ROBERT C. Labor in the Transportation Industries. Washington, D.C.: U.S. Department of Transportation, 1973. 136 pp.

MATTESON, PORTER. Whose Featherbed? Rochester, N.Y.: Mohawk, 1966. 80 pp.

OLIVER, ELI. "Job and Income Security in Railway Mergers and Abandonments." In Automation and Major Technological Change: Collective Bargaining Problems, pp. 21–27. Papers presented at a conference held under the auspices of the Industrial Union Department, AFL-CIO, April 22, 1958.

RAILWAY LABOR EXECUTIVES' ASSOCIATION. The Move toward Railroad Mergers: A Great National Problem. Washington, D.C.: The Association, 1962. 102 pp.

RISHER, HOWARD W., JR., and MARJORIE C. DENISON. The Negro in the Railroad Industry. Philadelphia: Industrial Research Unit, Department of Industry, Wharton School of Finance and Commerce, University of Pennsylvania, 1971. 202 pp.

ROSEN, SHERWIN. "Short-Run Employment Variation on Class I Railroads in the United States, 1947–1963." Ph.D. dissertation, University of Chicago, 1966.

UHL, ALEXANDER. Trains and the Men Who Run Them. Washington, D.C.: Public Affairs Institute, 1954. 100 pp.

5. Working Conditions

General

JONES, HARRY E. Railroad Wages and Labor Relations, 1900–1952: An Historical Survey and Summary of Results. New York: Bureau of Information of the Eastern Railways, 1953. 375 pp.

SHAW, ROBERT B. Down Brakes: A History of Railroad Accidents, Safety Precautions and Operating Practices in the U.S.A. London: P. R. Macmillan, 1961. 487 pp.

1850–98

ADAMS, CHARLES FRANCIS, JR. Notes on Railroad Accidents. New York: Putnam, 1879. 280 pp.

BROTHERHOOD OF LOCOMOTIVE FIREMEN AND ENGINEMEN. Research Department. Relative Rates of Wages of Railroad Employees, 1840–1891. n.p.: The Brotherhood, 1923. 3 pp.

25

BOOKS, PAMPHLETS, THESES

CLARK, CHARLES HUGH. "The Railroad Safety Movement in the United States: Origins and Developments, 1869–1893." Ph.D. dissertation, University of Illinois, 1966. 395 pp.

JONES, HARRY E. *Railroad Wages and Labor Relations, 1900–1952: An Historical Survey and Summary of Results.* New York: Bureau of Information of the Eastern Railways, 1953. 375 pp.

KIRKLAND, EDWARD C. *Men, Cities and Transportation: A Study in New England History, 1820–1900.* 2 vols. Cambridge, Mass.: Harvard University Press, 1948. 1005 pp.

KIRKMAN, M. M. *Treatise on the Method of Paying Large Bodies of Men: How Railroad Employes Should Be Paid; A Paymasters' Manual.* Chicago, 1886. 78 pp.

SHAW, ROBERT B. *Down Brakes: A History of Railroad Accidents, Safety Precautions and Operating Practices in the U.S.A.* London: P. R. Macmillan, 1961. 487 pp.

WILKINSON, S. E., and W. A. SHEAHAN. *Rates of Pay and Regulations Governing Employees in Train and Yard Service on the Principal Railroads of the United States, Canada, and Mexico.* Galesburg, Ill.: Brotherhood of Railroad Trainmen, 1892. 192 pp.

WORSFELD, W. *A Special Danger near Switches on Railroad Tracks.* Lansing, [Mich.?], 1878. 6 pp.

1898–1926

ATTERBURY, W. W. *Railroad Rates and Railroad Wages.* Philadelphia: Pennsylvania Railroad System, 1921. 4 pp.

BROTHERHOOD OF LOCOMOTIVE FIREMEN AND ENGINEMEN. *General Wage and Rule Agreements, Decisions, Awards, and Orders Governing Employees Engaged in Engine Service on Railroads in the United States, 1907–1914.* Cleveland: The Brotherhood, 1941. 596 pp.

————. Research Department. *Some Railroad Statistics and How They Affect Railroad Employees.* n.p.: The Brotherhood, 1923. 11 pp.

BROTHERHOOD OF MAINTENANCE OF WAY EMPLOYES. *Rates of Pay of Railroad Maintenance of Way Employes as of December 1, 1925.* 5 vols. Detroit: The Brotherhood, 1925. 1306 pp.

BUREAU OF INFORMATION OF THE EASTERN RAILWAYS. *Wage and Service Data: Various Classes of Railroad Employees, Oct. 1915, Oct. 1917, March 1920, and Decision No. 147.* New York: The Bureau, 1922. 118 pp.

————. *Wages and Labor Relations in the Railroad Industry, 1900–1941.* New York: The Bureau, 1942. 358 pp.

BUREAU OF RAILWAY ECONOMICS. *Effect of Recent Wage Advances upon Railway Employees' Compensation during the Year Ending June 30, 1911; Variations in the Number of Railway Employees, 1909–1910–1911; Relation of the Number of Employees and Their Compensation to Traffic and Revenue, 1909–1910–1911.* Bulletin 28. Washington, D.C.: The Bureau, 1912. 47 pp.

————. *Railway Trainmen's Earnings, 1916.* Bulletin 107. Washington, D.C.: The Bureau, 1919. 18 pp.

DUNCAN, C. S. *Getting Railroad Facts Straight about Wages, about Maintenance, about Valuation: An Answer to Frank V. Warne, Witness for the Railroad Unions before the U.S. Senate Committee on Interstate Commerce.* New York: Association of Railway Executives, 1922. 51 pp.

26

INTERNATIONAL CONGRESS ON HYGIENE AND DEMOGRAPHY. "Organized Relief [for railroad employees]." In *Transactions*, vol. 5, pt. 1, 1912, pp. 145–49. Washington, D.C.: GPO, 1913.

————. "Prevention of Accidents, Examination, Education, and Care of Employees of Common Carriers." In *Transactions*, vol. 5, pt. 1, 1912, pp. 141–45. Washington, D.C.: GPO, 1913.

JONES, HARRY E. *Railroad Wages and Labor Relations, 1900–1952: An Historical Survey and Summary of Results.* New York: Bureau of Information of the Eastern Railways, 1953. 375 pp.

KERR, K. AUSTIN. *American Railroad Politics, 1914–1920: Rates, Wages, and Efficiency.* Pittsburgh: University of Pittsburgh Press, 1968. 250 pp.

KUNDIG, A. *Automatic Couplings and the Safety of Railway Workers: Report on Statistics of Accidents Due to Coupling and Uncoupling Operations.* Geneva: International Labour Office, 1924. 62 pp.

NATIONAL INDUSTRIAL CONFERENCE BOARD. *"Money" Earnings and "Real" Earnings, Class 1 Railroads, U.S.: Changes Relative to July 1914 as Base 100.* NICB Wall Chart Service No. 19. New York, 1922. 1 sheet.

————. *Railroad Wages and Working Rules.* New York: Century, 1922. 130 pp.

————. *Wages — Class 1 Railroads, U.S.* NICB Wall Chart Service No. 18. New York, 1922. 1 sheet.

————. *Wages, Hours, and Employment of Railroad Workers.* Research Report 70. New York, 1924. 80 pp.

RAILWAY ACCOUNTING OFFICERS ASSOCIATION. *Wage Statistics Inquiries: Memorandum of Unofficial Instructions Issued by the Bureau of Statistics, Interstate Commerce Commission, in Answer to Inquiries Regarding Report of Employees, Service and Compensation.* Washington, D.C.: The Association, 1921. 38 pp.

SHAW, ROBERT B. *Down Brakes: A History of Railroad Accidents, Safety Precautions, and Operating Practices in the U.S.A.* London: P. R. Macmillan, 1961. 487 pp.

WALBER, J. G. *Summary of Wage Orders Issued during Periods of Federal Control of Railroads.* New York: Bureau of Information of the Eastern Railways, 1921. 18 pp.

1926–46

ASSOCIATION OF AMERICAN RAILROADS. *The Six-Hour Day Proposed for Railroads: An Impossible Burden.* Washington, D.C.: The Association, 1937. 12 pp.

BACUS, HOWARD A. "The Railway Labor Problem in the U.S.: Public Regulation of Hours of Service of Railroad Employees." Ph.D. dissertation, American University, 1936.

BROTHERHOOD OF LOCOMOTIVE FIREMEN AND ENGINEMEN. General Grievance Committee. *The Pennsylvania Railroad: Schedule of Regulations and Rates of Pay for the Government of Engineers, Firemen, and Hostlers in Road and Yard Service.* n.p.: The Brotherhood, 1928. 1063 pp.

BROTHERHOOD OF RAILROAD TRAINMEN. *Shorter Workday: A Plea in the Public Interest.* n.p.: The Brotherhood, 1937. 55 pp.

BROTHERHOOD OF RAILWAY AND STEAMSHIP CLERKS, FREIGHT HANDLERS, EXPRESS AND

STATION EMPLOYES. *Railway Wages and the War: Facts on the Non-operating Railway Employees' Dispute.* n.p.: The Brotherhood, 1943. 34 pp.

BUREAU OF INFORMATION OF THE EASTERN RAILWAYS. *Railroads and Railroad Wages, 1938.* New York: The Bureau, 1938. 16 pp.

————. *Wages and Labor Relations in the Railroad Industry, 1900–1941.* New York: The Bureau, 1942. 358 pp.

CARRIERS' JOINT CONFERENCE COMMITTEE. *Railroads and Railroad Wages.* Washington, D.C., 1938. 16 pp.

CLEVELAND RAILWAY COMPANY. *The Accident-prone Employee: A Study of Electric Railway Operation Undertaken by the Cleveland Railway Company with the Cooperation of Policyholders Service Bureau, Metropolitan Life Insurance Company.* Cleveland, 1929. 28 pp.

COTTRELL, WILLIAM F. *The Railroader.* Stanford, Calif.: Stanford University Press, 1940. 145 pp.

EMPLOYEES' NATIONAL COMMITTEE. *Railway Wages and the War: Facts on the Non-operating Railway Employees' Dispute by Fifteen Cooperating Railway Labor Organizations.* Washington, D.C.: The Committee, 1944. 34 pp.

FOX, BERTRAND. "Railway Wage Statistics of the Interstate Commerce Commission: An Analysis and Interpretation." Ph.D. dissertation, Harvard University, 1934.

INTERNATIONAL LABOUR OFFICE. *Generalisation of the Reduction of Hours of Work. Fifth Item on the Agenda.* 4 vols. Geneva: International Labour Office, 1938.

JONES, HARRY E. *Railroad Wages and Labor Relations, 1900–1952: An Historical Survey and Summary of Results.* New York: Bureau of Information of the Eastern Railways, 1953. 375 pp.

MCDOUGALL, J. L. *Railway Wage-Rates, Employment, and Pay.* n.p.: Longmans, 1944. 34 pp.

MONROE, JOSEPH ELMER. *Railroad Men and Wages.* Washington, D.C.: Bureau of Railway Economics, Association of American Railroads, 1947. 155 pp.

SHAW, ROBERT B. *Down Brakes: A History of Railroad Accidents, Safety Precautions and Operating Practices in the U.S.A.* London: P.R. Macmillan, 1961. 487 pp.

STEWART, LOTYS BENNING. *The Railroad Industry.* Indianapolis: National Youth Administration for Indiana, 1940. 119 pp.

TRANSPORTATION ASSOCIATION OF AMERICA. *The Shipper Pays: The Proposed Six-Hour Day for Railroad Labor.* n.p., 1937. 15 pp.

WHITNEY, ALEXANDER F. *Report of A. F. Whitney, President, Brotherhood of Railroad Trainmen, on Railroad Rules-Wage Movement, U. S., 1944–45–46.* Cleveland: Brotherhood of Railroad Trainmen, 1946. 182 pp.

————. *Wartime Wages and Railroad Labor: A Report on the 1942–43 Wage Movement of the Transportation Brotherhoods.* Cleveland: Brotherhood of Railroad Trainmen, 1944. 228 pp.

1946–Present

BURGESS, E. H. *Railroad Wages, 1947.* Chicago: Eastern Railroad Press Conference, 1947. 50 pp.

COTTRELL, FRED. *Technological Change and Labor in the Railroad Industry: A Comparative Study.* Lexington, Mass.: Heath, 1970. 159 pp.

GIFFORD, ADAM. "The Impact of Unionism on Annual Earnings: A Case Study Involving Locomotive Engineers and Firemen, and Telephone Linesmen and Servicemen." Ph.D. dissertation, University of Washington at Seattle, 1955. 272 pp.

JONES, HARRY E. *Railroad Wages and Labor Relations, 1900–1952: An Historical Survey and Summary of Results.* New York: Bureau of Information of the Eastern Railways, 1953. 375 pp.

KROLICK, REUBEN HARRISON. "A Study of the Changing Economic Status of Skilled Occupations: Railroad Engineers and Airline Pilots." Ph.D. dissertation, Stanford University, 1966. 356 pp.

SHAW, ROBERT B. *Down Brakes: A History of Railroad Accidents, Safety Precautions and Operating Practices in the U.S.A.* London: P. R. Macmillan, 1961. 487 pp.

UNITED TRANSPORTATION UNION. *Basic Day and Seniority Rules as a Claim Basis for Schedule Violations.* PR Series No. 3. Cleveland: The Union, 1969. 180 pp.

WHITNEY, ALEXANDER F. *Report of A. F. Whitney, President, Brotherhood of Railroad Trainmen, on Railroad Rules-Wage Movement, U.S., 1944–45–46.* Cleveland: Brotherhood of Railroad Trainmen, 1946. 182 pp.

6. Unions and Workers

General

BROTHERHOOD OF LOCOMOTIVE FIREMEN AND ENGINEMEN. *An Historical Sketch of the Brotherhood.* Cleveland: The Brotherhood, 1937. 256 pp.

BROTHERHOOD OF MAINTENANCE OF WAY EMPLOYES. *Pictorial History, 1877–1951.* Detroit: The Brotherhood, 1952. 52 pp.

BROTHERHOOD OF RAILROAD SIGNALMEN. *Fifty Years of Railroad Signaling: A History of the Brotherhood of Railroad Signalmen of America.* Chicago: The Brotherhood, n.d. 32 pp.

COMMONS, JOHN R., DAVID J. SAPOSS, HELEN L. SUMNER, E. B. MITTELMAN, H. E. HOAGLAND, JOHN B. ANDREWS, and SELIG PERLMAN. *History of Labour in the United States.* 4 vols. New York: Macmillan, 1921–35.

DENTON, NIXSON. *History of the Brotherhood of Railway and Steamship Clerks, Freight Handlers, Express and Station Employees.* Cincinnati: George M. Harrison Biographical Committee, 1965. 299 pp.

DEWHURST, HENRY STEPHEN. *The Railroad Police, 1865–1955.* Springfield, Ill.: C. C. Thomas, 1955. 211 pp.

ESTES, GEORGE. *Railroad Employees United: A Story of Railroad Brotherhoods.* Portland, Ore., 1931. 79 pp.

HAMMOND, ROBERT EMANUEL. *Memories of a Retired Pullman Porter.* New York: Exposition, 1954. 191 pp.

HENIG, HARRY. *The Brotherhood of Railway Clerks.* New York: Columbia University Press, 1937. 300 pp.

BOOKS, PAMPHLETS, THESES

HERTEL, DENVER WILLARD. *History of the Brotherhood of Maintenance of Way Employes: Its Birth and Growth, 1887–1955.* Washington, D.C.: Randsdell, 1955. 308 pp.

KEATING, EDWARD. *The Story of "Labor," Thirty-three Years on Rail Workers' Fighting Front.* Washington, D.C., 1953. 305 pp.

MCCALEB, WALTER F. *Brotherhood of Railroad Trainmen: With Special Reference to the Life of Alexander F. Whitney.* New York: Boni & Liveright, 1936. 273 pp.

MCISAAC, ARCHIBALD M. *The Order of Railroad Telegraphers: A Study in Trade Unionism and Collective Bargaining.* Princeton, N.J.: Princeton University Press, 1933. 284 pp.

MARSHALL, F. RAY. "Railroad Workers and Longshoremen," chap. 4, pp. 50–70. *Labor in the South.* Cambridge, Mass.: Harvard University Press, 1967.

MARSHALL, ROSS S. *Working on the Railroad.* Cleveland: Gates Legal, 1956. 179 pp.

MIDDLETON, PHILIP HARVEY. *Railways and Organized Labor.* Chicago: Railway Business Association, 1941. 136 pp.

NOBLE, JOSEPH A. *From Cab to Caboose: Fifty Years of Railroading.* Oklahoma City: University of Oklahoma Press, 1964. 204 pp.

PAINTER, LEONARD. *Through Fifty Years with the Brotherhood Railway Carmen of America.* Kansas City, Mo.: Brotherhood Railway Carmen of America, 1941. 228 pp.

RICHARDSON, REED C. *The Locomotive Engineer, 1863–1963: A Century of Railway Labor Relations and Work Rules.* Ann Arbor: Bureau of Industrial Relations, University of Michigan, 1963. 456 pp.

WHITTEMORE, L. H. *The Man Who Ran the Subways: The Story of Mike Quill.* New York: Holt, Rinehart, 1968. 308 pp.

1850–98

AMERICAN ASSOCIATION OF RAILROAD CLERKS. *Souvenir of the Third Annual National Convention.* Philadelphia: Burk & McFetridge, 1892. 128 pp.

ARTHUR, P. M. "The Rise of Railroad Organization." In *The Labor Movement: The Problem of Today,* edited by G. E. McNeill, chap. 12. Boston, 1887. 115 pp.

ASHLEY, OSSIAN DOOLITTLE. *Railways and Their Employees.* Chicago: Railway Age and Northwestern Railroader, 1895. 213 pp.

BRADBURY, JAMES WARE. "Railroad Reminiscences." Paper read before the . . . Society, March 26, 1896. In *Collections and Proceedings of the Maine Historical Society,* vol. 7, pp. 379–90. Portland, 1896.

BROTHERHOOD OF LOCOMOTIVE FIREMEN AND ENGINEMEN. *An Historical Sketch of the Brotherhood.* Cleveland: The Brotherhood, 1937. 256 pp.

————. *Fiftieth Anniversary, Brotherhood of Locomotive Firemen and Enginemen, December 1, 1873–December 1, 1923.* Kansas City, Mo.: The Brotherhood, 1923.

BROTHERHOOD OF MAINTENANCE OF WAY EMPLOYES. *Pictorial History, 1877–1951.* Detroit: The Brotherhood, 1952. 52 pp.

BROTHERHOOD OF RAILROAD SIGNALMEN. *Fifty Years of Railroad Signaling: A History of the Brotherhood of Railroad Signalmen of America.* Chicago: The Brotherhood, n.d. 32 pp.

30

UNIONS AND WORKERS

BUCKNAM, WILTON F., ed. *A History of Boston Division, Number Sixty-one, Brotherhood of Locomotive Engineers.* Boston: A. T. Bliss, 1906. 201 pp.

COMMONS, JOHN R., DAVID J. SAPOSS, HELEN L. SUMNER, E. B. MITTELMAN, H. E. HOAG-LAND, JOHN B. ANDREWS, and SELIG PERLMAN. *History of Labour in the United States.* 4 vols. New York: Macmillan, 1921–35.

DEBS, EUGENE V. *Writings and Speeches of Eugene V. Debs.* New York: Hermitage, 1948. 486 pp.

DENTON, NIXSON. *History of the Brotherhood of Railway and Steamship Clerks, Freight Handlers, Express and Station Employees.* Cincinnati: George M. Harrison Biographical Committee, 1965. 299 pp.

DEPEW, C. M. *Address at the Grand Central Depot, January 4, 1887.* Delivered at the tenth anniversary of the Railroad Branch of the Young Men's Christian Association of New York City. New York, 1887. 8 pp.

————. *Address before the Twenty-seventh Annual Convention of the Brotherhood of Locomotive Engineers at Pittsburgh, October 16, 1890.* n.p., n.d. 12 pp.

DEWHURST, HENRY STEPHEN. *The Railroad Police, 1865–1955.* Springfield, Ill.: C. C. Thomas, 1955. 211 pp.

ESTES, GEORGE. *Railroad Employees United: A Story of Railroad Brotherhoods.* Portland, Ore., 1931. 79 pp.

FAGAN, JAMES OCTAVIUS. *The Autobiography of an Individualist.* Boston: Houghton Mifflin, 1912. 290 pp.

————. *Confessions of a Railroad Signalman.* Boston: Houghton Mifflin, 1908. 181 pp.

————. *Labor and the Railroads.* Boston: Houghton Mifflin, 1909. 164 pp.

FEICK, FRED. *The Life of Railway Men.* Chicago: H. O. Shepard, 1905. 184 pp.

FULTON, JUSTIN D. "The Brotherhood of Locomotive Engineers," chap. 8, pp. 83–109. *Sam Hobart.* New York: Funk & Wagnalls, 1883.

GEORGE, C. B. *Reminiscences of a Veteran Conductor: Forty Years on the Rail.* New York, 1888. 262 pp.

GINGER, RAY. *The Bending Cross: A Biography of Eugene V. Debs.* New Brunswick, N.J.: Rutgers University Press, 1949. 516 pp.

HALL, JOHN A. *The Great Strike on the "Q," with a History of the Organization and Growth of the Brotherhood of Locomotive Firemen, and Switchmen's Mutual Aid Association of North America.* Chicago: Elliott & Beezley, 1889. 124 pp.

HAMMOND, ROBERT EMANUEL. *Memories of a Retired Pullman Porter.* New York: Exposition, 1954. 191 pp.

HENIG, HARRY. *The Brotherhood of Railway Clerks.* New York: Columbia University Press, 1937. 300 pp.

HERTEL, DENVER WILLARD. *History of the Brotherhood of Maintenance of Way Employes: Its Birth and Growth, 1887–1955.* Washington, D.C.: Randsdell, 1955. 308 pp.

KEATING, EDWARD. *The Story of "Labor," Thirty-three Years on Rail Workers' Fighting Front.* Washington, D.C., 1953. 305 pp.

LATHROP, GILBERT A. *Little Engines and Big Men.* Caldwell, Idaho: Caxton, 1954. 326 pp.

LIGHTNER, DAVID LEE. "Labor on the Illinois Central Railroad, 1852–1900." Ph.D. dissertation, Cornell University, 1969. 419 pp.

McCaleb, Walter F. *Brotherhood of Railroad Trainmen: With Special Reference to the Life of Alexander F. Whitney.* New York: Boni & Liveright, 1936. 273 pp.

McIsaac, Archibald M. *The Order of Railroad Telegraphers: A Study in Trade Unionism and Collective Bargaining.* Princeton, N.J.: Princeton University Press, 1933. 284 pp.

Marot, Helen. "The Railroad Brotherhoods," chap. 3, pp. 29–47. *American Labor Unions.* New York: Henry Holt, 1914.

Marshall, F. Ray. "Railroad Workers and Longshoremen," chap. 4, pp. 50–70. *Labor in the South.* Cambridge, Mass.: Harvard University Press, 1967.

Marshall, Ross S. *Working on the Railroad.* Cleveland: Gates Legal, 1956. 179 pp.

Middleton, Philip Harvey. *Railways and Organized Labor.* Chicago: Railway Business Association, 1941. 136 pp.

Painter, Leonard. *Through Fifty Years with the Brotherhood Railway Carmen of America.* Kansas City, Mo.: Brotherhood Railway Carmen of America, 1941. 228 pp.

Perlman, Jacob. "A History of the Brotherhood of Locomotive Engineers up to 1903." Ph.D. dissertation, University of Wisconsin, 1926.

Reed, J. Harvey. *Forty Years a Locomotive Engineer: Thrilling Tales of the Rail.* Prescott, Wash.: Chas. H. O'Neil, 1912.

Reinhardt, Richard. *Workin' on the Railroad: Reminiscences from the Age of Steam.* Palo Alto, Calif.: American West, 1970. 318 pp.

Richardson, Reed C. *The Locomotive Engineer, 1863–1963: A Century of Railway Labor Relations and Work Rules.* Ann Arbor: Bureau of Industrial Relations, University of Michigan, 1963. 456 pp.

Robbins, Edwin C. *Railway Conductors: A Study in Organized Labor.* New York: Columbia University, 1914. 185 pp.

Southern Pacific Company's Employes' Library. *Constitution and By-Laws.* Tucson, Ariz., 1885. 10 pp.

Stevenson, George James. "The Brotherhood of Locomotive Engineers and Its Leaders, 1863–1920." Ph.D. dissertation, Vanderbilt University, 1954. 519 pp.

Tussey, Jean Y., ed. *Eugene V. Debs Speaks.* New York: Pathfinder, 1970. 320 pp.

Warman, Cy. *Snow on the Headlight: A Story of the Great Burlington Strike.* New York: D. Appleton, 1899. 248 pp.

Whittemore, L. H. *The Man Who Ran the Subways: The Story of Mike Quill.* New York: Holt, Rinehart, 1968. 308 pp.

Winkler, Fred Andrew. *Railroad Conductor.* Spokane, Wash.: Pacific Book, 1948. 201 pp.

1898–1926

Brazeal, Brailsford. *The Brotherhood of Sleeping Car Porters: Its Origin and Development.* New York: Harper, 1946. 258 pp.

Brotherhood of Locomotive Firemen and Enginemen. *Fiftieth Anniversary, Brotherhood of Locomotive Firemen and Enginemen, December 1, 1873–December 1, 1923.* Kansas City, Mo.: The Brotherhood, 1923.

—————. *An Historical Sketch of the Brotherhood.* Cleveland: The Brotherhood, 1937. 256 pp.

UNIONS AND WORKERS

BROTHERHOOD OF MAINTENANCE OF WAY EMPLOYES. *Pictorial History, 1877–1951.* Detroit: The Brotherhood, 1952. 52 pp.

BROTHERHOOD OF RAILROAD SIGNALMEN. *Fifty Years of Railroad Signaling: A History of the Brotherhood of Railroad Signalmen of America.* Chicago: The Brotherhood, n.d. 32 pp.

BUCKNAM, WILTON F., ed. *A History of Boston Division, Number Sixty-one, Brotherhood of Locomotive Engineers.* Boston: A. T. Bliss, 1906. 201 pp.

CARLSON, RUTH INGLOF. "The Railway Employees Department of the American Federation of Labor, 1908–1918." M.A. thesis, Cornell University, 1929. 82 pp.

COMMONS, JOHN R., DAVID J. SAPOSS, HELEN L. SUMNER, E. B. MITTELMAN, H. E. HOAGLAND, JOHN B. ANDREWS, and SELIG PERLMAN. *History of Labour in the United States.* 4 vols. New York: Macmillan, 1921–35.

DEBS, EUGENE V. *Writings and Speeches of Eugene V. Debs.* New York: Hermitage, 1948. 486 pp.

DENTON, NIXSON. *History of the Brotherhood of Railway and Steamship Clerks, Freight Handlers, Express and Station Employees.* Cincinnati: George M. Harrison Biographical Committee, 1965. 299 pp.

DEWHURST, HENRY STEPHEN. *The Railroad Police, 1865–1955.* Springfield, Ill.: C. C. Thomas, 1955. 211 pp.

DUFOUR, WILLIAM DAMIAN, JR. "The Early Black Labor Movement: The Case of the Brotherhood of Sleeping Car Porters." M.A. thesis, West Virginia University, 1972. 89 pp.

ESTES, GEORGE. *Railroad Employees United: A Story of Railroad Brotherhoods.* Portland, Ore., 1931. 79 pp.

FAGAN, JAMES OCTAVIUS. *The Autobiography of an Individualist.* Boston: Houghton Mifflin, 1912. 290 pp.

————. *Confessions of a Railroad Signalman.* Boston: Houghton Mifflin, 1908. 181 pp.

————. *Labor and the Railroads.* Boston: Houghton Mifflin, 1909. 164 pp.

FEICK, FRED. *The Life of Railway Men.* Chicago: H. O. Shepard, 1905. 184 pp.

GINGER, RAY. *The Bending Cross: A Biography of Eugene V. Debs.* New Brunswick, N.J.: Rutgers University Press, 1949. 516 pp.

HAMMOND, ROBERT EMANUEL. *Memories of a Retired Pullman Porter.* New York: Exposition, 1954. 191 pp.

HENIG, HARRY. *The Brotherhood of Railway Clerks.* New York: Columbia University Press, 1937. 300 pp.

HERTEL, DENVER WILLARD. *History of the Brotherhood of Maintenance of Way Employes: Its Birth and Growth, 1887–1955.* Washington, D.C.: Randsdell, 1955. 308 pp.

HOGAN, EDMOND K. *The Work of the Railway Carman.* Kansas City, Mo.: Brotherhood Railway Carmen of America, 1921. 201 pp.

KEATING, EDWARD. *The Story of "Labor," Thirty-three Years on Rail Workers' Fighting Front.* Washington, D.C., 1953. 305 pp.

KERLEY, JAMES WILLIAM. "The Failure of Railway Labor Leadership: A Chapter in Railroad Labor Relations, 1900–1932." Ph.D. dissertation, Columbia University, 1959. 268 pp.

BOOKS, PAMPHLETS, THESES

LATHROP, GILBERT A. *Little Engines and Big Men.* Caldwell, Idaho: Caxton, 1954. 326 pp.

MCCALEB, WALTER F. *Brotherhood of Railroad Trainmen: With Special Reference to the Life of Alexander F. Whitney.* New York: Boni & Liveright, 1936. 273 pp.

MCISAAC, ARCHIBALD M. *The Order of Railroad Telegraphers: A Study in Trade Unionism and Collective Bargaining.* Princeton, N.J.: Princeton University Press, 1933. 284 pp.

MAROT, HELEN. "The Railroad Brotherhoods," chap. 3, pp. 29–47. *American Labor Unions.* New York: Henry Holt, 1914.

MARSHALL, F. RAY. "Railroad Workers and Longshoremen," chap. 4, pp. 50–70. *Labor in the South.* Cambridge, Mass.: Harvard University Press, 1967.

MARSHALL, ROSS S. *Working on the Railroad.* Cleveland: Gates Legal, 1956. 179 pp.

MIDDLETON, PHILIP HARVEY. *Railways and Organized Labor.* Chicago: Railway Business Association, 1941. 136 pp.

MILES, JOHN EDWARD. *The Railroads, Their Employes and the Public: A Discourse upon the Rights, Duties and Obligations of Each toward the Other.* Plymouth, Mass.: Memorial, 1906. 199 pp.

MINTON, BRUCE B., and JOHN STUART. "A. Philip Randolph: Negro Labor's Champion," chap. 6, pp. 143–71. *Men Who Lead Labor.* New York: Modern Age Books, 1937. 270 pp.

NADWORNY, MILTON J. *Scientific Management and the Unions, 1900–1932: A Historical Analysis.* Cambridge, Mass.: Harvard University Press, 1955. 187 pp.

NOBLE, JOSEPH A. *From Cab to Caboose: Fifty Years of Railroading.* Oklahoma City: University of Oklahoma Press, 1964. 204 pp.

PAINTER, LEONARD. *Through Fifty Years with the Brotherhood Railway Carmen of America.* Kansas City, Mo.: Brotherhood Railway Carmen of America, 1941. 228 pp.

PERLMAN, JACOB. "A History of the Brotherhood of Locomotive Engineers Up to 1903." Ph.D. dissertation, University of Wisconsin, 1926.

Railway Employes Respected by President Roosevelt. n.p., [1904 ?]. 8 pp.

REED, J. HARVEY. *Forty Years a Locomotive Engineer: Thrilling Tales of the Rail.* Prescott, Wash.: Chas. H. O'Neil, 1912.

REINHARDT, RICHARD. *Workin' on the Railroad: Reminiscences from the Age of Steam.* Palo Alto, Calif.: American West, 1970. 318 pp.

RICHARDSON, REED C. *The Locomotive Engineer, 1863–1963: A Century of Labor Relations and Work Rules.* Ann Arbor: Bureau of Industrial Relations, University of Michigan, 1963. 456 pp.

ROBBINS, EDWIN C. *Railway Conductors: A Study in Organized Labor.* New York: Columbia University, 1914. 185 pp.

STEVENSON, GEORGE JAMES. "The Brotherhood of Locomotive Engineers and Its Leaders 1863–1920." Ph.D. dissertation, Vanderbilt University, 1954. 519 pp.

TROY, LEO. "Company Unions on the Railroads," chap. 2. pp. 31–67. "The Course of Company and Local Independent Unions." Ph.D. dissertation, University of Michigan, 1958.

TUSSEY, JEAN Y., ed. *Eugene V. Debs Speaks.* New York: Pathfinder, 1970. 320 pp.

WHITTEMORE, L. H. *The Man Who Ran the Subways: The Story of Mike Quill.* New York: Holt, Rinehart, 1968. 308 pp.

1926–46

BRAZEAL, BRAILSFORD. *The Brotherhood of Sleeping Car Porters: Its Origin and Development.* New York: Harper, 1946. 258 pp.

BROTHERHOOD OF LOCOMOTIVE FIREMEN AND ENGINEMEN. *An Historical Sketch of the Brotherhood.* Cleveland: The Brotherhood, 1937. 256 pp.

BROTHERHOOD OF MAINTENANCE OF WAY EMPLOYES. *Pictorial History, 1877–1951.* Detroit: The Brotherhood, 1952. 52 pp.

BROTHERHOOD OF RAILROAD SIGNALMEN. *Fifty Years of Railroad Signaling: A History of the Brotherhood of Railroad Signalmen of America.* Chicago: The Brotherhood, n.d. 32 pp.

CAYTON, HORACE R. *Black Workers and the New Unions.* Chapel Hill: University of North Carolina Press, 1939. 467 pp.

COMMONS, JOHN, DAVID J. SAPOSS, HELEN L. SUMNER, E. B. MITTELMAN, H. E. HOAGLAND, JOHN B. ANDREWS, and SELIG PERLMAN. *History of Labour in the United States.* 4 vols. New York: Macmillan, 1921–35.

COTTRELL, WILLIAM F. *The Railroader.* Stanford, Calif.: Stanford University Press, 1940. 145 pp.

DENTON, NIXSON. *History of the Brotherhood of Railway and Steamship Clerks, Freight Handlers, Express and Station Employees.* Cincinnati: George M. Harrison Biographical Committee, 1965. 299 pp.

DEWHURST, HENRY STEPHEN. *The Railroad Police, 1865–1955.* Springfield, Ill.: C. C. Thomas, 1955. 211 pp.

DUFOUR, WILLIAM DAMIAN, JR. "The Early Black Labor Movement: The Case of the Brotherhood of Sleeping Car Porters." M.A. thesis, West Virginia University, 1972. 89 pp.

ESTES, GEORGE. *Railroad Employees United: A Story of Railroad Brotherhoods.* Portland, Ore., 1931. 79 pp.

FOSTER, WILLIAM Z. *Railroad Workers Forward!* n.p.: Workers Library, 1937. 61 pp.

GALENSON, WALTER. "Railroad Unionism," chap. 18, pp. 566–82. *The CIO Challenge to the AFL.* Cambridge, Mass.: Harvard University Press, 1960.

HAMMOND, ROBERT EMANUEL. *Memories of a Retired Pullman Porter.* New York: Exposition, 1954. 191 pp.

HARRIS, HERBERT. "The Railroad Unions," pp. 225–66. *American Labor.* New Haven, Conn.: Yale University Press, 1938.

HENIG, HARRY. *The Brotherhood of Railway Clerks.* New York: Columbia University Press, 1937. 300 pp.

HERTEL, DENVER WILLARD. *History of the Brotherhood of Maintenance of Way Employes: Its Birth and Growth, 1887–1955.* Washington, D.C.: Randsdell, 1955. 308 pp.

KEATING, EDWARD. *The Story of "Labor," Thirty-three Years on Rail Workers' Fighting Front.* Washington, D.C., 1953. 305 pp.

KERLEY, JAMES WILLIAM. "The Failure of Railway Labor Leadership: A Chapter in Railroad Labor Relations, 1900–1932." Ph.D. dissertation, Columbia University, 1959. 268 pp.

KNOWLTON, THOMAS ANSON. "Railroad Labor Organizations and the Contraction of Job Opportunities." Ph.D. dissertation, University of Wisconsin, 1940. 233 pp.

McCALEB, WALTER F. *Brotherhood of Railroad Trainmen: With Special Reference to the Life of Alexander F. Whitney.* New York: Boni & Liveright, 1936. 273 pp.

McISAAC, ARCHIBALD M. *The Order of Railroad Telegraphers: A Study in Trade Unionism and Collective Bargaining.* Princeton, N.J.: Princeton University Press, 1933. 284 pp.

MARSHALL, F. RAY. "Railroad Workers and Longshoremen," chap. 4, pp. 50–70. *Labor in the South.* Cambridge, Mass.: Harvard University Press, 1967.

MARSHALL, ROSS S. *Working on the Railroad.* Cleveland: Gates Legal, 1956. 179 pp.

MIDDLETON, PHILIP HARVEY. *Railways and Organized Labor.* Chicago: Railway Business Association, 1941. 136 pp.

MINTON, BRUCE B., and JOHN STUART. A. Philip Randolph: Negro Labor's Champion," chap. 6, pp. 143–71. *Men Who Lead Labor.* New York: Modern Age Books, 1937. 270 pp.

NOBLE, JOSEPH A. *From Cab to Caboose: Fifty Years of Railroading.* Oklahoma City: University of Oklahoma Press, 1964. 204 pp.

PAINTER, LEONARD. *Through Fifty Years with the Brotherhood Railway Carmen of America.* Kansas City, Mo.: Brotherhood Railway Carmen of America, 1941. 228 pp.

RAILROAD BROTHERHOOD UNITY MOVEMENT. *Revolt in the Railroad Unions.* Chicago, 1935.

RICHARDSON, REED C. *The Locomotive Engineer, 1863–1963: A Century of Railway Labor Relations and Work Rules.* Ann Arbor: Bureau of Industrial Relations, University of Michigan, 1963. 456 pp.

TROY, LEO. "Company Unions on the Railroads," chap. 2, pp. 31–67. "The Course of Company and Local Independent Unions." Ph.D. dissertation, University of Michigan, 1958.

WHITTEMORE, L. H. *The Man Who Ran the Subways: The Story of Mike Quill.* New York: Holt, Rinehart, 1968. 308 pp.

1946–Present

AMERICAN FEDERATION OF LABOR. Railway Employes' Department. *Report to the American Federation of Labor.* n.p., 1955.

BROOKS, GEORGE W., and SARA GAMM. "The Causes and Effects of Union Mergers during the Sixties and Seventies." Forthcoming.
     Includes unions in the railroad, printing, paper, and steel industries.

BROTHERHOOD OF MAINTENANCE OF WAY EMPLOYES. *Pictorial History, 1877–1951.* Detroit: The Brotherhood, 1952. 52 pp.

COLLINS, DANIEL W., and GOULD P. COLMAN. *Joint Railway-Labor History Project: A Report to the Delegates of the First UTU Convention.* August 1971. Ithaca: Cornell University, 1971. 9 pp.

DENTON, NIXSON. *History of the Brotherhood of Railway and Steamship Clerks, Freight*

Handlers, Express and Station Employees. Cincinnati: George M. Harrison Biographical Committee, 1965. 299 pp.

DEWHURST, HENRY STEPHEN. *The Railroad Police, 1865–1955.* Springfield, Ill.: C. C. Thomas, 1955. 211 pp.

GIFFORD, ADAM. "The Impact of Unionism on Annual Earnings: A Case Study Involving Locomotive Engineers and Firemen, and Telephone Linesmen and Servicemen." Ph.D. dissertation, University of Washington at Seattle, 1955. 272 pp.

HAMMOND, ROBERT EMANUEL. *Memories of a Retired Pullman Porter.* New York: Exposition, 1954. 191 pp.

HERTEL, DENVER WILLARD. *History of the Brotherhood of Maintenance of Way Employes: Its Birth and Growth, 1887–1955.* Washington, D.C.: Randsdell, 1955. 308 pp.

INDUSTRIAL WORKERS OF THE WORLD. *A Union for All Railroad Workers; Join Railroad Workers Industrial Union No. 520 of the I.W.W.* Chicago, n.d. [1948?]. 32 pp.

KALISHER, SIMPSON. *Railroadmen: A Book of Photographs and Collected Stories.* New York: Clarke & Way, 1961. 83 pp.

KEATING, EDWARD. *The Story of "Labor," Thirty-three Years on Rail Workers' Fighting Front.* Washington, D.C., 1953. 305 pp.

LEIGHTY, GEORGE E. *Impact of Transportation Policy on Railroad Labor.* Ithaca, N.Y.: New York State School of Industrial and Labor Relations, Cornell University, 1960. 21 pp.

LIEB, ROBERT C. *Labor in the Transportation Industries.* Washington, D.C.: U.S. Department of Transportation, 1973. 136 pp.

MARSHALL, ROSS S. *Working on the Railroad.* Cleveland: Gates Legal, 1956. 179 pp.

NOBLE, JOSEPH A. *From Cab to Caboose: Fifty Years of Railroading.* Oklahoma City: University of Oklahoma Press, 1964. 204 pp.

RAILWAY LABOR EXECUTIVES' ASSOCIATION. *Labor and Transportation Labor in the Post-War Period: A Report Issued by the Railway Labor Executives' Association.* Washington, D.C.: The Association, 1946. 52 pp.

RICHARDSON, REED C. *The Locomotive Engineer, 1863–1963: A Century of Railway Labor Relations and Work Rules.* Ann Arbor: Bureau of Industrial Relations, University of Michigan, 1963. 456 pp.

SEIDMAN, JOEL. *The Brotherhood of Railroad Trainmen: The Internal Political Life of a National Union.* New York: Wiley, 1962. 207 pp.

SUMMA, JOSEPH. "The UTU Merger: Its History, Causes, and Effects." M.S. thesis, Cornell University, forthcoming.

UHL, ALEXANDER. *Trains and the Men Who Run Them.* Washington, D.C.: Public Affairs Institute, 1954.

WHITTEMORE, L. H. *The Man Who Ran the Subways: The Story of Mike Quill.* New York: Holt, Rinehart, 1968. 308 pp.

WILLIAMS, CLIFFORD GLYN. "Railroad Union Policies in the Postwar Period." Ph.D. dissertation, University of Virginia, 1962. 325 pp.

WOOD, NORMAN J. "Restriction of Output by the Railroad Unions." Ph.D. dissertation, Columbia University, 1954. 185 pp.

7. Labor Legislation

General

SIGMUND, ELWIN WILBER. "Federal Laws concerning Railroad Labor Disputes: A Legislative and Legal History, 1877–1934." Ph.D. dissertation, University of Illinois, 1961. 294 pp.

1850–98

EGGERT, GERALD G. *Railroad Labor Disputes: The Beginnings of Federal Strike Policy.* Ann Arbor: University of Michigan Press, 1967. 313 pp.

The Legal Rights of Capital, Labor and the Public. Chicago, 1893. 77 pp.

SIGMUND, ELWIN WILBER. "Federal Laws concerning Railroad Labor Disputes: A Legislative and Legal History, 1877–1934." Ph.D. dissertation, University of Illinois, 1961. 294 pp.

1898–1926

BUREAU OF RAILWAY ECONOMICS. *The Arguments for and against Train-Crew Legislation.* Bulletin 53. Washington, D.C.: The Bureau, 1913. 44 pp.

KIRBY, JOHN, JR. *Labor Provisions of the House and Senate Railroad Bills.* National Industrial Council Bulletin 35. Dayton, Ohio: National Industrial Council, 1919. 4 pp.

NATIONAL TRANSPORTATION CONFERENCE. *Program of Railroad Legislation.* Washington, D.C., 1919. 185 pp.

SHEPHERD, ALLEN LAVERNE. "Federal Railway Labor Policy, 1913–1926." Ph.D. dissertation, University of Nebraska, 1972. 355 pp.

SIGMUND, ELWIN WILBER. "Federal Laws concerning Railroad Labor Disputes: A Legislative and Legal History, 1877–1934." Ph.D. dissertation, University of Illinois, 1961. 294 pp.

SISSON, F. H. *Russianizing the Railroads: The Real Issue Raised in the Brotherhoods' Plan for Class Control of Transportation.* New York: Guaranty Trust, 1919. 15 pp.

WOLF, HARRY D. *The Railroad Labor Board.* Chicago: University of Chicago Press, 1927. 473 pp.

1926–46

BENNETT, JAMES W., JR. "The Railway Labor Act of 1926." Ph.D. dissertation, University of Florida at Gainesville, 1955.

BROTHERHOOD OF LOCOMOTIVE FIREMEN AND ENGINEMEN. *Federal Legislation, etc., Affecting Railroad Employees.* n.p., 1940. 247 pp.

————. *State Railroad Laws Relating to Full Crew Qualifications of Personnel Train Lengths.* Cleveland: The Brotherhood, 1939. 46 pp.

FOSTER, WILLIAM Z. *The Railroaders' Next Step.* Labor Herald Pamphlet No. 1. Chicago: Trade Union Educational League, 1921. 48 pp.

—————. *The Watson-Parker Law: The Latest Scheme to Hamstring Railroad Union-ism.* Chicago: Trade Union Educational League, 1927. 48 pp.

SIGMUND, ELWIN WILBER. "Federal Laws concerning Railroad Labor Disputes: A Legislative and Legal History, 1877–1934." Ph.D. dissertation, University of Illinois, 1961. 294 pp.

1946–Present

BACKMAN, JULES. *Economics of New York State Full-Crew Laws.* New York: New York State Association of Railroads, 1964. 52 pp.

REYNOLDS, ROY R. "Public Policy with Respect to the Settlement of Labor Disputes in the Canadian Railway Industry." Ph.D. dissertation, Massachusetts Institute of Technology, 1951. 354 pp.

UHL, ALEXANDER. *Trains and the Men Who Run Them.* Washington, D.C.: Public Affairs Institute, 1954.

8. Labor Relations

General

DISHMAN, ROBERT BURNS. "The President and Labor Disputes: A Case History of Executive Intervention in Railway Labor Relations, 1877–1946." Ph.D. dissertation, Princeton University, 1948. 411 pp.

JONES, HARRY EDWIN. *Railroad Wages and Labor Relations, 1900–1952: An Historical Survey and Summary of Results.* New York: Bureau of Information of the Eastern Railways, 1953. 375 pp.

LEVINSON, HAROLD M., *et al. Collective Bargaining and Technological Change in American Transportation.* Evanston, Ill.: Transportation Center, Northwestern University, 1971. 723 pp.
See especially Part 2, "Collective Bargaining and Technological Change on American Railroads," by Charles M. Rehmus, pp. 85–242.

RAILROAD WORKERS JOINT ACTION COMMITTEE. *Action and Reaction on the Railroad.* Hibbing, Minn.: n.d. 23 pp.

1850–98

ADAMS, B. B., JR. "The Treatment of Railroad Employees." *Compendium of Transportation Theories.* Washington, D.C., 1893.

ALLEN, RUTH A. *The Great Southwest Strike.* Austin: University of Texas Press, 1942. 174 pp.

ASHLEY, OSSIAN DOOLITTLE. *Railways and Their Employees.* Chicago: Railway Age and Northwestern Railroader, 1895. 213 pp.

ASHLEY, WILLIAM J. *The Railroad Strike of 1894.* Cambridge, Mass.: Church Social Union. 1895.

BANCROFT, EDGAR A. *The Chicago Strike of 1894.* Chicago: Gunthrop-Warren, 1895.

BARNARD, HARRY. *Eagle Forgotten: The Life of John Peter Altgeld.* Indianapolis: Bobbs-Merrill, 1938. 484 pp.

BOOKS, PAMPHLETS, THESES

BARNARD, WILLIAM THEODORE. *The Relations of Railway Managers and Employees*. Baltimore, 1886. 42 pp.

BOYLE, OHIO D. *History of Railroad Strikes: A History of the Railroad Revolt of 1877; the American Railroad Union Strike on the Great Northern in 1894 and Its Participation in the Pullman Car Strikes of the Same Year; the Eight-Hour-Day Strike of 1917 and the Runaway Switchmen's Strike of 1920*. Washington, D.C.: Brotherhood Publishing, 1935. 110 pp.

BRUCE, ROBERT V. *1877: Year of Violence*. Indianapolis: Bobbs-Merrill, 1959. 384 pp.

BUDER, STANLEY. *Pullman: An Experiment in Industrial Order and Community Planning, 1880–1930*. New York: Oxford University Press, 1967. 263 pp.

BURBANK, DAVID T. *City of Little Bread: The St. Louis General Strike of 1877, the History of an American Strike*. St. Louis: David T. Burbank, 1957. 7 microcards.

————. *Reign of the Rabble: The St. Louis General Strike of 1877*. New York: A.M. Kelley, 1966. 208 pp.

BURNS, WILLIAM F. *The Pullman Boycott*. St. Paul: McGill, 1894.

CARWARDINE, WILLIAM H. *The Pullman Strike*. Chicago: Charles Kerr, 1894.

CHICAGO CIVIC FEDERATION. *Congress on Industrial Conciliation and Arbitration*. Chicago, 1895. 96 pp.

CLEVELAND, GROVER. *The Government in the Chicago Strike of 1894*. Princeton, N.J.: Princeton University Press, 1913. 49 pp.

DACUS, JOSEPH A. *Annals of the Great Strikes*. 1877. Reprint. New York: Arno and the New York Times, 1969. 480 pp.
Introduction by Leon and Philip Taft.

DISHMAN, ROBERT BURNS. "The President and Labor Disputes: A Case History of Executive Intervention in Railway Labor Relations, 1877–1946." Ph.D. dissertation, Princeton University, 1948. 411 pp.

EGGERT, GERALD G. *Railroad Labor Disputes: The Beginnings of Federal Strike Policy*. Ann Arbor: University of Michigan Press, 1967. 313 pp.

GINGER, RAY. *Altgeld's America: The Lincoln Ideal versus Changing Realities*. New York: Funk & Wagnalls, 1958. 376 pp.

HALL, JOHN A. *The Great Strike on the "Q," with a History of the Organization and Growth of the Brotherhood of Locomotive Firemen, and Switchmen's Mutual Aid Association of North America*. Chicago: Elliott & Beezley, 1889. 124 pp.

HEADLEY, JOEL T. *Pen and Pencil Sketches of the Great Riots: An Illustrated History of the Railroad and Other Great American Riots*. New York: E. B. Treat, 1877. 560 pp.

HEYWOOD, EZRA H. *The Great Strike: Its Relation to Labor, Property and Government*. Princeton, Mass.: Cooperative Publishing, 1878.

ILLINOIS CENTRAL RAILROAD COMPANY. *Illinois Central System's Appreciation of Its Faithful Employees*. Chicago: Broadside, 1853.

————. *Rules Governing Employes. Issued in Accordance with the Recommendation of the American Railway Association*. Chicago: American Railway Association, 1891. 24 pp.

JONES, HARRY EDWIN. *Railroad Wages and Labor Relations, 1900–1952: An Historical Survey and Summary of Results*. New York: Bureau of Information of the Eastern Railways, 1953. 375 pp.

LEVINSON, HAROLD M., et al. *Collective Bargaining and Technological Change in American Transportation.* Evanston, Ill.: Transportation Center, Northwestern University, 1971. 723 pp.
See especially Part 2, "Collective Bargaining and Technological Change on American Railroads," by Charles M. Rehmus, pp. 85–242.

LINDSEY, ALMONT. *The Pullman Strike.* Chicago: University of Chicago Press, 1942. 385 pp.

LOGAN, SAMUEL C. *A City's Danger and Defense: Or, Issues and Results of the Strikes of 1877. Containing the Origin and History of the Scranton City Guard.* Philadelphia: J. B. Rodgers, 1887. 355 pp.

McCABE, JAMES DABNEY [Edward W. Martin, pseud.]. *The History of the Great Riots.* Philadelphia: National, 1877. 516 pp.

McMURRAY, DONALD L. *The Great Burlington Railroad Strike of 1888: A Case History in Labor Relations.* Cambridge, Mass.: Harvard University Press, 1956. 337 pp.

MANNING, THOMAS G. *The Chicago Strike of 1894: Industrial Labor in the Late Nineteenth Century.* New York: Holt, 1960.

MISSOURI PACIFIC RAILWAY. *Report of Transactions Relative to the Strike of the Knights of Labor, on the Missouri Pacific, in 1886.* New York, 1886. 52 pp.

PINKERTON, ALLEN. *Strikers, Communists, Tramps and Detectives: Railroad Strike of 1877.* New York: G. W. Carleton, 1900. 412 pp.

PORTER, H. H. *The Relations of Organized Labor to the Railroads, and the Relations of the Public to Organized Labor and the Railroads.* Chicago, 1893. 8 pp.

PULLMAN, GEORGE. *The Strike at Pullman.* Cambridge, Mass.: Church Social Union, 1895.

RAILROAD WORKERS JOINT ACTION COMMITTEE. *Action and Reaction on the Railroad.* Hibbing, Minn., n.d. 23 pp.

SALMONS, C. H. *The Burlington Strike: Its Motives and Methods.* Aurora, Ill.: Bunnell & Ward, 1889. 480 pp.

VOORHEES, T. *The Buffalo Strike.* New York, 1892. 11 pp.

WARD, ROBERT DAVID, and WILLIAM WARREN ROGERS. *Labor Revolt in Alabama: The Great Strike of 1894.* Southern Historical Publication No. 9. University: University of Alabama Press, 1965. 172 pp.

WARNE, COLSTON ESTEY, ed. *The Pullman Boycott of 1894: The Problem of Federal Intervention.* Boston: D. C. Heath, 1955. 112 pp.

YELLEN, SAMUEL. "The Railroad Uprisings of 1877," chap. 1, pp. 3–38; "Strike at Pullman," chap. 4, pp. 101–35. *American Labor Struggles.* New York: S. A. Russell, 1956.

1898–1926

ALABAMA AND VICKSBURG RAILWAY, et al. *Brief for the Brotherhood of Railway and Steamship Clerks, Freight Handlers, Express and Station Employes: Before the U.S. Railroad Labor Board. Alabama and Vicksburg Railway, et al., vs. Brotherhood of Railway and Steamship Clerks, et al., Docket No. 1300.* Chicago, 1922. 102 pp.

AMERICAN FEDERATION OF LABOR. Railway Employes' Department. *Before the U.S. Railroad Labor Board: Argument for a Wage Increase, Presented by B. M. Jewell, President, in Behalf of the Federated Shop Crafts.* Chicago: The Federation, 1922. 334 pp.

—————. Railway Employes' Department. *Before the U.S. Railroad Labor Board: Inadequacies of Railway Management, Presented by W. J. Lauck in Behalf of B. M. Jewell, President.* Chicago: The Federation, 1921.

—————. Railway Employes' Department. *Before the U.S. Railroad Labor Board: Industrial Relations on Railroads Prior to 1917, Presenting Evidence Relating to Certain Conditions Existing under Non-Contractual Relations in 1899 to 1900 and on the Pennsylvania Railroad in 1914–1915, Presented by W. J. Lauck in Behalf of B. M. Jewell, President.* Chicago: The Federation, 1921. 36 pp.

—————. Railway Employes' Department. *Before the U.S. Railroad Labor Board: Occupation Hazard of Railway Shopmen.* Chicago: The Federation, 1921. 14 pp.

—————. Railway Employes' Department. *Before the U.S. Railroad Labor Board: The Problem of Piecework, Prepared by the Bureau of Research in Behalf of B. M. Jewell, President.* Chicago: The Federation, 1921. 506 pp.

—————. Railway Employes' Department. *Before the U.S. Railroad Labor Board: Punitive Overtime, Presented by W. J. Lauck in Behalf of B. M. Jewell, President.* Chicago: The Federation, 1921. 11 pp.

—————. Railway Employes' Department. *Before the U.S. Railroad Labor Board: Railroad Boards of Labor Adjustment, Presented by W. J. Lauck in Behalf of B. M. Jewell, President.* Chicago: The Federation, 1921. 13 pp.

—————. Railway Employes' Department. *Before the U.S. Railroad Labor Board: The Sanction of the Eight-Hour Day, Presented by W. J. Lauck in Behalf of B. M. Jewell, President.* Chicago: The Federation, 1921. 36 pp.

—————. Railway Employes' Department. *Before the U.S. Railroad Labor Board: Specific Cases Cited by Mr. Whiter and Employees Rebuttal in Connection Therewith.* Chicago: The Federation, 1921. 140 pp.

—————. Railway Employes' Department. *Before the U.S. Railroad Labor Board: The Unity of the American Railway System, Presented by W. J. Lauck in Behalf of B. M. Jewell, President.* 1921. 32 pp.

—————. Railway Employes' Department. *Before the U.S. Railroad Labor Board: The Work of the Railway Carmen, Prepared in Behalf of B. M. Jewell, President.* Chicago: The Federation, 1921. 201 pp.

—————. Railway Employes' Department. *The Case of the Railway Shopmen: A Brief Statement of Facts concerning the Controversies Which Precipitated the Strike.* Washington, D.C.: The Department, 1922.

—————. Railway Employes' Department. *Presentation Made before the U.S. Railroad Labor Board, Chicago, Illinois, 1921, in Reply to the Objections of the Railroads as Presented by the Conference Committee of Managers of the Association of Railway Executives: National Agreement, Federated Shop Crafts.* Chicago: The Federation, 1921. 2319 pp.

ASSOCIATED RAILWAY EMPLOYEES ORGANIZATIONS. *These Two Recent Decisions of the U.S. Railroad Labor Board Are of Tremendous Importance to Every Citizen of America.* Chicago: The Organizations, 1921. 32 pp.

Decisions referred to are Order in Docket 404; Order relating to the petition of the Pennsylvania system requesting the Labor Board to vacate and set aside Decision 218; Decision 224, Docket 426.

LABOR RELATIONS

ASSOCIATION OF WESTERN RAILWAYS. Executive Committee. *Business Men Protest against Railway Strikes.* Chicago: The Association, 1916. 12 pp.

BERNHARDT, JOSHUA. *The Railroad Labor Board: Its History, Activities and Organization.* Baltimore: Johns Hopkins Press, 1923. 83 pp.

BOYLE, OHIO D. *History of Railroad Strikes: A History of the Railroad Revolt of 1877; the American Railroad Union Strike on the Great Northern in 1894 and Its Participation in the Pullman Car Strikes of the Same Year; the Eight-Hour-Day Strike of 1917 and the Runaway Switchmen's Strike of 1920.* Washington, D.C.: Brotherhood Publishing, 1935. 110 pp.

BRADLEY, WALTER F., comp. *An Industrial War: History of the Missouri and North Arkansas Railroad Strike. An Unprecedented Result of a Common Occurrence in American Industry and Its Aftermath.* Harrison, Ark.: Bradley & Russell, 1923. 144 pp.

BROTHERHOOD OF LOCOMOTIVE FIREMEN AND ENGINEMEN. *Eastern Concerted Wage Movement, 1912–1913. Supplemental Report.* Cleveland: The Brotherhood, 1913. 1283 pp.

————. *General Wage and Rule Agreements, Decisions, Awards, and Orders Governing Employees Engaged in Engine Service on Railroads in the United States, 1907–1914.* Cleveland: The Brotherhood, 1941. 596 pp.

————. Research Department. *Testimonials for the Eight-Hour Day: Exhibit U.S. Railroad Labor Board.* n.p., 1923. 266 pp.

BROTHERHOOD OF MAINTENANCE OF WAY EMPLOYES. *Rates of Pay of Railroad Maintenance of Way Employes as of December 1, 1925.* 5 vols. Detroit: The Brotherhood, 1925. 1306 pp.

BUDER, STANLEY. *Pullman: An Experiment in Industrial Order and Community Planning, 1880–1930.* New York: Oxford University Press, 1967. 263 pp.

BUREAU OF INFORMATION OF THE EASTERN RAILWAYS. *Wages and Labor Relations in the Railroad Industry, 1900–1941.* New York: The Bureau, 1942. 358 pp.

BUREAU OF INFORMATION OF THE SOUTHEASTERN RAILWAYS. *Index-digest of Decisions of United States Railroad Labor Board to May 1, 1922 (Decisions Numbers 1 to 949, Inclusive).* Washington, D.C.: Railway Accounting Officers Association, 1922. 327 pp.

DISHMAN, ROBERT BURNS. "The President and Labor Disputes: A Case History of Executive Intervention in Railway Labor Relations, 1877–1946." Ph.D. dissertation, Princeton University, 1948. 411 pp.

ESTABROOK, HENRY D. *Pending Controversy between Railways and Their Train Service Employees.* New York, 1916. 8 pp.

FISH, F. P. "Railroads and Railroad Labor." Address given at the annual dinner of the Railway Business Association. New York, 1922. 16 pp.

FISHER, THOMAS RUSSEL. *Industrial Disputes and Federal Legislation, with Special Reference to the Railroad, Coal, Steel and Automobile Industries in the U.S. since 1900.* New York: Columbia University Press, 1940. 370 pp.

GOODEN, ORVILLE THRASHER. *The Missouri and North Arkansas Railroad Strike.* New York: Columbia University Press, 1926. 274 pp.

ILLINOIS CENTRAL RAILROAD COMPANY. *The Concern of the Railroad Employes in the Existing Railroad Situation.* Chicago: Bureau of Railway Economics, 1910. 14 pp.

JONES, HARRY EDWIN. *Railroad Wages and Labor Relations, 1900–1952: An Historical*

Survey and Summary of Results. New York: Bureau of Information of the Eastern Railways, 1953. 375 pp.

KERLEY, JAMES WILLIAM. "The Failure of Railway Labor Leadership: A Chapter in Railroad Labor Relations, 1900–1932." Ph.D. dissertation, Columbia University, 1959. 268 pp.

LEVINSON, HAROLD M., *et al. Collective Bargaining and Technological Change in American Transportation.* Evanston, Ill.: Transportation Center, Northwestern University, 1971. 723 pp.
See especially Part 2, "Collective Bargaining and Technological Change on American Railroads," by Charles M. Rehmus, pp. 85–242.

LOGAN, ROBERT S. *The Railway Problem from the Viewpoint of Both Capital and Labor.* n.p., 1908. 11 pp.

MILES, JOHN EDWARD. *The Railroads, Their Employes and the Public: A Discourse upon the Rights, Duties and Obligations of Each toward the Other.* Plymouth, Mass.: Memorial, 1906. 199 pp.

NATIONAL CONFERENCE COMMITTEE OF THE RAILWAYS. *Minutes of Meetings Held between the National Conference Committee of the Railways and the Brotherhood of Locomotive Engineers.* New York: Master Reporting, 1916. 551 pp.

NATIONAL INDUSTRIAL CONFERENCE BOARD. *Railroad Wages and Working Rules.* New York: Century, 1922. 130 pp.

PENNSYLVANIA RAILROAD SYSTEM. *Speaking for 80,000: Addresses Made at the Conference between the Officers of the Pennsylvania Railroad and Representatives of the Employees.* West Philadelphia: Pennsylvania Railroad System, 1921. 26 pp.

PERSON, CARL E. *The Lizard's Trail: A Story from the Illinois Central and Harriman Lines Strike of 1911 to 1915 Inclusive.* Chicago: Lake, 1918. 462 pp.

PHILADELPHIA RAPID TRANSIT COMPANY. "A Plan for Collective Bargaining and Cooperative Welfare." In *Trade Unionism and Labor Problems,* edited by John R. Commons, chap. 21, pp. 270–87. 2nd series. New York: A. M. Kelley, 1967.

RAILROAD WORKERS JOINT ACTION COMMITTEE. *Action and Reaction on the Railroad.* Hibbing, Minn., n.d. 23 pp.

STOCKETT, JOSEPH NOBLE. *The Arbitral Determination of Railway Wages.* Boston: Houghton Mifflin, 1918. 198 pp.

TAFT, WILLIAM HOWARD. *Ex-President Taft on the Issues Involved in the Railroad Labor Controversy.* New York: Association of Railroad Executives, 1921. 1 p.

TOWNE, H. R. *Report of the Committee on Public Utilities and Law and Railroad Strikes: Their Menace and Their Lesson.* New York: N.Y. Merchants Association, 1916. 19 pp.

TROY, LEO. "Company Unions on the Railroads," chap. 2, pp. 31–67. "The Course of Company and Local Independent Unions." Ph.D. dissertation, University of Michigan, 1958.

WARD, FRANK B. *The United States Railroad Labor Board and Railway Labor Disputes.* Philadelphia: University of Pennsylvania Press, 1929. 93 pp.

WOLF, HARRY D. *The Railroad Labor Board.* Chicago: University of Chicago Press, 1927. 473 pp.

WOOD, LOUIS A. *Union-Management Cooperation on the Railroads.* New Haven, Conn.: Yale University Press, 1931. 326 pp.

1926–46

ADLER, PHILIP. "A Historical Study of Management-Labor Relations Pertaining to the Dieselization of Railroads in the U.S." Ph. D. dissertation, Ohio State University, 1966. 283 pp.

AGNEW, ROBERT J. "The Diesel-Electric Locomotive and Railway Employees." Ph.D. dissertation, Massachusetts Institute of Technology, 1953.

AMERICAN FEDERATION OF LABOR. Railway Employes' Department. *Presentation in Behalf of the Shop Craft Employes, Chesapeake and Ohio Railway Company before the Federal Arbitration Board.* Richmond, Va., 1928. 142 pp.

ASSOCIATION OF AMERICAN RAILROADS. *1938 National Railway Wage Reduction Controversy, Brief on Behalf of the Carriers: Before the Presidential Emergency Board Appointed under the Terms of Section 10 of the Railway Labor Act, October 17, 1938.* 167 pp.

BEYER, OTTO S., JR. "Experiences with Cooperation between Labor and Management in the Railroad Industry." In *Wertheim Lectures in Industrial Relations, 1928.* Cambridge, Mass.: Harvard University Press, 1929. 229 pp.

BROTHERHOOD OF LOCOMOTIVE FIREMEN AND ENGINEMEN. General Grievance Committee. *The Pennsylvania Railroad: Schedule of Regulations and Rates of Pay for the Government of Engineers, Firemen, and Hostlers in Road and Yard Service.* n.p.: The Brotherhood, 1928. 1063 pp.

BROTHERHOOD OF RAILROAD TRAINMEN. *Enemy Hours: The Waste of Manpower on American Railroads Occasioned by Managerial Mispractices in Utilization of Personnel.* Cleveland: The Brotherhood, 1945. 264 pp.

—————. *The Five Wrong Men: Why Railroad Labor Cannot Accept the Recommendations of the President's Emergency Board.* Cleveland: The Brotherhood, 1941. 210 pp.

—————. *Main Street Not Wall Street: A Reply to the Railroads' Demands for a Wage Reduction.* Cleveland: The Brotherhood, 1938. 482 pp.

BROTHERHOOD OF RAILWAY AND STEAMSHIP CLERKS, FREIGHT HANDLERS, EXPRESS AND STATION EMPLOYES. *Railway Wages and the War: Facts on the Non-Operating Railway Employees' Dispute.* n.p.: The Brotherhood, 1934. 34 pp.

BUREAU OF INFORMATION OF THE EASTERN RAILWAYS. *Wages and Labor Relations in the Railroad Industry, 1900–1941.* New York: The Bureau, 1942. 358 pp.

CARRIERS' JOINT CONFERENCE COMMITTEE. *Railroads and Railroad Wages.* Washington, D.C., 1938. 16 pp.

CHEN, CHI-TA. "The Awards of the National Railroad Adjustment Board." Ph.D. dissertation, University of Michigan, 1954. 317 pp.

DISHMAN, ROBERT BURNS. "The President and Labor Disputes: A Case History of Executive Intervention in Railway Labor Relations, 1877–1946." Ph.D. dissertation, Princeton University, 1948. 411 pp.

EMPLOYEES' NATIONAL COMMITTEE. *Railway Wages and the War: Facts on the Non-Operating Railway Employees' Dispute by Fifteen Cooperating Railway Labor Organizations.* Washington, D.C.: The Committee, 1944. 34 pp.

FEDERAL COUNCIL OF THE CHURCHES OF CHRIST IN AMERICA. Department of Research and Education. *The Enginemen's Strike on the Western Maryland Railroad.* New York: Davis, 1927. 130 pp.

BOOKS, PAMPHLETS, THESES

FISHER, THOMAS RUSSEL. *Industrial Disputes and Federal Legislation, with Special Reference to the Railroad, Coal, Steel and Automobile Industries in the U.S. since 1900.* New York: Columbia University Press, 1940. 370 pp.

JONES, HARRY EDWIN. *Inquiry of the Attorney General's Committee on Administrative Procedure Relating to the National Railroad Adjustment Board . . . Historical Background and Growth of Machinery Set Up for Handling of Railroad Labor Disputes.* New York: Eastern, 1941. 251 pp.

————. *Railroad Wages and Labor Relations, 1900–1952: An Historical Survey and Summary of Results.* New York: Bureau of Information of the Eastern Railways, 1953. 375 pp.

KAUFMAN, JACOB JOSEPH. *Collective Bargaining in the Railroad Industry.* New York: King's Crown, 1954. 235 pp.

KERLEY, JAMES WILLIAM. "The Failure of Railway Labor Leadership: A Chapter in Railroad Labor Relations, 1900–1932." Ph.D. dissertation, Columbia University, 1959. 268 pp.

LECHT, LEONARD A. *Experience under Railway Labor Legislation.* New York: Columbia University Press, 1955. 254 pp.

LEVINSON, HAROLD M., et al. *Collective Bargaining and Technological Change in American Transportation.* Evanston, Ill.: Transportation Center, Northwestern University, 1971. 723 pp.
See especially Part 2, "Collective Bargaining and Technological Change on American Railroads," by Charles M. Rehmus, pp. 85–242.

MILLER, S. L. "The Railways and Labor: What Price Peace?" Address before the Associated Traffic Clubs of America. Jacksonville, Fla.: Associated Traffic Clubs of America, 1941. 50 pp.

NATIONAL INDUSTRIAL CONFERENCE BOARD. *Individual and Collective Bargaining in Public Utilities and on Railroads.* New York: The Board, 1934. 16 pp.

PIERSON, FRANK C. "The National Railroad Adjustment Board," pp. 36–39. *Collective Bargaining Systems: A Study of Union-Employer Responsibilities and Problems.* Washington, D.C.: American Council on Public Affairs, 1942. 227 pp.

RAILROAD WORKERS JOINT ACTION COMMITTEE. *Action and Reaction on the Railroad.* Hibbing, Minn., n.d. 23 pp.

SHURMAN, BERNARD. "The History and Operation of Railway Emergency Boards [under the Railway Labor Act], 1926–1952." Ph.D. dissertation, Columbia University, 1958.

SPENCER, WILLIAM H. *The National Railroad Adjustment Board.* Chicago: University of Chicago Press, 1938. 65 pp.

TRANSPORTATION ASSOCIATION OF AMERICA. *Rail Labor and the Public Welfare.* n.p., 1941. 11 pp.

TROY, LEO. "Company Unions on the Railroads," chap. 2, pp. 31–67. "The Course of Company and Local Independent Unions." Ph.D. dissertation, University of Michigan, 1958.

WARD, FRANK B. *The United States Railroad Labor Board and Railway Labor Disputes.* Philadelphia: University of Pennsylvania Press, 1929. 93 pp.

WOLF, HARRY D. "Railroads," chap. 7, pp. 318–80. In Harry A. Millis, *How Collective Bargaining Works.* New York: Twentieth Century Fund, 1945. 986 pp.

46

Wood, Louis A. *Union-Management Cooperation on the Railroads.* New Haven, Conn.: Yale University Press, 1931. 326 pp.

1946–Present

Adler, Philip. "A Historical Study of Management-Labor Relations Pertaining to the Dieselization of Railroads in the U.S." Ph.D. dissertation, Ohio State University, 1966. 283 pp.

Agnew, Robert J. "The Diesel-Electric Locomotive and Railway Employees." Ph.D. dissertation, Massachusetts Institute of Technology, 1953.

Association of American Railroads. *Facts about Featherbedding in the Railway Industry.* Washington, D.C.: The Association, 1960. 43 pp.

————. Railroad Committee for the Study of Transportation, Subcommittee on Labor and Personnel. *Railroad Personnel Practices: A Report.* Washington, D.C.: The Association, 1946. 93 pp.

Backman, Jules. *Featherbedding, the Economics of Waste.* Richmond, Calif.: Lynmar, 1961. 7 pp.

Brooks, George W., and Sara Gamm. "The Causes and Effects of Union Mergers during the Sixties and Seventies." Forthcoming.
  Includes unions in the railroad, printing, paper, and steel industries.

Brotherhood of Railroad Trainmen. *Federal Laws, General Wage and Rule Agreements, Decisions, Awards and Orders Governing Employees Engaged in Train, Yard and Dining Car Service on Railroads in the U.S.* Cleveland: The Brotherhood, 1954. 909 pp.

————. *Negotiating Manual.* Cleveland: The Brotherhood, 1957. 288 pp.

————. *Personal Injury Suits and Seniority Rights.* Cleveland: The Brotherhood, 1959. 98 pp.

Chen, Chi-Ta. "The Awards of the National Railroad Adjustment Board." Ph.D. dissertation, University of Michigan, 1954. 317 pp.

Coates, Norman. "The Discontinuance of the Use of Firemen on Diesel Locomotives in Freight and Yard Service on the Canadian Pacific Railway Company." M.S. thesis, Cornell University, 1959. 191 pp.

Dishman, Robert Burns. "The President and Labor Disputes: A Case History of Executive Intervention in Railway Labor Relations, 1877–1946." Ph.D. dissertation, Princeton University, 1948. 411 pp.

Duriez, Philip. "The Effects of Make-Work Rules on Railroad Revenue." Ph.D. dissertation, Louisiana State University, 1962. 184 pp.

Horowitz, Morris A. *Manpower Utilization in the Railroad Industry: An Analysis of Working Rules and Practices.* Boston: Bureau of Business and Economic Research, Northeastern University, 1960. 68 pp.

Jones, Harry Edwin. *Railroad Wages and Labor Relations, 1900–1952: An Historical Survey and Summary of Results.* New York: Bureau of Information of the Eastern Railways, 1953. 375 pp.

Kaufman, Jacob Joseph. *Collective Bargaining in the Railroad Industry.* New York: King's Crown, 1954. 235 pp.

BOOKS, PAMPHLETS, THESES

KENNEDY, W. P. *Automation in the Railroad Industry: The Twentieth Century Challenge to Management and Labor.* Washington, D.C.: Public Affairs Institute, n.d. 29 pp.

LAZAR, JOSEPH. *Due Process on the Railroads: Disciplinary Grievance Procedures before the National Railroad Adjustment Board.* Los Angeles: Institute of Industrial Relations, University of California, 1958. 66 pp.

LECHT, LEONARD A. *Experience under Railway Labor Legislation.* New York: Columbia University Press, 1955. 254 pp.

LEIGHTY, GEORGE E. *The Truth about the Railroads, '59.* Washington, D.C.: Railway Labor Executives' Association, 1959. 23 pp.

LEVINSON, HAROLD M., et al. *Collective Bargaining and Technological Change in American Transportation.* Evanston, Ill.: Transportation Center, Northwestern University, 1971. 723 pp.
See especially Part 2, "Collective Bargaining and Technological Change on American Railroads," by Charles M. Rehmus, pp. 85–242.

LYON, A. E. *Railway Labor Relations.* Washington, D.C.: Railway Labor Executives' Association, 1948. 31 pp.

MATTESON, PORTER. *Whose Featherbed?* Rochester, N.Y.: Mohawk, 1966. 80 pp.

NORTHRUP, HERBERT R. "Industrial Relations on the Railroads." In *Labor in Postwar America,* edited by Colston Warne, chap. 20, pp. 449–60. Brooklyn: Remsen Press, 1949.

ORAM, JAMES W. *Anti-Productivity: Management's Dilemma.* Philadelphia: Public Relations Department, Pennsylvania Railroad, 1959.

RAILROAD WORKERS JOINT ACTION COMMITTEE. *Action and Reaction on the Railroad.* Hibbing, Minn., n.d. 23 pp.

RISHER, HOWARD WESLEY. "The Crisis in Railroad Collective Bargaining: A Study of the Institutional Impediments to Change in the Industrial Relations System." Ph.D. dissertation, University of Pennsylvania, 1972. 572 pp.

ROBB, DEAN A. *Rights of Railroad Workers.* Detroit: Advocates, 1968. 417 pp.

SHURMAN, BERNARD. "The History and Operation of Railway Emergency Boards [under the Railway Labor Act], 1926–1952." Ph.D. dissertation, Columbia University, 1958.

SIGMUND, ELWIN W. *Railroad Strikers in Court.* Springfield: Illinois State Historical Society, 1956. 19 pp.

UHL, ALEXANDER. *Trains and the Men Who Run Them.* Washington, D.C.: Public Affairs Institute, 1954.

UNITED TRANSPORTATION UNION. *Railroad Investigations and Discipline.* PR Series No. 1. Cleveland: The Union, 1969. 242 pp.

WOOD, NORMAN J. "Restriction of Output by the Railroad Unions." Ph.D. dissertation, Columbia University, 1954. 185 pp.

9. Retirement, Protective Programs

1850–98

BALTIMORE AND OHIO EMPLOYES' RELIEF ASSOCIATION. *First through Eighth Annual Reports.* 8 vols. Baltimore, 1881–88.

BALTIMORE AND OHIO RAILROAD. Relief Department. *Statement of Receipts and Disbursements for the Month of February, 1894.* Baltimore, 1894.

BARR, S. R. *Baltimore and Ohio Employes' Relief Association — Its Relations to its Members and to Other Insurance Organizations.* [Baltimore, 1888 ?]. 20 pp.

CENTRAL PACIFIC RAILROAD HOSPITAL. *Condensed History and Statement of the Workings of the Hospital.* Sacramento, Calif., 1880. 14 pp.

CENTRAL AND SOUTHERN PACIFIC RAILROAD EMPLOYEES' MUTUAL BENEFIT ASSOCIATION. *Proceedings of the Third Annual Meeting, May 7, 1883.* n.p., n.d.

HOME FOR THE AGED AND DISABLED RAILROAD EMPLOYES OF THE UNITED STATES AND CANADA. *Constitution and General Rules, in Effect on and after January 1, 1895.* Chicago, 1895. 16 pp.

KIRKMAN, MARSHALL M. *Mutual Guarantee Company; Which It Is Proposed to Organize by Railway Men for the Benefit of Railway Men.* Chicago, 1886. 28 pp.

1898–1926

KENT, OTIS BEALL. *A Digest of Decisions under the Federal Safety Appliance and Hours of Service Acts.* Washington, D.C.: GPO, 1915. 281 pp.

POLNER, WALTER. "Development of the Railroad Retirement System, 1900–1937." Ph.D. dissertation, University of Wisconsin, 1955. 105 pp.

1926–46

CLEVELAND RAILWAY COMPANY. *The Accident-prone Employee: A Study of Electric Railway Operation Undertaken by the Cleveland Railway Company with the Cooperation of Policyholders Service Bureau, Metropolitan Life Insurance Company.* Cleveland, 1929. 28 pp.

INDUSTRIAL RELATIONS COUNSELORS, INCORPORATED. *Pensions for Industrial and Business Employees.* Preliminary Report. 3 vols. New York, 1928–29. 156 pp.

POLNER, WALTER. "Development of the Railroad Retirement System, 1900–1937." Ph.D. dissertation, University of Wisconsin, 1955. 105 pp.

RESEARCH COUNCIL FOR ECONOMIC SECURITY. *Social Security for Railroad Workers: A Study of the Probable Effects of the New Railroad Retirement Act, an Estimate of the Future Cost and a Comparison with Foreign Experience.* Chicago, 1946. 8 pp.

ROBBINS, RAINARD BENTON. *Railroad Social Insurance: Favored Treatment versus Uniform Social Insurance.* New York: American Enterprise Association, 1945. 82 pp.

1946–Present

BROTHERHOOD OF RAILROAD TRAINMEN. *Personal Injury Suits and Seniority Rights.* Cleveland: The Brotherhood, 1959. 98 pp.

BOOKS, PAMPHLETS, THESES

HASTINGS, LAWRENCE V. *Rights of the Injured Railroad Worker under the F.E.L.A., Federal Employer's Liability Act.* Miami, Fla., 1972. 43 pp.

ROBB, DEAN A. *Rights of Railroad Workers.* Detroit: Advocates, 1968. 417 pp.

UNITED TRANSPORTATION UNION. *The Injured Man, His Rights and Wrongs.* PR Series No. 4. Cleveland: The Union, 1969. 344 pp.

PART IV

PERIODICAL LITERATURE

1. Railroads and Government

1850–98

MILLER, GEORGE H. "Origins of the Iowa Granger Law." *Mississippi Valley Historical Review* 40, no. 4 (March 1954): 657–80.

WRIGHT, CARROLL D. "Steps toward Government Control of Railroads." *Forum* 18, no. 6 (February 1895): 704–13.

1898–1926

AMSTER, NATHAN L. "A Plan for Railway Regulation." *Nation* 109, no. 2824 (August 16, 1919): 214–15.

BIKLE, HENRY WOLF. "Mr. Justice Brandeis and the Regulation of Railroads." *Harvard Law Review* 45, no. 1 (November 1931): 4–32.

CABOT, PHILIP. "A Practical Way Out of the Railroad Trouble." *World's Work* 41, no. 4 (February 1921): 410–16.

CLAGETT, BRICE. "Organization of American Railroads under Government Control." *Quarterly Journal of Economics* 33 (November 1918): 188–95.

CLARK, WALTER. "Government Ownership: The Inevitable, If Not the Immediate, Result of the Strike." *American Law Review* 56 (September–October 1922): 776–83.

"Commissioner Eastman in Favor of Government Management." *Nation* 109, no. 2824 (August 16, 1919): 208.

"Compulsory Extension of Railroads under the Transportation Act of 1920." *Harvard Law Review* 46, no. 8 (June 1933): 1301–7.

CUMMINS, ALBERT B. "The Railway Problem." *American Review of Reviews* 60, no. 1 (July 1919): 61–66.

————. "The Senate Committee Railroad Bill." *Proceedings of the Academy of Political Science* 8, no. 4 (January 1920): 518–39.

CUNNINGHAM, WILLIAM V. "The Railroads under Government Operation: I. The Period to the Close of 1918." *Quarterly Journal of Economics* 35 (February 1921): 288–340.

DAGGETT, C. E. "The Esch-Cummins Act." *American Law Review* 59 (September–October 1925): 678–706.

"Direct Action and the Plumb Plan, An Editorial to the Railroad Workers: Brotherhood Plan or What?" *New Republic* 20, no. 250 (August 20, 1919): 69–77.

DIXON, FRANK HAIGH. "Federal Operation of Railroads during the War." *Quarterly Journal of Economics* 33 (August 1919): 577–631.

PERIODICAL LITERATURE

————. "Mann-Elkins Act, Amending the Act to Regulate Commerce." *Quarterly Journal of Economics* 24 (August 1910): 593–633.

————. "The Railroad Situation: An Appraisal." *American Economic Review, Supplement* 11, no. 1 (March 1921): 5–18.

ELLIOTT, HOWARD. "A Live and Let Live Railroad Policy." *Forum* 61, no. 6 (June 1919): 690–700.

"Esch Railroad Bill Reported to the House." *Commercial and Financial Chronicle* 109, no. 2838 (November 15, 1919): 1855–59.

HINES, WALTER D. "The Director-General's Position." *Nation* 109, no. 2824 (August 16, 1919): 202–3.

HOWE, FREDERIC C. "Labor and the Democratic Control of Railroads." *Proceedings of the Academy of Political Science* 8, no. 4 (January 1920): 696–702.

HUNTINGTON, SAMUEL P. "The Marasmus of the I.C.C.: The Commission, the Railroads, and the Public Interest." *Yale Law Journal* 61, no. 4 (April 1952): 467–509.

JOHNSON, EMORY R. "A Federal Transportation Board: Its Powers and Duties." *Nation* 109, no. 2824 (August 16, 1919): 209–11.

————. "The Scope and Functions of a Federal Transportation Board." *Proceedings of the Academy of Political Science* 8, no. 4 (January 1920): 572–77.

KERR, K. AUSTIN. "Decision for Federal Control: Wilson, McAdoo, and the Railroads, 1917." *Journal of American History* 54, no. 3 (December 1967): 550–60.

"The Lovett Proposal: For and Against." *Nation* 109, no. 2824 (August 16, 1919): 213–14.

MILLER, GEORGE H. "Origins of the Iowa Granger Law." *Mississippi Valley Historical Review* 40 (March 1954): 657–80.

MORGAN, CHARLES P. "A Critique of 'The Marasmus of the I.C.C.: The Commission, the Railroads, and the Public Interest.'" *Yale Law Journal* 62, no. 2 (January 1953): 171–225.

MORRIS, RAY. "The New Railroad Law." *World's Work* 39, no. 6 (April 1920): 547–52.

NOXON, FRANK W. "Objects of Railway Legislation." *Proceedings of the Academy of Political Science* 8, no. 4 (January 1920): 566–71.

"Objections of Director-General Hines to Refunding and Other Features of Esch Railroad Bill" *Commercial and Financial Chronicle* 109, no. 2838 (November 15, 1919) :1861–62.

OLDS, LELAND. "Guild Socialism and the Railway Brotherhoods." *Intercollegiate Socialist* 7 (April 1919): 20–23.

PERLEY, ALLAN H. "Emergency Railroad Transportation Act of 1933." *American Bar Association Journal* 20, no. 7 (July 1934): 444–48.

PLUMB, GLENN E. "Plan of Organized Employes for Railroad Organization." *Public* 22, no. 1099 (April 26, 1919): 427–29.

————. "What the Plumb Plan Means." *Forum* 62 (September 1919): 358–69.

"The Plumb Plan to the Front." *Nation* 109, no. 2824 (August 16, 1919): 196.

POMERENE, ATLEE. "Our Recent Federal Railroad Legislation." *American Law Review* 55 (May–June 1921): 364–92.

"The Railroad Situation — Discussion." *American Economic Review, Supplement* 11, no. 1 (March 1921): 18–21.

"The Railroad Wage Question in the United States." *Labour Gazette* 19 (September 1919): 1069–71.

"Railway Executives on Federal Ownership." *Railway Review* 65, no. 7 (August 16, 1919): 240–42.

"The Railway Problem — Discussion." *American Economic Review, Supplement* 10, no. 1 (March 1920): 186–212.

RAPEER, LOUIS W. "The Railway Problem Boiled Down." *Nation* 109, no. 2824 (August 16, 1919): 203–4.

"Review of Railway Labor Problems: Addresses before the Academy of Political Science, New York, December 7, 1918." *Railway Review* 63, no. 24 (December 14, 1918): 836–39, 856–59.

RICH, EDGAR J. "The Transportation Act of 1920." *American Economic Review* 10 (September 1920): 507–27.

ROBERTSON, WILLIAM ALLMAND. "An Argument against Government Railroads in the United States." *Annals of the Academy of Political and Social Science* 29 (March 1907): 342–51.

RUGGLES, C. O. "Railway Service and Regulation." *Quarterly Journal of Economics* 33 (November 1918): 129–74.

SEAGER, HENRY R. "Railroad Labor and the Labor Problem." *Proceedings of the Academy of Political Science* 10, no. 1 (July 1922): 15–18.

SNOW, FRANKLIN. "After Eight Years [of the Transportation Act of 1920]." *North American Review* 225, no. 842 (April 1928): 452–60.

THOMAS, DAVID Y. "The Next Step in Railway Legislation." *Unpopular Review* 9, no. 17 (January 1918): 47–57.

VANMETRE, T. W. "The Railroad Predicament: How It Arose and How to Get Out of It." *Annals of the American Academy of Political and Social Science* 97, no. 186 (September 1921): 93–98.

————. "Railroad Regulation under the Transportation Act." *Proceedings of the Academy of Political Science* 40, no. 1 (July 1922): 3–12.

WARBURG, PAUL M. "The Re-establishment of Railroad Credit." *Nation* 109, no. 2824 (August 16, 1919): 205–7.

WARFIELD, S. DAVIES. "Railroad Necessities and the Transportation Act." *Proceedings of the Academy of Political Science* 10, no. 4 (January 1924): 751–57.

WARREN, BENTLEY W. "Wage Arbitration and Contracts." *AERA* [American Electric Railway Association] 5, no. 7 (February 1917): 767–75.

WATKINS, EDGAR. "Status of Existing Railroad Laws and Regulative Agencies under Federal Control." *Annals of the American Academy of Political and Social Science* 76, no. 165 (March 1918): 121–24.

"What a Digest of Several Railroad Settlement Plans Shows." *Literary Digest* 61, no. 2 (April 12, 1919): 144–47.

WILLARD, DANIEL. "Railroads on a Sound Basis." *World's Work* 42, no. 2 (June 1921): 135–41.

1926–46

DANIELS, WINTHROP MOORE. "The Railroad Employees' Interest in Rate Regulation." *American Federationist* 36 (March 1929): 343–46.

"Demands of Railway Labor Unions: Nationalization of the Rail Lines Sought by Four Brotherhoods — the Plumb Plan." *Current History Magazine of the New York Times* 10, part 2 (September 1919): 445–50.

"Emergency Railroad Transportation Act, 1933." *Monthly Labor Review* 37, no. 1 (July 1933): 91.

"Engineers on the Railroad Problem: Point Out the Glaring Misrepresentations Made by Supporters of the Plumb Plan." *Public Service* 27, no. 4 (October 1919): 92–94.

"Federal Agencies and Unions Defined." *Congressional Digest* 26, no. 3 (March 1947): 73–76.

FLETCHER, ROBERT V. "Restrictive Legislation, Rates, Wages and Taxation." *Proccedings of the Academy of Political Science* 17, no. 2 (January 1937): 189–201.

HARBESON, R. W. "The Emergency Railroad Transportation Act of 1933." *Journal of Political Economy* 42, no. 1 (February 1934): 106–26.

HULTGREN, THOR. "American Railroads in Wartime." *Political Science Quarterly* 57, no. 3 (September 1942): 321–37.

HUNTINGTON, SAMUEL P. "The Marasmus of the I.C.C.: The Commission, the Railroads, and the Public Interest." *Yale Law Journal* 61, no. 4 (April 1952): 467–509.

HUTCHINS, F. LINCOLN. "A Solution of the Railroad Problem." *Nation* 109, no. 2824 (August 16, 1919): 217–18.

JACOBS, NATHAN L. "The Interstate Commerce Commission and Interstate Railroad Reorganizations." *Harvard Law Review* 45, no. 5 (March 1932): 855–89.

LOCKLIN, D. P. "Railroad Legislation of 1933." *Journal of Land and Public Utility Economics* 10, no. 1 (February 1934): 13–21.

LOWENTHAL, MAX. "The Railroad Reorganization Act." *Harvard Law Review* 47, no. 1 (November 1933): 18–58.

MORGAN, CHARLES P. "A Critique of 'The Marasmus of the I.C.C.: The Commission, the Railroads, and the Public Interest.'" *Yale Law Journal* 62, no. 2 (January 1953): 171–225.

NEWCOMB, H. T. "Regimenting the Railroads." *American Mercury* 38, no. 151 (July 1936): 327–33.

PLUMB, GLENN E. "Labor's Solution of the Railroad Problem." *Nation* 109, no. 2824 (August 16, 1919): 200–201.

"Present Federal Agencies Dealing with the Railroads." *Congressional Digest* 18, nos. 8–9 (August–September 1939): 196–97.

SNOW, FRANKLIN. "After Eight Years [of the Transportation Act of 1920]." *North American Review* 225, no. 842 (April 1928): 452–60.

"State versus Federal Regulation of Railroads." *Monthly Labor Review* 24, no. 1 (January 1927): 130–31.

1946–Present

"Anti-trust Laws for Railroads: Reed-Bullwinkle Bill." *Forum* 108, no. 2 (August 1947): 91–103.

BENKERT, AMBROSE W. "Railroads and America's Future." *Vital Speeches of the Day* 15, no. 21 (August 15, 1949): 664–66.

BIAGGINI, B. F. "The Railroad Industry: Is Nationalization the Answer?" *Vital Speeches of the Day* 37, no. 7 (January 15, 1971): 212–16.

BROWN, GUY L. "A Challenge for the 1960's." *Vital Speeches of the Day* 26, no. 16 (June 1, 1960): 500–504.

BUFORD, CURTIS D. "Railroads Have Quit Slumbering." *Annals of the American Academy of Political and Social Science* 345 (January 1963): 58–65.

DEWEY, RALPH L. "The Maintenance of Railroad Credit." *American Economic Review* 36, no. 2 (May 1946): 451–65.

FRIEDLAENDER, ANN F. "The Social Costs of Regulating Railroads." *American Economic Review* 61, no. 2 (May 1971): 226–34.

GOODFELLOW, THOMAS M. "Countdown for America's Railroads, ASTRO Recommendations." *Vital Speeches of the Day* 37, no. 2 (November 1, 1970): 56–58.

HAND, C. H., and G. C. CUMMINGS. "The Railroad Modification Law." *Columbia Law Review* 48, no. 7 (July 1948): 689–712.

HUNTINGTON, SAMUEL P. "The Marasmus of the I.C.C.: The Commission, the Railroads, and the Public Interest." *Yale Law Journal* 61, no. 4 (April 1952): 467–509.

LOCKLIN, D. PHILIP. "Reorganization of the Railroad Rate Structure." *American Economic Review* 36, no. 2 (May 1946): 466–78.

MORGAN, CHARLES P. "A Critique of the 'Marasmus of the I.C.C.: The Commission, the Railroads, and the Public Interest.'" *Yale Law Journal* 62, no. 2 (January 1953): 171–225.

REED, JOHN S. "Is Anyone Listening?" *Vital Speeches of the Day* 37, no. 18 (July 1, 1971): 569–72.

ROBERTS, MERRILL J. "Transport Regulation and the Railroad Problem." *Southern Economic Journal* 23, no. 3 (January 1957): 256–71.

SMITH, ELMER A. "The Interstate Commerce Commission, the Department of Justice, and the Supreme Court." *American Economic Review* 36, no. 2 (May 1946): 479–93.

STEVENS, W. H. S., et al. "Postwar Railroad Problems — Discussion." *American Economic Review* 36, no. 2 (May 1946): 494–519.

SYMES, JAMES M. "A Tide in the Affairs of Railroads." *Vital Speeches of the Day* 25, no.3 (November 15, 1958): 87–90.

THOMPSON, EDWARD T. "What Hope for the Railroads?" *Fortune* 57, no. 2 (February 1958): 136–39, 146, 148.

WILLIAMS, ERNEST W., JR. "An Evaluation of Public Policy toward the Railway Industry." *American Economic Review* 41, no. 2 (May 1951): 506–18.

WRIGHT, V. HANDLY. "A Tale of Two Crises." *Vital Speeches of the Day* 30, no. 4 (December 1, 1963): 122–25.

2. Management

1850-98

DEPEW, CHAUNCEY M. "Railway Men in Politics." *North American Review* 151, no. 404 (July 1890): 86–89.

McMURRAY, DONALD L. "Labor Policies of the General Managers' Association of Chicago, 1886–1894." *Journal of Economic History* 13, no. 2 (Spring 1953): 160–78.

STOREY, BRIT ALLAN. "William Jackson Palmer: The Technique of a Pioneer Railroad Promoter in Colorado, 1871–1880." *Journal of the West* 5 (April 1966): 263–74.

1898-1926

BALDWIN, WILLIAM H., JR. "The Interest of Labor in the Economies of Railroad Consolidation." *Supplement to the Annals of the American Academy of Political and Social Science* 15 (May 1900): 137–49.

BASFORD, GEORGE M. "American Railroad Operation." *Engineering Magazine* 31, no. 5 (August 1906): 745–48.

BESLER, W. G. "Relations of Railroads and Their Employees." *Proceedings of the Academy of Political Science* 8, no. 9 (January 1920): 677–89.

COUNTY, A. J. "Consolidation of Railroads into Systems." *American Economic Review, Supplement* 14, no. 1 (March 1924): 73–87.

DEWING, ARTHUR S. "The Theory of Railroad Reorganization." *American Economic Review* 8 (December 1918): 774–95.

FLINT, CHARLES R. "Industrial Consolidations: What They Have Accomplished for Capital and Labor." *North American Review* 172, no. 534 (May 1901): 664–77.

HANEY, LEWIS H. "Advantages and Disadvantages of Railway Consolidation." *American Economic Review, Supplement* 14, no. 1 (March 1924): 88–99.

HEISERMAN, C. B. "Labor Policies of the Transportation Act from the Point of View of Railway Management." *Proceedings of the Academy of Political Science* 10, no. 1 (July 1922): 29–38.

HOOPER, WILLIAM E. "Plans for Railroad Consolidations." *American Monthly Review of Reviews* 67, no. 5 (May 1923): 529–35.

PAINE, GEORGE HEBARD. "Railway Discipline." *Munsey's Magazine* 23, no. 3 (June 1900): 396–400.

"Railroad Consolidation — Discussion." *American Economic Review, Supplement* 14, no. 1 (March 1924): 100–108.

STROTHER, FRENCH. "A New Day for the Railroads." *World's Work* 40, no. 2 (June 1920): 194–201.

TRUMBULL, FRANK. "The Adamson Law: The Employers' Viewpoint." *Proceedings of the Academy of Political Science* 7, no. 1 (January 1917): 179–84.

1926–46

DOAK, W. N. "Consolidation from the Railroad Employees' Viewpoint." *Proceedings of the Academy of Political Science* 13, no. 3 (June 1929): 406–15.

FITZGIBBON, THOMAS O'GORMAN. "The Present Status of the Six Months' Rule." *Columbia Law Review* 34, no. 2 (February 1934): 230–54.

HARRIMAN, W. A. "Transportation and the Railroads, Progressive Management." *Vital Speeches of the Day* 3, no. 4 (December 1, 1936): 118–21.

PELLEY, JOHN J. "American Railroads in and after the War." *Annals of the American Academy of Political and Social Science* 230 (November 1943): 22–28.

"Present Federal Agencies Dealing with the Railroads." *Congressional Digest* 18, nos. 8–9 (August–September 1939): 196–97.

"Salaries of Railway Officials Revealed." *Commercial and Financial Chronicle* 135, no. 3499 (July 16, 1932): 355–57.

"United States Board of Mediation." *Congressional Digest* 20, no. 4 (April 1941): 103.

WILLIAMSON, FREDERICH E. "Railroad Problems of 1935." *Vital Speeches of the Day* 1, no. 9 (January 28, 1935): 275–77.

1946–Present

BENKERT, AMBROSE W. "Railroads and America's Future." *Vital Speeches of the Day* 15, no. 21 (August 15, 1949): 664–66.

"A Clear Track for the Rails." *Dun's Review and Modern Industry, Special Supplement II* 85 (June 1965): 98–101, 239–48.

FLETCHER, ROBERT V. "Our Railroads: A Balance Sheet." *Atlantic Monthly* 179, no. 3 (March 1947): 73–78.

"People Are Management!" *Railway Age* 135, no. 18 (May 3, 1954): 34–37.

"Renaissance on the Rails." *Dun's Review and Modern Industry* 79, no. 6 (June 1962): 48–71.

THOMPSON, EDWARD T. "What Hope for the Railroads?" *Fortune* 57, no. 2 (February 1958): 136–39, 146–48.

"What Kind of Diesel Shops?" *Railway Age* 136, no. 25 (June 21, 1954): 33–35.

"What's Good Diesel Maintenance?" *Railway Age* 137, no. 4 (July 26, 1954): 32–35.

3. Labor Force

1850–98

LIGHTNER, DAVID. "Construction Labor on the Illinois Central Railroad." *Illinois State Historical Society Journal* 66 (1973): 285–301.

1898–1926

"Annual Report of Women's Service Section, United States Railroad Administration." *Monthly Labor Review* 10, no. 3 (March 1920): 750–52.

PERIODICAL LITERATURE

BASFORD, GEORGE M. "The Education of Railroad Employees, Methods of Providing Technically Trained Men for Responsible Positions in Railroad Service." *Engineering Magazine* 29, no. 5 (August 1905): 749–51.

"A Brotherhood Interpretation of the Adamson Act." *Railway Review* 59, no. 17 (October 21, 1916): 543–46.

CLARKE, VICTOR S. "Occupations in Which Mexicans Are Employed — Railway Laborers." *Bulletin of the Bureau of Labor* 17, no. 78 (September 1907): 477–82.

"Condition of Railroad Employment Defined by Director General of Railroads." *Monthly Review of the U.S. Bureau of Labor Statistics* 6, no. 4 (April 1918): 837–38.

CROSS, C. W. "The Apprentice System on the New York Central Lines." *Annals of the American Academy of Political and Social Science* 33, no. 1 (January 1909): 163–74.

"Employment and Earnings of Railroad Employees, July 1921 to August 1922." *Monthly Labor Review* 15, no. 6 (December 1922): 1301–5.

"The Expert Train Dispatcher." *Scientific American Supplement* 56, no. 1442 (August 22, 1903): 23102–3.

FAGAN, JAMES O. "Labor and the Railroads." *Atlantic Monthly* 103, no. 2 (February 1909): 145–53.

————. "Railroads and Education." *Atlantic Monthly* 103, no. 3 (March 1909): 326–35.

————. "The Railroads and Efficiency of Service." *Atlantic Monthly* 103, no. 4 (April 1909): 543–52.

GOLDMARK, PAULINE. "Women in the Railroad Service." *Proceedings of the Academy of Political Science* 8, no. 2 (February 1919): 151–56.

————. "Women in the Railroad World." *Annals of the American Academy of Political and Social Science* 86, no. 197 (November 1919): 214–21.

HARRIS, HENRY J. "The Occupation Hazard of Locomotive Firemen." *Quarterly Publications of the American Statistical Association* 14, no. 107 (September 1914): 177–202.

HINE, CHARLES DeLANO. "What a Train-Dispatcher Does." *Century Magazine* 62, no. 4 (August 1901): 594–603.

HUNGERFORD, EDWARD. "The Fellows Out upon the Line." *Outing Magazine* 54, no. 3 (June 1909): 267–77.

LINDSAY, SAMUEL McCUNE. "Railway Employees in the United States." *Bulletin of the Department of Labor* 6, no. 37 (November 1901): 1023–114.

NORRIS, H. H. "What One Railway Is Doing along Educational Lines." *AERA* [American Electric Railway Association] 14, no. 6 (January 1926): 1061–68.

"Practical Air-Brake Instruction for Railroad Men." *Scientific American Supplement* 55, no. 1426 (May 2, 1903): 22853–54.

"Railroad Employment of Reservists." *United Service* 19, no. 849 (August 1899): 528–33.

"Railroad Labor Accomplishment, 1922 and 1923." *Monthly Labor Review* 20, no. 3 (March 1925): 550–53.

"Review of Railway Labor Problems: Addresses before the Academy of Political Science, New York, Dec. 7, 1918." *Railway Review* 63, no. 24 (December 14, 1918): 836–39, 856–59.

WARREN, FREDERIC BLOUNT. "A Railroad University: Altoona and ITS Methods." *Engineering Magazine* 33, no. 2 (May 1907): 170–83.

"Women in Railroad Work in the United States." *Monthly Labor Review* 9, no. 3 (September 1919): 867–69.

"Work of Women's Service Section, United States Railroad Administration." *Monthly Labor Review* 8, no. 3 (March 1919): 825–28.

1926–46

ASHTON, HERBERT. "Some Consideration in the Measurement of Productivity of Railroad Workers." *Journal of Political Economy* 46, no. 5 (October 1938): 714–20.

BEYER, OTTO S., JR. "How as Well as What." *American Federationist* 33, (August 1926): 938–46.

————. "Unemployment Compensation in the Transportation Industry." *Annals of the American Academy of Political and Social Science* 187 (September 1935): 94–105.

BOWDEN, WITT. "Productivity, Hours, and Compensation of Railroad Labor: Part I, All Employees." *Monthly Labor Review* 37, no. 6 (December 1933): 1275–89.

————. "Productivity, Hours, and Compensation: Part II, Classes Other Than Transportation Employees." *Monthly Labor Review* 38, no. 1 (January 1934): 43–65.

————. "Productivity, Hours, and Compensation of Railroad Labor: Part III, Transportation Employees." *Monthly Labor Review* 38, no. 2 (February 1934): 269–88.

CAMPBELL, C. D. "The Business Cycle and Accidents to Railroad Employees in the United States." *Journal of the American Statistical Association* 26, no. 175 (September 1931): 295–302.

COTTRELL, W. F. "Of Time and the Railroader." *American Sociological Review* 4, no. 2 (April 1939): 190–98.

"Decrease in Railroad Employment." *Monthly Labor Review* 32, no. 1 (January 1931): 54–60.

DEEMS, M. "Full Speed Ahead!" *Independent Woman* 21, no. 12 (December 1942): 360–62, 381.

DOAK, W. N. "Consolidation from the Railroad Employees' Viewpoint." *Proceedings of the Academy of Political Science* 13, no. 3 (June 1929): 406–15.

DUNLAP, WALTER H. "Productivity of Railroad Labor." *Monthly Labor Review* 24, no. 3 (March 1927): 471–78.

————. "Stability of Railroad Employment." *Monthly Labor Review* 27, no. 2 (August 1928): 227–36.

"Employees' Service and Compensation for 1941." *Monthly Review of the Railroad Retirement Board* 4, no. 1 (January 1943): 4–8.

GOSHEN, EDWARD E. "Apprenticeship Training Revitalized." *Railway Age* 124, no. 14 (April 3, 1948): 664–66, 716–17.

HARRISON, GEORGE M. "Unemployment Reserves for the Transportation Industry." *American Federationist* 40 (March 1933): 246–51.

HUBER, CLYDE M. "Displacement of Labor by Installation of Automatic Grade-Crossing Devices." *Monthly Labor Review* 34, no. 4 (April 1932): 759–69.

"Increased Operating Efficiency of Railroads." *Monthly Labor Review* 28, no. 2 (February 1928): 235–36.

PERIODICAL LITERATURE

JOHNSON, CHARLES S. "Negroes in the Railway Industry — Part I." *Phylon* 3, no. 1 (First Quarter 1942): 5–14.

————. "Negroes in the Railway Industry — Part II: Mechanization." *Phylon* 3, no. 2 (Second Quarter 1942): 196–205.

"Manpower Problems of the Railroad Industry." *Monthly Review of the Railroad Retirement Board* 5, no. 4 (May 1944): 58–61, 68.

MARSHAK, IRA. "Service, Compensation, and Age of Railroad Employees, 1941." *Social Security Bulletin* 6, no. 3 (March 1943): 36–42.

MATER, DAN H. "The Development and Operation of the Railroad Seniority System." *Journal of Business of the University of Chicago* 13, no. 4 (October 1940): 387–419.

————. "The Development and Operations of the Railroad Seniority System." *Journal of Business of the University of Chicago* 14, no. 1 (January 1941): 36–67.

————. "Effects of Seniority upon the Welfare of the Employee, the Employer and Society." *Journal of Business of the University of Chicago* 14, no. 4 (October 1941): 384–418.

MIDDLETON, KENNETH A. "Wartime Labor Productivity in Railroad Transportation." *Monthly Labor Review* 57, no. 3 (September 1943): 444–51.

"New Entrants to the Railroad Industry, 1941." *Monthly Review of the Railroad Retirement Board* 4, no. 4 (September 1943): 184–90.

"Occupational Status of Negro Railroad Employees." *Monthly Labor Review* 56, no. 3 (March 1943): 484–85.

"Operations under Railroad Unemployment Insurance Act, 1939." *Monthly Labor Review* 50, no. 3 (March 1940): 640–42.

"Program for Stabilization of Railroad Shop Employment." *Monthly Labor Review* 31, no. 2 (August 1930): 292–94.

"Railroad Unemployment Insurance and Employment Service, 1943–44." *Social Security Bulletin* 7, no. 8 (August 1944): 31–32.

RANDOLPH, A. PHILIP. "The Crisis of Negro Railroad Workers." *American Federationist* 46 (August 1939): 807–21.

"Recent Developments in Railroad Employment." *Monthly Review of the Railroad Retirement Board* 4, no. 6 (June 1943): 111–15.

"Recruiting and Placing Railroad Workers." *Monthly Review of the Railroad Retirement Board* 4, no. 2 (February 1943): 30–34.

"Recruitment of Mexican Workers for Railroad Jobs." *Monthly Review of the Railroad Retirement Board* 5, no. 4 (May 1944): 63–68.

"Report of Special Committee of Association of Railway Executives on Desirability of Stability of Employment on Railroads — Adequate Rate of Return Essential Factor." *Commercial and Financial Chronicle* 125, no. 3237 (July 9, 1927): 199–200.

"Rules for Admission of Mexican Workers as Railroad Track Laborers." *Monthly Labor Review* 57, no. 2 (August 1943): 240–41.

STEVENS, MARGARET TALBOT. "Now They Are Working on the Railroads." *Independent Woman* 14, no. 11 (November 1935): 368–69, 385–86.

————. "Women and the Railroad." *American Federationist* 36 (April 1929): 479–82.

STEWART, ETHELBERT. "Displacement of Railroad Labor." *American Federationist* 36 (April 1929): 464–70.

U.S. BUREAU OF LABOR STATISTICS. "Decrease in Railroad Employment." *Monthly Labor Review* 32, no. 1 (January 1931): 54–60.

————. "Displacement of Railroad Labor." *Monthly Labor Review* 28, no. 3 (March 1929): 467–70.

————. "Stability of Railroad Unemployment." *Monthly Labor Review* 27, no. 2 (August 1928): 227–36.

U.S. NATIONAL YOUTH ADMINISTRATION FOR INDEPENDENCE. "Working on the Railroad." *Railroad Independent* (August 1940): 32–107.

"Wartime Railroad Employment." *Monthly Labor Review* 62, no. 5 (May 1946): 753–54.

WILLIAMS, JEROME H. "Interborough Provides Practical Training Courses for Its Power Department Men." *AERA* [American Electric Railway Association] 20 (November 1929): 644–50.

"Women Employed by Class I Steam Railways, April 1945." *Monthly Labor Review* 61, no. 3 (September 1945): 506–7.

1946–Present

AFROS, JOHN L. "Guaranteed Employment Plan of Seaboard Railroad." *Monthly Labor Review* 65, no. 2 (August 1947): 167–71.

ASSOCIATION OF AMERICAN RAILROADS. "Why Railroad Featherbeds Must Go." *Railway Digest of Developments and Comments* 14 (April 1959): 32 pp.

ATEN, FRED N. "Apprentice Training in the Railroad Industry." *American Federationist* 55 (January 1948): 14–15, 25–26.

BACKMAN, JULES. "The Size of Crews." *Labor Law Journal* 12, no. 9 (September 1961): 805–15.

"Benefit Exhaustions, 1948–49: Railroad Unemployment Insurance." *Monthly Labor Review* 70, no. 3 (March 1950): 299–301.

BRAND, HORST. "Problems of Measuring Railroad Productivity." *Monthly Labor Review* 97, no. 10 (October 1974): 26–32.

BROMLEY, DOROTHY DUNBAR. "The Railroads and the Fourteenth Amendment." *Nation* 172, no. 19 (May 12, 1951): 441–43.

BURCK, GILBERT. "Great Featherbed Fight." *Fortune* 61 (March 1960): 151–53+.

CARSON, DANIEL. "Occupational Mobility and Occupational Outlook." *Southern Economic Journal* 14, no. 4 (April 1948): 411–19.

DUNAND, GEORGE. "Technical Progress and Job Security on the U.S. Railroads." *International Labour Review* 89, no. 5 (May 1964): 482–95.

"Economic Protection for Railroad Workers." (In 8 parts.) *Monthly Review of the Railroad Retirement Board* 23, no. 12 (December 1962): 11–13; 24, no. 1 (January 1963): 6–9; 24, no. 3 (March 1963): 15–17; 24, no. 4 (April 1963): 9–11; 24, no. 5 (May 1963): 12–13; 24, no. 6 (June 1963): 11–13; 24, no. 9 (September 1963): 12–14; 24, no. 11 (November 1963): 12–14.

ELKIN, JACK M. "The 1946 Amendments to the Railroad Retirement and Railroad Unemployment Insurance Acts." *Social Security Bulletin* 9, no. 12 (December 1946): 23–33, 49–50.

GOMBERG, WILLIAM. "Featherbedding: An Assertion of Property Rights." *Annals of the American Academy of Political and Social Science* 333 (January 1961): 119–29.

HABER, WILLIAM, and MARK L. KAHN. "Maintenance of Way Employment: Part I — Technological Displacement in Employment and Possible Moderating Measures." *Monthly Labor Review* 80, no. 10 (October 1957): 1177–82.

————. "Maintenance of Way Employment: Part II — Cyclical and Seasonal Instability and Possible Remedial Measures." *Monthly Labor Review* 80, no. 11 (November 1957): 1315–20.

HOROWITZ, MORRIS A. "The Diesel Firemen Issue on the Railroads." *Industrial and Labor Relations Review* 13, no. 4 (July 1960): 550–58.

"Is It Endsville for the Railroads?" *Forbes* 104, no. 8 (October 15, 1969): 30–34, 39–40.

JAKUBAUSKAS, EDWARD B. "Technological Change and Recent Trends in the Composition of Railroad Employment." *Quarterly Review of Economics and Business* 2, no. 4 (November 1962): 81–90.

LEIGHTY, GEORGE E. "Are Railroad Workers 'Featherbedding'?" *Vital Speeches of the Day* 26, no. 6 (January 1, 1960): 175–79.

LEVINE, MARVIN J. "The Railroad Crew Size Controversy Revisited." *Labor Law Journal* 20, no. 6 (June 1969): 373–86.

LEVINE, MORTON. "Adjusting to Technology on the Railroads." *Monthly Labor Review* 92, no. 11 (November 1969): 36–42.

LIPSON, H. MICHAEL. "The Great Train Robbery: Railroad Full Crew Laws." *George Washington Law Review* 37 (October 1968): 153–67.

LOFTUS, JOSEPH A. "Streamlining Railroad Work Rules." *Challenge* 10, no. 10 (July 1962): 33–36.

"Occupations of Railroad Employees in 1961." *Monthly Review of the Railroad Retirement Board* 23, no. 10 (October 1962): 7–12.

"Postwar Decrease in Railroad Employment of Women." *Monthly Labor Review* 63, no. 1 (July 1946): 90–91.

"Railroad Retirement and Unemployment Insurance in 1953–54." *Monthly Labor Review* 78, no. 5 (May 1955): 560–61.

RICHE, MARTHA F. "Railroad Unemployment Insurance." *Monthly Labor Review* 90, no. 11 (November 1967): 9–18.

"Sickness and Unemployment Benefits for Railroad Workers." *Monthly Labor Review* 78, no. 8 (August 1955): 907–9.

"Technological Change and the Railroads." *Railway Age* 159, no. 18 (November 8, 1965): 16–21.

"Unemployment Insurance Operations [1946–47]." *Monthly Review of the Railroad Retirement Board* 8, no. 5 (August 1947): 183–86.

WEIDY, GARY R. "The Crew Consist Issue since 1959." *Industrial and Labor Relations Forum* 9, no. 3 (October 1973): 1–44.

"Women in the Railroad Industry." *Monthly Review of the Railroad Retirement Board* 9, no. 4 (April 1948): 66–70.

"Women in the Railroad Industry." *Monthly Review of the Railroad Retirement Board* 27, no. 4 (April 1966): 5–7.

WOOD, HELEN, *et al.* "Employment Outlook in Railroad Occupations." *Bulletin of the U.S. Bureau of Labor Statistics*, no. 961 (1949): 1–52.

"Work Rules Report: Board Asks End to Featherbedding." *Railway Age* 152, no. 9 (March 5, 1962): 9–10, 38–39, 52–56, 58.

YABROFF, BERNARD, and WILLIAM J. KELLY. "Employment Changes in Railroad Occupations, 1947–60." *Monthly Labor Review* 85, no. 10 (October 1962): 1129–35.

4. Working Conditions

1850–98

"Accidents, Their Causes and Means of Prevention." *Journal of the Franklin Institute*, 3rd ser. 25, no. 4 (April 1853): 217–22; 25, no. 5 (May 1853): 289–93.

ADAMS, CHARLES FRANCIS, JR. "The Railroad Death-Rate." *Atlantic Monthly* 37, no. 220 (February 1876): 207–19.

————. "Of Some Railroad Accidents." *Atlantic Monthly* 36, no. 217 (November 1875): 571–82.

ADAMS, HENRY C. "The Slaughter of Railway Employees." *Forum* 13, no. 4 (June 1892): 500–506.

BRUNLEES, JAMES. "On Railway Accidents — Their Causes and Means of Prevention; Showing the Bearing Which Existing Legislation Has upon Them." *Journal of the Franklin Institute*, 3rd ser. 44, no. 1 (July 1862): 19–21.

CRISSEY, FORREST. "Railroad Employees as Shareholders." *Outlook* 62, no. 2 (May 13, 1899): 122–25.

CRUM, FREDERICK S. "Accidents to Railroad Employees in New Jersey, 1888–1907." *Bulletin of the Bureau of Labor* 19, no. 84 (September 1909): 183–337.

GALTON, DOUGLAS. "On Railway Accidents." *Journal of the Franklin Institute*, 3rd ser. 44, no. 1 (July 1862): 78–81.

GODKIN, E. L. "Railroad Wages." *Nation* 25, no. 633 (August 16, 1877): 99–100.

HADLEY, A.T. "The Responsibility for Railroad Accidents." *Nation* 45, no. 1170 (December 1, 1887): 430–31.

HENDERSON, JOHN. "Railroad Accidents in Ohio and Other States." *Merchants' Magazine and Commercial Review* 54 (March 1866): 174–83.

HUISH, MARK. "Railway Accidents; Their Cause, and Means of Prevention." *Journal of the Franklin Institute*, 3rd ser. 25, no. 2 (February 1853): 96–107; 3rd ser. 25, no. 3 (March 1853): 145–96.

"On the Causes of Railway Accidents." *Temple Bar* 1, no. 1 (March 1861): 344–55.

PITCHER, JAMES R. "Accidents and Accident Insurance." *Forum* 12 (September 1891): 131–37.

"The Prevention of Railroad Accidents." *Merchants' Magazine and Commercial Review* 57 (July 1867): 66–68.

"Railroad Accidents." *Journal of the Franklin Institute,* 3rd ser. 30, no. 5 (November 1855): 347–49.

"Railroad Casualties." *Popular Science Monthly* 16, no. 3 (January 1880): 413–16.

ROBBINS, EDWIN CLYDE. "The Trainmen's Eight-Hour Day — I." *Political Science Quarterly* 31, no. 4 (December 1916): 541–57.

————. "The Trainmen's Eight-Hour Day — II." *Political Science Quarterly* 32, no. 3 (September 1917): 412–28.

THOMSON, WILLIAM. "The Sight and Hearing of Railway Employees." *Popular Science Monthly* 26, no. 4 (February 1885): 433–41.

1898–1926

AN OLD TIMER. "The Engineer's Side of It." *Independent* 59, no. 2960 (August 24, 1905): 443–46.

"Annual Report of Women's Service Section, United States Railroad Administration." *Monthly Labor Review* 10, no. 3 (March 1920): 750–52.

"Asleep at His Post." *Outlook* 83 (July 21, 1907): 656–58.

"Average Daily and Monthly Wage Rates of Railroad Employees on Class I Carriers, 1917 to 1921." *Monthly Labor Review* 14, no. 4 (April 1922): 690–93.

"Average Daily Wage Rates of Railroad Employees on Class I Carriers, July, 1923." *Monthly Labor Review* 18, no. 6 (June 1924): 1272–76.

BEYER, OTTO S., JR., and EDWIN M. FITCH. "Annual Earnings of Railroad Employees, 1924 to 1933." *Monthly Labor Review* 41, no. 1 (July 1935): 1–12.

BRAY, F. C. "Social Centers for Railroad Men." *Chautauquan* 39, no. 4 (July 1904): 364–67.

BUCHANAN, J. R. "No More Railway Accidents." *Harper's Weekly* 47, no. 2427 (June 27, 1903): 1068–69.

CARTER, W. S. "The Adamson Law: The Employees' Viewpoint." *Proceedings of the Academy of Political Science* 7, no. 1 (January 1917): 170–78.

————. "Effect of Federal Control on Railway Labor." *Proceedings of the Academy of Political Science* 8, no. 2 (February 1919): 198–210.

CEASE, D. L. "Attitude of Railroad Transportation Organizations toward Federal Compensation." *Monthly Labor Review* 9, no. 5 (November 1919): 1613–18.

————. "The Death and Disability Roll of Our Railway Employees." *Charities and the Commons* 19 (December 7, 1907): 1217–19.

————. "Railway Accidents and Railway Employees." *World To-day* 13 (July 1907): 735–37.

CLARK, LINDLEY D. "Rights and Status of Employees Injured in Commerce." *Monthly Labor Review* 15, no. 2 (August 1922): 399–409.

————. "When a Railroad Employee Is Hurt: The Legal Tangle." *Journal of Political Economy* 24, no. 8 (October 1916): 805–10.

————. "Workmen's Compensation and the Federal Congress." *Journal of Political Economy* 23, no. 8 (October 1915): 814–21.

COES, HAROLD VINTON. "Can Railroad Collisions Be Reduced to a Theoretical Minimum?" *Engineering Magazine* 34, no. 4 (January 1908): 632–42.

WORKING CONDITIONS

COLBY, BAINBRIDGE. "The Adamson Law: The Public Viewpoint." *Proceedings of the Academy of Political Science* 7, no. 1 (January 1917): 185–88.

CRUM, FREDERICK S. "Accidents to Railroad Employees in New Jersey, 1888–1907." *Bulletin of the Bureau of Labor* 19, no. 84 (September 1909): 183–337.

CUNNINGHAM, WILLIAM J. "Standardizing the Wages of Railroad Trainmen." *Quarterly Journal of Economics* 25 (November 1910): 139–60.

DIXON, FRANK HAIGH. "Public Regulation of Railway Wages." *American Economic Review, Supplement* 5, no. 1 (March 1915): 245–69.

————. "Railroad Accidents." *Atlantic Monthly* 99, no. 5 (May 1907): 577–90.

"Easing the Life Problems of Railroad Men." *World's Work* 9, no. 4 (February 1907): 5882.

"Effect of the Eight-Hour Law upon Wages and Hours of Railroad Employees." *Monthly Review of the U.S. Bureau of Labor Statistics* 6, no. 3 (March 1918): 628–31.

"Employment and Earnings of Railroad Employees, July 1921 to August 1922." *Monthly Labor Review* 15, no. 6 (December 1922): 1301–5.

ESCH, JOHN J. "Should the Safety of Employees and Travellers on Railroads Be Promoted by Legislation?" *North American Review* 179, no. 5 (November 1904): 671–84.

GARDNER, W. A. "Railroad Rewards and Pensions." *Independent* 53, no. 2730 (March 28, 1901): 729–30.

GARRETSON, A. B. "Long Hours in Railroading." *American Labor Legislation Review* 4, no. 1 (March 1914): 120–28.

GOLDMARK, PAULINE. "Women in the Railroad Service." *Proceedings of the Academy of Political Science* 8, no. 2 (February 1919): 151–56.

HARRIS, HENRY J. "The Occupation Hazard of Locomotive Firemen." *Quarterly Publications of the American Statistical Association*, n.s. 14, no. 107 (September 1914): 177–202.

HASKELL, F. W. "The Causes of Accidents on American Railways." *Engineering Magazine* 28, no. 3 (December 1904): 321–32.

HENDERSON, CHARLES RICHMOND. "Insurance Plans of Railroad Corporations." *American Journal of Sociology* 13, no. 5 (March 1908): 584–616.

HINE, CHARLES DELANO, and GUSTAVE KOBBE. "Heroes of the Railway Service." *Century Magazine* 57 (n.s. 35), no. 5 (March 1899): 653–63.

HOWARD, CHARLES A. "Safety in American Railway Transport." *Cassier's Magazine* 34, no. 1 (May 1908): 3–9.

"Increase of Wages in Mechanical Departments of Railroads under Federal Control." *Monthly Labor Review* 7, no. 3 (September 1918): 607–10.

JACOBS, H. W. "The Square Deal to the Railroad Employee." *Engineering Magazine* 33, no. 3 (June 1907): 328–52.

JANDRON, FRANCIS LYSTER. "Efficiency and the Railway Wage Problem." *Engineering Magazine* 44, no. 2 (November 1912): 241–47.

KEYES, CHARLES R. "Psychology of the Railroad Accident." *American Monthly Review of Reviews* 35, no. 4 (April 1907): 465–68.

"Labor Results of Federalized Railroads." *Monthly Labor Review* 8, no. 3 (March 1919): 908–10.

PERIODICAL LITERATURE

LAUCK, W. JETT. "The Case of Railroad Employees for an Eight-Hour Day." *Annals of the American Academy of Political and Social Science* 69, no. 158 (January 1917): 13–22.

————. "Eight Hours for Railway Crews." *New Republic* 6, no. 72 (March 18, 1916): 173–75.

LINDSAY, SAMUEL M'CUNE. "Railway Employees in the United States." *Bulletin of the Department of Labor* 6, no. 37 (November 1901): 1023–114.

MCTAVISH, ARTHUR. "Can the Railroad Death Rate Be Reduced?" *American Monthly Review of Reviews* 35, no. 4 (April 1907): 456–62.

MENKEL, WILLIAM. "Welfare Work on American Railroads." *American Monthly Review of Reviews* 38, no. 4 (October 1907): 449–63.

"Methods of Computing Wages of Railroad Employees Fixed by Director General." *Monthly Labor Review* 8, no. 2 (February 1919): 468–71.

MOSELEY, EDWARD A. "The Penalty of Progress." *Independent* 64, no. 3106 (June 11, 1908): 1340–44.

————. "Railroad Accidents in the United States." *American Monthly Review of Reviews* 30, no. 5 (November 1904): 592–96.

"Mr. Roosevelt's Letter on Railroad Wages." *Independent* 64, no. 3091 (February 27, 1907): 435–36.

"New System of Wage Adjustment for Railways." *Monthly Labor Review* 10, no. 5 (May 1920): 1120–23.

"New Wage Order Issued by Director General of Railroads." *Monthly Labor Review* 8, no. 3 (March 1919): 779–82.

"New Wage Orders Issued by the Director General of Railroads." *Monthly Labor Review* 7, no. 4 (October 1918): 966–75.

"Order of Director General of Railroads Fixing Wages of Railroad Employees." *Monthly Review of the U.S. Bureau of Labor Statistics* 6, no. 6 (June 1918): 1363–83.

PAINE, GEORGE HEBARD. "Railway Discipline." *Munsey's Magazine* 23, no. 3 (June 1900): 396–400.

PARMELEE, JULIUS H. "Labor: Report of the Railroad Wage Commission." *American Economic Review* 8 (September 1918): 654–59.

————. "The Problem of Railway Trainmen's Wages." *Annals of the American Academy of Political and Social Science* 69, no. 158 (January 1917): 1–12.

"Payment of Wages — Semimonthly Pay Day for Railroad Companies — Constitutionality of Statute." *Bulletin of the Bureau of Labor* 20, no. 86 (January 1910): 340–47.

"Public Regulation of Railway Wages: Discussion." *American Economic Review, Supplement* 5, no. 1 (March 1915): 278–99.

"Railroad Labor Board's Reports on Wages of Railroad Employees, 1920." *Monthly Labor Review* 11, no. 5 (November 1920): 959–65.

"Railway Liability to Employees." *Outlook* 88, no. 3 (January 18, 1908): 104–5.

"Railway Workmen and Disbursements." *Scientific American* 86, no. 6 (February 8, 1902): 84–85.

RANDALL, WYATT. "Railway Accidents and Railway Personnel." *American Monthly Review of Reviews* 35, no. 4 (April 1907): 462–65.

"Recent Wage Studies and the Demands of the Locomotive Firemen." *Monthly Review of the U.S. Bureau of Labor Statistics* 6, no. 4 (April 1918): 916–20.

"Report of the Eight-Hour Commission." *Railway Review* 62, no. 5 (February 2, 1918): 169–72.

"Report of the Railroad Wage Commission." *Monthly Review of the U.S. Bureau of Labor Statistics* 6, no. 6 (June 1918): 1383–407.

RICHARDS, RALPH C. "Safety First — I: Accident Prevention on Railroads." *Scientific American, Supplement* 74, no. 1921 (October 26, 1912): 271–72.

————. "Safety First — II: Accident Prevention on Railroads." *Scientific American, Supplement* 74, no. 1922 (November 2, 1912): 287–88.

RIEBENACK, M. "Pennsylvania Railroad Pension Departments: Systems East and West of Pittsburgh and Erie, Pa.: Status to and Including the Year 1907." *Annals of the American Academy of Political and Social Science* 33, no. 2 (March 1909): 258–64.

ROBBINS, EDWIN CLYDE. "The Trainmen's Eight-Hour Day — I." *Political Science Quarterly* 31, no. 4 (December 1916): 541–57.

————. "The Trainmen's Eight-Hour Day — II." *Political Science Quarterly* 32, no. 3 (September 1917): 412–28.

RUSSELL, CHARLES EDWARD. " 'Gravity Yard' and Other Shambles." *Independent* 64, no. 3087 (January 30, 1908): 233–38.

SINES, G. H. "Adjustments of Wages and Conditions of Employment under Governmental Control of Industry." *Proceedings of the Academy of Political Science* 8, no. 2 (February 1919): 229–34.

TRUMBULL, FRANK. "The Adamson Law: The Employers' Viewpoint." *Proceedings of the Academy of Political Science* 7, no. 1 (January 1917): 179–84.

VILLARD, O. G. "Railway Accidents and the Unions." *Nation* 86, no. 2223 (February 6, 1908): 119–20.

VREELAND, H. H. "Pensioning Street Railway Employees." *Outlook* 70, no. 13 (March 29, 1902): 766–67.

VROOMAN, CARL S. "The Ultimate Issue Involved in Railroad Accidents." *Arena* 39, no. 218 (January 1908): 14–19.

"Wage Movement of Organized Railway Employees, 1919–1920." *Monthly Labor Review* 10, no. 5 (May 1920): 1123–26.

"Wages and Hours of Labor in the Building and Repairing of Steam Railroad Cars: 1890–1912." *Bulletin of the U.S. Bureau of Labor Statistics*, no. 137 (December 1, 1913): 1–89.

"Wages and Hours of Labor: Decisions of the Railroad Labor Board." *Monthly Labor Review* 11, no. 3 (September 1920): 504–7.

WELSH, CHARLES. "[Railroad] Workmen's Homes and Workmen's Trains." *New England Magazine* 20, no. 6 (August 1899): 764–66.

WILLEY, DAY ALLEN. "Safety in American Railway Travel." *Cassier's Magazine* 28, no. 1 (May 1907): 55–62.

1926–46

"Accident Experience of American Steam Railroads in 1934." *Monthly Labor Review* 42, no. 2 (February 1936): 373–75.

PERIODICAL LITERATURE

"Annual Earnings of Railroad Employees." *Labor Information Bulletin*, July 1935: 4–7.

"Annual Earnings of Railroad Employees, 1926." *Monthly Labor Review* 24, no. 2 (February 1927): 310–12.

BELMAN, ALBERT A. "Wage Chronology: Railroads — Non-operating Employees, 1920–61." *Monthly Labor Review* 84, no. 9 (September 1961): 966–83.

BEYER, OTTO S., JR. "Unemployment Compensation in the Transportation Industry." *Annals of the American Academy of Political and Social Science* 187 (September 1936): 95–105.

BEYER, OTTO S., JR., and EDWIN M. FITCH. "Annual Earnings of Railroad Employees, 1924 to 1933." *Monthly Labor Review* 41, no. 1 (July 1935): 1–12.

————. "Cost of Accidents to Railroad Employees, 1932." *Monthly Labor Review* 41, no. 3 (September 1935): 552–58.

BORTZ, N. M. "Hourly Earnings in the Railroad Industry, 1929–1937." *Labor Information Bulletin*, July 1937: 5–7.

BOWDEN, WITT. "Changes in Railroad Wages, 1943–44." *Monthly Labor Review* 58, no. 3 (March 1944): 611–27.

————. "Productivity, Hours, and Compensation of Railroad Labor: Part I, All Employees." *Monthly Labor Review* 37, no. 6 (December 1933): 1275–89.

————. "Productivity, Hours, and Compensation: Part II, Classes Other Than Transportation Employees." *Monthly Labor Review* 38, no. 1 (January 1934): 43–65.

————. "Productivity, Hours, and Compensation of Railroad Labor: Part III, Transportation Employees." *Monthly Labor Review* 38, no. 2 (February 1934): 269–88.

————. "Productivity, Hours, and Compensation of Railroad Labor, 1933 to 1936." *Monthly Labor Review* 45, no. 1 (July 1937): 78–101.

BRINTON, HUGH P. "Regional Variation in Disabling Sickness among a Group of Negro Male Railroad Employees." *Social Forces* 20, no. 2 (December 1941): 264–70.

BROWN, PHILIP KING. "Tuberculosis Control in a Railway Health Insurance Program." *American Journal of Public Health and the Nation's Health* 25, no. 6 (June 1935): 741–48.

BURCK, G. H. "Another Golden Age Goes Haywire." *American Mercury* 26, no. 103 (July 1932): 315–22.

CAMPBELL, C. D. "The Business Cycle and Accidents to Railroad Employees in the United States." *Journal of the American Statistical Association* 26, no. 175 (September 1931): 295–302.

"Casualties to Trainmen on Class I Railroads, 1916–1924." *Monthly Labor Review* 22, no. 2 (February 1926): 430–33.

CLARK, LINDLEY D. "Workmen's Compensation and the Railroads: A Hesitating Revolution." *Journal of Political Economy* 41, no. 6 (December 1933): 806–20.

COTTRELL, FRED W. "The Seniority Curse." *Personnel Journal* 18, no. 5 (November 1937): 177–83.

"Dismissal Compensation for Railway Employees Displaced by Railroad Consolidations." *Monthly Labor Review* 82, no. 6 (June 1936): 1503–5.

DOAK, W. N. "The Attitude of the Railroad Brotherhoods toward Workmen's Compensation and the Reason for Such Attitude." *Bulletin of the U.S. Bureau of Labor Statistics*, no. 564 (April 1932): 53–61.

———. "Consolidation from the Railroad Employee's Viewpoint." *Proceedings of the Academy of Political Science* 13, no. 3 (June 1929): 406–15.

"Earnings and Living Standards of Railway Employees during the Depression." *Monthly Labor Review* 39, no. 4 (October 1934): 853–56.

"Employees Service and Compensation for 1941." *Monthly Review of the Railroad Retirement Board* 4, no. 1 (January 1943): 4–8.

"Extent of Low Wages and Long Hours among Railroad Employees." *Monthly Labor Review* 41, no. 3 (September 1935): 690–97.

"Extent of Low Wages and Long Hours in the Railroad Industry." *Labor Information Bulletin,* January 1937: 8–9.

"Fatalities and Injuries among Railway Maintenance-of-Way Employees, 1928." *Monthly Labor Review* 30, no. 6 (June 1930): 1288–89.

"Financing Railroad Pension Plans." *Monthly Labor Review* 31, no. 4 (October 1930): 911–14.

FLETCHER, ROBERT U. "Restrictive Legislation, Rates, Wages and Taxation." *Proceedings of the Academy of Political Science* 17, no. 2 (January 1937): 189–201.

FOX, BERTRAND. "The Effect of Methods of Compensation upon Railroad Wage Costs." *Review of Economic Statistics* 17, no. 3 (March 15, 1935): 60–67.

HARRISON, GEORGE M. "Railroad Workers Ask for Justice." *American Federationist* 52 (December 1945): 13–14.

HART, JAMES A. "Railway Wage Changes, 1941–46." *Monthly Labor Review* 63, no. 3 (September 1946): 335–41.

"Heads of Railroad Brotherhoods Endorse Six-Hour Day with No Reduction in Daily Wage Rate — Conference with Railroad Presidents and Others Scheduled for December 4, 1930." *Commercial and Financial Chronicle* 131, no. 3414 (November 29, 1930): 3469–70.

HOFFMAN, H. G. "Earnings, Hours, Employment: Class I Railroads, August 1940–July 1941." *Conference Board Economic Record* 3, no. 21 (November 11, 1941): 466–70.

"The International Regulation of Hours of Work on Railways." *International Labour Review* 29, no. 5 (May 1934): 633–55.

MARSHAK, IRA. "Service, Compensation, and Age of Railroad Employees, 1941." *Social Security Bulletin* 6, no. 3 (March 1943): 36–42.

MATER, DAN H. "The Development and Operation of the Railroad Seniority System." *Journal of Business of the University of Chicago* 13, no. 4 (October 1940): 387–419; 14, no. 1 (January 1941): 36–67.

———. "Effects of Seniority upon the Welfare of the Employee, the Employer and Society." *Journal of Business of the University of Chicago* 14, no. 4 (October 1941): 384–418.

———. "A Statistical Study of the Effect of Seniority upon Employee Efficiency." *Journal of Business of the University of Chicago* 14, no. 2 (April 1941): 169–204.

"Mileage Pay Basis Abolished on Delaware and Hudson Railroad." *Monthly Labor Review* 35, no. 5 (November 1932): 1119–21.

"Minimum Wages for Railway Porters." *International Labour Review* 43, no. 4 (April 1941): 444–45.

MYERS, ROBERT J. "Security for Railway Workers." *American Federationist* 44 (December 1937): 1315–19.

————. "Why Railway Benefits Are Larger." *American Federationist* 43 (August 1936): 809–13.

ODELL, P. E. "You Can't Make Safety a Side Issue." *National Safety News* 23, no. 1 (January 1931): 27–28, 63.

"100 Percent Safety." *Fortune* 3, no. 4 (April 1931): 81–88.

"Operations under Railroad Unemployment Insurance Act, 1939." *Monthly Labor Review* 50, no. 3 (March 1940): 640–42.

"Pennsylvania Railroad Wage Data." *Bulletin of the U.S. Bureau of Labor Statistics*, no. 514 (May 1930): 1–209.

"Railroad Accidents in the United States, 1930 to 1939." *Monthly Labor Review* 51, no. 5 (November 1940): 1171–75.

"Railroad Wages, Taxes and Freight Rates: The Wage Question." *Economic Conditions, Government Finance, United States Securities*, October–November 1932: 154–59, 169–73.

"Railroad Unemployment Insurance and Employment Service, 1943–44." *Social Security Bulletin* 7, no. 3 (August 1944): 31–32.

RANDOLPH, A. PHILIP. "The Crisis of Negro Railroad Workers." *American Federationist* 46 (August 1939): 807–21.

"Report on Proposed Six-Hour Day for Railroad Employees." *Monthly Labor Review* 36, no. 2 (February 1933): 367–69.

ROBERTSON, D. B. "The Stake of Railroad Labor in the Transportation Problem." *Annals of the American Academy of Political and Social Science*, September 1936: 88–94.

SCHOENE, LESTER R., and FRANK WATSON. "Workmen's Compensation in Interstate Railways." *Harvard Law Review* 47, no. 3 (January 1934): 389–424.

TAIT, JOHN W. "Making Democracy Safer for Railway Servants — How Toilers on Rails Broadened the Constitution." *George Washington Law Review* 10, no. 3 (January 1942): 272–301.

"Union Scales of Wages and Hours of Labor, May 15, 1929." *Bulletin of the U.S. Bureau of Labor Statistics*, no. 515 (July 1930): 250–73.

U.S. NATIONAL YOUTH ADMINISTRATION FOR INDEPENDENCE. "Working on the Railroad." *Railroad Independent*, August 1940: 32–107.

"Wage Cut. How Capital Won $210,000,000 from Labor; a Drama in Three Acts, Featuring Daniel Willard (B&O), David Brown Robertson (Locomotive Firemen), and Mr. Elisha Lee, Who Was Heard but Not Seen; Time: The Depression; Place, Chicago." *Fortune* 5, no. 4 (April 1932): 20–25, 57–59.

"Wage Increase for Steam Railroad Employees." *Monthly Labor Review* 45, no. 5 (November 1937): 1218–22.

"Wages of Railroad Section Men." *Monthly Labor Review* 60, no. 5 (May 1945): 1067–70.

"Wages and Service of Employees in 1939." *Monthly Review of the Railroad Retirement Board* 2, no. 2 (February 1941): 5–10.

WHITING, DANIEL. "Wages of Railroad Labor." *Editorial Research Report* 2, no. 14 (October 13, 1931): 685–96.

1946–Present

BELMAN, ALBERT A. "Wage Chronology: Railroads — Non-operating Employees, 1920–61." *Monthly Labor Review* 84, no. 9 (September 1961): 966–83.

"Benefit Exhaustions, 1948–49, Railroad Unemployment Insurance." *Monthly Labor Review* 70, no. 3 (March 1950): 299–301.

BURCK, GILBERT. "Great Featherbed Fight." *Fortune* 61 (March 1960): 151–53+.

CARSON, DANIEL. "Sickness Benefits for Railroad Employees." *American Economic Security* 6, no. 8 (December 1948): 29–35.

DUNAND, GEORGE. "Technical Progress and Job Security on the U.S. Railroads." *International Labour Review* 89, no. 5 (May 1964): 482–95.

ELKIN, JACK M. "The 1946 Amendments to the Railroad Retirement and Railroad Unemployment Insurance Acts." *Social Security Bulletin* 9, no. 12 (December 1947): 23–33, 49–50.

FOX, MICHAEL. "Progress on the Railroads." *American Federationist* 63 (August 1956): 12–13, 29.

HARRISON, GEORGE M. "Rail Labor Seeks Wage Boost." *American Federationist* 54 (September 1947): 8–9, 32.

HOROWITZ, MORRIS A. "The Railroad's Dual System of Payment: A Make-Work Rule?" *Industrial and Labor Relations Review* 8, no. 2 (January 1955): 177–94.

——————. "Wage Guarantees of Road Service Employees of American Railroads." *American Economic Review* 45, no. 5 (December 1955): 853–66.

——————. "Wage Guarantees of Road Service Employees of American Railroads: Reply." *American Economic Review* 46, no. 4 (September 1956): 659–62.

"Is It Endsville for the Railroads?" *Forbes* 104, no. 8 (October 15, 1969): 30–34, 39–40.

LABOR-MANAGEMENT COMMITTEE [of the Railroad Industry]. Task Force on Terminals. St. Louis Terminal Project. "Evaluation of Changes in Terminal Operations: A Progress Report to Task Force on Terminals." Multicopied report. May 15, 1974. 41 pp.

——————. "Program of Experiments Involving Changes in Terminal Operations: 1974 Progress Report."

LOFTUS, JOSEPH A. "Streamlining Railroad Work Rules." *Challenge* 10, no. 10 (July 1962): 33–36.

MONROE, J. ELMER. "A Review of Railway Operations in 1953." *Railway Age* 136, no. 2 (January 11, 1954): 110–32.

POPE, ROBERT E. "Pay and Fringe Benefits of Railroad Employees." *Monthly Labor Review* 91, no. 9 (September 1968): 45–48.

"Railroad Retirement and Unemployment Insurance in 1953–54." *Monthly Labor Review* 78, no. 5 (May 1955): 560–61.

RICHE, MARTHA F. "Railroad Unemployment Insurance." *Monthly Labor Review* 90, no. 11 (November 1967): 9–18.

"Sickness Benefits for Railroad Workers, 1947." *Monthly Labor Review* 66, no. 4 (April 1948): 402.

"Sickness and Maternity Benefits for Railroad Workers." *Monthly Labor Review* 65, no. 3 (August 1947): 194–95.

71

"Sickness and Unemployment Benefits for Railroad Workers." *Monthly Labor Review* 78, no. 8 (August 1955): 907–9.

"Technological Change and the Railroads." *Railway Age* 159, no. 18 (November 8, 1965): 16–21.

UNTERBERGER, S. HERBERT. "Wage Guarantees of Road Service Employees of American Railroads: Comment." *American Economic Review* 46, no. 4 (September 1956): 656–59.

"Wage Chronology: Railroads — Nonoperating Employees, Supplement No. 1, 1961–62." *Monthly Labor Review* 86, no. 4 (April 1963): 409–10.

WHITING, DANIEL. "Railway Safety." *Editorial Research Reports,* January 31, 1951: 65–80.

5. Unions and Workers

1850–98

ADAMS, CHARLES FRANCIS, JR. "The Brotherhood of Locomotive Engineers." (In 2 parts.) *Nation* 24, no. 611 (March 15, 1877): 158–59; 24, no. 612 (March 22, 1877): 173–74.

"The A.R.U." *American Monthly Review of Reviews* 10, no. 2 (August 1894): 190–91.

BROOKS, HAROLD C. "Story of the Founding of the Brotherhood of Locomotive Engineers." *Michigan History Magazine* 27, no. 4 (October–December 1943): 611–19.

FRUMERMAN, HARRY. "The Railroad Strikes of 1885–1886." *Marxist Quarterly* 1, no. 3 (October–December 1937): 394–407.

GODKIN, E. L. "Railroad Discipline." *Nation* 51, no. 1314 (September 4, 1890): 184–85.

MCMURRY, DONALD L. "Federation of the Railroad Brotherhoods, 1889–1894." *Industrial and Labor Relations Review* 7, no. 1 (October 1953): 73–92.

RHODES, JAMES FORD. "The Railroad Riots of 1877." *Scribner's Magazine* 50, no. 1 (July 1911): 86–96.

ROBBINS, EDWIN CLYDE. "The Trainmen's Eight-Hour Day — I." *Political Science Quarterly* 31, no. 4 (December 1916): 541–57.

SLANER, PHILIP A. "The Railroad Strikes of 1877." *Marxist Quarterly* 1, no. 2 (April–June 1937): 214–36.

1898–1926

AN OLD TIMER. "The Engineers' Side of It." *Independent* 59, no. 2960 (August 24, 1905): 443–46.

BALDWIN, WILLIAM H., JR. "The Interest of Labor in the Economies of Railroad Consolidation." *Supplement to the Annals of the American Academy of Political and Social Science* 15 (May 1900): 137–49.

BALLOU, WILLIAM HOSEA. "The Railway Employee." *Harper's Weekly* 45, no. 2318 (May 25, 1901): 533.

BLANSHARD, PAUL, SAMUEL REA, and N. P. GOOD. "Company Unions or National Unions? — A Debate." *Nation* 117, no. 3028 (July 25, 1873): 79–82.

BROOKS, HAROLD C. "Story of the Founding of the Brotherhood of Locomotive Engineers." *Michigan History Magazine* 27, no. 4 (October–December 1943): 611–19.

CADWALLADER, STARR. "Organizations of Railway Employees." *Chautauquan* 39, no. 4 (June 1904): 340–46.

CARTER, CHARLES F. "The Brotherhood of Locomotive Engineers." *Century Magazine* 80, no. 5 (September 1910): 728–35.

————. "Railroad Heroes and Such." *Collier's* 42, no. 15 (January 2, 1909): 10–11.

CEASE, D. L. "Organization of Railway Employees." *Outlook* 86, no. 10 (July 6, 1907): 503–10.

CONVERSE, JOHN W. "Progressive Non-Union Labour." *Cassier's Magazine* 23, no. 5 (March 1903): 656–66.

COPELAND, CHARLES E. "Brotherhood of Railroad Patrolmen." *American Federationist* 28 (September 1921): 772–73.

CUNNIFF, M. G. "Social Clubs for Railroad Men." *World's Work* 3, no. 6 (April 1902): 2002–5.

"The Expert Train Dispatcher." *Scientific American Supplement* 56, no. 1442 (August 22, 1903): 23102–3.

FAGAN, JAMES O. "Confessions of a Railroad Signalman." (In 6 parts.) *Atlantic Monthly* 101, no. 1 (January 1908): 80–87; 101, no. 2 (February 1908): 225–32; 101, no. 4 (April 1908): 497–505; 101, no. 5 (May 1908): 684–92; 101, no. 6 (June 1908): 805–15; 102, no. 1 (July 1908): 109–20.

FITZGERALD, E. V. "With Ranks Unbroken." *American Federationist* 28 (September 1921): 773.

GARRETSON, A. B. "The Attitude of the Railroad Brotherhoods toward Hours and Wages." *Annals of the American Academy of Political and Social Science* 69, no. 158 (January 1917): 265–67.

HINE, CHARLES DeLANO. "What a Train-Dispatcher Does." *Century* 62, no. 4 (August 1901): 594–603.

HINE, CHARLES DeLANO, and GUSTAV KOBBE. "Heroes of the Railway Service." *Century* 57 (n.s. 35), no. 5 (March 1899): 653–63.

HOFFMAN, ARTHUR SULLIVANT. "The Tzar of the Sleeping Car." *Chautauquan* 39, no. 4 (June 1904): 361–64.

HUNGERFORD, EDWARD. "The Fellows Out upon the Line." *Outing Magazine* 154, no. 3 (June 1909): 267–77.

————. "Getting the Traffic Through." *Harper's Monthly Magazine* 119, no. 714 (November 1909): 876–87.

————. "The Terminal." *Harper's Monthly Magazine* 118, no. 705 (February 1909): 413–25.

HYATT, GILBERT E. "Railroad Union Bustin' Is Expensive." *American Federationist* 33 (February 1927): 169–71.

JEWELL, BERT M. "The Railroad Labor Institute of 1925." *American Federationist* 32 (October 1925): 935–38.

MANION, E. J. "The Order of Railroad Telegraphers." *American Federationist* 28 (September 1921): 768–69.

OAKLEY, THORNTON. "Vignettes of the Road." *Harper's Monthly Magazine* 115, no. 685 (June 1907): 140–46.

OSBORN, CHRISTABEL. "Railway Brotherhoods in the United States." *Economic Journal* 18, no. 32 (December 1898): 577–79.

PROUT, H. G. "Railroading as a Profession." *Munsey's Magazine* 22, no. 6 (March 1900): 874–78.

"Railroad Union Buys Interest in New York Bank: Arrangement between Locomotive Engineers and Empire Trust Company; An Important Development of Union Policy." *Industrial Relations; Bloomfield's Labor Digest* 14, no. 2 (January 27, 1923): 1406.

"Railroad Unions Agree to Settle Wage Demand through Cummins-Esch Bill — President's Letter to Unions." *Commercial and Financial Chronicle* 110, no. 2854 (March 6, 1920): 929–32.

ROBBINS, EDWIN CLYDE. "The Trainmen's Eight-Hour Day — I." *Political Science Quarterly* 31, no. 4 (December 1916): 541–57.

SHANLEY, J. J. "The Way Station Agent: Suggesting an Epic." *Chautauquan* 39, no. 4 (June 1904): 359–61.

TAYLOR, GRAHAM ROMEYN. "The Man Who Throws the Switch." *Charities and the Commons* 17, no. 18 (February 2, 1907): 807–10.

"Two Views of the Railroad Question — Part I, Brotherhoods and Efficiency," by William J. Cunningham; "Part II, Authority and Efficiency," by James O. Fagan. *Atlantic Monthly* 104, no. 3 (September 1909): 289–302, 302–15.

WARBURTON, G. A. "The Railroad Branch of the Y.M.C.A." *Chautauquan* 39, no. 4 (June 1904): 351–58.

WEISS, GEORGE. "Labor and the Railroads." *Forum* 56, no. 3 (September 1916): 370–84.

WILLETS, GILSON. "The Power of the Railroad Brotherhoods." *World's Work* 25, no. 6 (April 1913): 676–79.

YOUNG, GARY. "The Railroad Brotherhoods and the Railway Labor Act: A Study in Progressive Political Action in the 1920's." *Industrial and Labor Relations Forum* 9, no. 3 (October 1973): 97–121.

1926–46

BEYER, OTTO S., JR. "How as Well as What." *American Federationist* 33 (August 1927): 938–46.

BROWN, GEORGE. "Railroad Workers Raise Struggle against Consolidation." *Communist* 15, no. 8 (August 1936): 698–706.

BURCK, GILBERT. "A Railroad Fireman." *Fortune* 19, no. 6 (June 1939): 78–84, 91.

COTTRELL, FRED W. "The Seniority Curse." *Personnel Journal* 18, no. 5 (November 1939): 177–83.

"Federal Agencies and Unions Defined." *Congressional Digest* 26, no. 3 (March 1947): 73–76.

HARRISON, GEORGE M. "Achievements of Railway Clerks." *American Federationist* 42 (September 1935): 921–24.

"Heads of Railroad Brotherhoods Endorse Six-Hour Day with No Reduction in Daily Wage Rate — Conference with Railroad Presidents and Others Scheduled for December 4, 1930." *Commercial and Financial Chronicle* 131, no. 344 (November 29, 1930): 3469–70.

JEWELL, BERT M. "Railroad Workers Do Their Part for Victory." *American Federationist* 52 (June 1945): 10–12.

McKILL, B. C. "Company Unions on the Railroads." *Nation* 142, no. 3679 (January 8, 1936): 48–50.

"Railroad Brotherhoods." *Congressional Digest* 20, no. 4 (April 1941): 105.

RANDOLPH, A. PHILIP. "The Case of the Pullman Porter." *American Federationist* 33 (November 1926): 1334–39.

―――. "The Crisis of Negro Railroad Workers." *American Federationist* 46 (August 1939): 807–21.

―――. "One Union's Story." *American Federationist* 60 (November 1953): 20–23.

―――. "An Open Letter to Mr. J. P. Morgan." *American Federationist* 40 (July 1933): 704–10.

―――. "Porters Fight Paternalism." *American Federationist* 37 (June 1930): 666–73.

―――. "Pullman Porters Vote for Organization They Want." *American Federationist* 42 (July 1935): 727–29.

―――. "Why a Trade Union: Letter to the Pullman Company." *American Federationist* 37 (December 1930): 1470–82.

RODNICK, DAVID. "Status Values among Railroad Men." *Social Forces* 20, no. 1 (October 1941): 89–96.

TAYLOR, ELVA M. "Employee Representation on American Railroads." (In 4 parts.) *American Federationist* 33 (September 1926): 1103–8; 33 (October 1926): 1201–17; 33 (November 1926): 1357–65; 33 (December 1926): 1483–91.

WILLIAMS, JEROME H. "Interborough Provides Practical Training Courses for Its Power Department Men." *AERA* [American Electric Railway Association] 20 (November 1929): 664–50.

WOODS, JOHN J. "Union Solves Depression Problem." *American Federationist* 42 (September 1935): 925–29.

YANCY, JOHN L. "Red Caps' Struggle for Employee Status." *American Federationist* 46 (March 1939): 259–63.

1946–Present

"BRAC's Dennis: Proposals Are Ready; BRT's Luna: Drive for Merger Is Near." *Railway Age* 163, no. 12 (September 25, 1967): 27–30, 39, 54.

CASHEN, THOMAS C. "Switchmen's Union." *American Federationist* 54 (May 1947): 19.

ELDRIDGE, PAUL W. "The Trainman Political Education League, 1948–1968." *Industrial and Labor Relations Forum* 11, no. 3 (October 1973): 45–68.

HOROWITZ, MORRIS AARON. "Labor's Role in the Declining Railroad Industry." *Labor Law Journal* 9 (July 1958): 473–77.

MEYERS, FREDERIC. "Organization and Collective Bargaining in the Local Mass Transportation Industry in the Southeast." *Southern Economic Journal* 15, no. 4 (April 1949): 425–40.

RANDOLPH, A. PHILIP. "One Union's Story." *American Federationist* 60 (November 1953): 20–23.

TAFT, PHILIP. "Independent Unions and the Merger." *Industrial and Labor Relations Review* 9, no. 3 (April 1956): 433–38.

TROY, LEE. "Labor Representation on American Railways." *Labor History* 2, no. 3 (Fall 1961): 295–322.

WICKERSHAM, EDWARD D. "Railroad Brotherhoods: Special Treatment, How Has the Effectiveness of the Brotherhoods in Serving Their Members Affected Railroad Management and the Public?" *Current History* 27, no. 155 (July 1954): 7–12.

6. Labor Legislation

1850–98

COOLEY, T. M. "Labor and Capital before the Law." *North American Review* 139, no. 337 (December 1884): 503–16.

"A Digest of Legislation to Adjust Railway Labor Disputes." *Industrial Relations; Bloomfield's Labor Digest* 20, no. 6 (February 6, 1926): 3368–69.

GODKIN, E. L. "The Congressional Remedy for Railroad Strikes." *Nation* 60, no. 1546 (February 14, 1895): 120–21.

TAYLOR, FREDERIC. "Uniform Laws for Railways." *Forum* 6 (September 1888): 81–91.

WALKER, ALDACE F. "Recent Labor Rulings by Federal Courts." *Forum* 15, no. 3 (May 1893): 311–22.

1898–1926

"Amendments to the McAdoo Award Affecting Telegraph Operators and Station Agents in the United States." *Labour Gazette* 19 (January 1919): 69–71.

"Analysis of Labor Provisions of the New Transportation Act." *Monthly Labor Review* 10, no. 4 (April 1920): 880–87.

"A Brotherhood Interpretation of the Adamson Act." *Railway Review* 59, no. 17 (October 21, 1916): 543–46.

CABOT, PHILIP. "A Practical Way Out of the Railroad Trouble." *World's Work* 41, no. 4 (February 1921): 410–16.

CARTER, W. S. "The Adamson Law: The Employees' Viewpoint." *Proceedings of the Academy of Political Science* 7, no. 1 (January 1917): 170–78.

————. "Effect of Federal Control on Railway Labor." *Proceedings of the Academy of Political Science* 8, no. 2 (February 1919): 198–210.

CHANDLER, ALBERT. "Compulsory Arbitration in Railroad Disputes." *American Monthly Review of Reviews* 55, no. 2 (February 1917): 190–92.

CLAPP, EDWIN J. "The Adamson Law." *Yale Review* 6, no. 2 (January 1917): 258–75.

CLARK, LINDLEY D. "Rights and Status of Employees Injured in Commerce." *Monthly Labor Review* 15, no. 2 (August 1922): 399–409.

————. "Workmen's Compensation and the Federal Congress." *Journal of Political Economy* 23, no. 8 (October 1915): 814–21.

COLBY, BAINBRIDGE. "The Adamson Law: The Public Viewpoint." *Proceedings of the Academy of Political Science* 7, no. 1 (January 1917): 185–88.

COMMONS, JOHN R. "The LaFollette Railroad Law in Wisconsin." *American Monthly Review of Reviews* 32, no. 1 (July 1905): 76–79.

CUMMINS, ALBERT B. "The Senate Committee Railroad Bill." *Proceedings of the Academy of Political Science* 8, no. 4 (January 1920): 518–39.

LABOR LEGISLATION

DAGGETT, C. E. "The Esch-Cummins Act." *American Law Review* 59 (September–October 1925): 678–706.

"Demands of Railway Labor Unions: Nationalization of the Rail Lines Sought by Four Brotherhoods — the Plumb Plan." *Current History Magazine of the New York Times* 10, part 2 (September 1919): 445–50.

"A Digest of Legislation to Adjust Railway Labor Disputes." *Industrial Relations; Bloomfield's Labor Digest* 20, no. 6 (February 6, 1926): 3368–69.

"Direct Action and the Plumb Plan: An Editorial to the Railroad Workers; Brotherhood Plan, or What?" *New Republic* 20, no. 250 (August 20, 1919): 69–77.

DIXON, FRANK H. "Functions and Policies of the Railroad Labor Board." *Proceedings of the Academy of Political Science* 10, no. 1 (July 1922): 19–28.

——————. "Public Regulation of Railway Wages." *American Economic Review, Supplement* 5, no. 1 (March 1915): 245–69.

——————. "Public Regulation of Railway Wages — Discussion." *American Economic Review, Supplement* 5, no. 1 (March 1915): 278–99.

——————. "The Railroad Situation: An Appraisal." *American Economic Review, Supplement* 11, no. 1 (March 1921): 5–18.

DOAK, W. N. "The Adjustment of Labor Controversies." *Proceedings of the Academy of Political Science* 8, no. 4 (January 1920): 690–95.

——————. "Labor Policies of the Transportation Act from the Point of View of Railroad Employees." *Proceedings of the Academy of Political Science* 10, no. 1 (July 1922): 39–48.

DUNN, SAMUEL O. "The Threatened Strike on the Railways." *North American Review* 204, no. 731 (October 1916): 575–88.

ELLIOTT, HOWARD. "A Live and Let Live Railroad Policy." *Forum* 61, no. 6 (June 1919): 690–700.

"Enforcement of Findings of United States Railroad Labor Board: Pennsylvania Railroad Case." *Monthly Labor Review* 20, no. 4 (April 1925): 900–902.

"Engineers on the Railroad Problem: Point Out the Glaring Misrepresentations Made by Supporters of the Plumb Plan." *Public Service* 27, no. 4 (October 1919): 92–94.

ESCH, JOHN J. "Should the Safety of Employees and Travellers on Railroads be Promoted by Legislation?" *North American Review* 179, no. 5 (November 1904): 671–84.

"Esch Railroad Bill Reported to the House." *Commercial and Financial Chronicle* 109, no. 2838 (November 15, 1919): 1855–59.

GIBSON, THOMAS. "The Railroad Labor Situation." *Moody's Magazine* 19, no. 10 (October 16, 1916): 501–4.

HACKETT, F. W. "Adamson Act Decision." *American Law Review* 52 (January–February 1918): 23–40.

HEISERMAN, C. B. "Labor Policies of the Transportation Act from the Point of View of Railway Management." *Proceedings of the Academy of Political Science* 10, no. 1 (July 1922): 29–38.

HOLLY, WILLIAM H. "Supreme Court's Decision on the Adamson Law." *Life and Labor* 7, no. 5 (May 1917): 74–75.

HOWE, FREDERIC C. "Labor and the Democratic Control of Railroads." *Proceedings of the Academy of Political Science* 8, no. 4 (January 1920): 696–702.

PERIODICAL LITERATURE

HUNGERFORD, EDWARD. "An American Railroad Program." *Century Magazine* 104, no. 1 (May 1922): 123–31.

JOHNSON, EMORY R. "Legislation concerning the Railroad Service." *American Academy of Political and Social Science* 69, no. 158 (January 1917): 247–55.

————. "The Scope and Functions of a Federal Transportation Board." *Proceedings of the Academy of Political Science* 8, no. 4 (January 1920): 572–77.

KENNEDY, WALTER B. "Law and the Railroad Labor Problem." *Yale Law Journal* 32, no. 6 (April 1923): 553–74.

"Labor Law Question: Wabash Railroad." *Outlook* 73, no. 11 (March 14, 1903): 599–600.

"Labor Legislation of 1913." *American Labor Legislation Review* 3, no. 3 (October 1913): 333–44.

"Labor's Protest against Esch Railroad Bill." *Commercial and Financial Chronicle* 109, no. 2838 (November 15, 1919): 1862–63.

LAUCK, W. JETT. "The Case of Railroad Employees for an Eight-Hour Day." *Annals of the American Academy of Political and Social Science* 69, no. 158 (January 1917): 13–22.

————. "Eight Hours for Railway Crews." *New Republic* 6, no. 72 (March 18, 1916): 173–75.

"The Loree Plan." *Nation* 109, no. 2824 (August 16, 1919): 212.

MAGNUSSON, LEIFUR, and MARGUERITE A. GADSBY. "Federal Intervention in Railroad Disputes." *Monthly Labor Review* 11, no. 1 (July 1920): 26–43.

MORRIS, RAY. "The New Railroad Law." *World's Work* 39, no. 6 (April 1920): 547–52.

MOSELEY, EDWARD A. "The Penalty of Progress." *Independent* 64, no. 3106 (June 11, 1908): 1340–44.

"New Agreement for Adjustment of Railroad Labor Disputes." *Monthly Review of the U.S. Bureau of Labor Statistics* 6, no. 5 (May 1918): 1228–30.

NOXON, FRANK W. "Objects of Railway Legislation." *Proceedings of the Academy of Political Science* 8, no. 4 (January 1920): 566–71.

"Objections of Director-General Hines to Refunding and Other Features of Esch Railroad Bill." *Commercial and Financial Chronicle* 109, no. 2838 (November 15, 1919): 1861–62.

OLDS, LELAND. "Guild Socialism and the Railway Brotherhoods." *Intercollegiate Socialist* 7 (April 1919): 20–23.

"Order of Director General of Railroads Fixing Wages of Railroad Employees." *Monthly Review of the U.S. Bureau of Labor Statistics* 6, no. 6 (June 1918): 1363–83.

PLUMB, GLENN E. "Plan of Organized Employes for Railroad Organization." *Public* 22, no. 1099 (April 26, 1919): 427–29.

————. "What the Plumb Plan Means." *Forum* 62 (September 1919): 358–69.

POMERENE, ATLEE. "Our Recent Federal Railroad Legislation." *American Law Review* 55 (May–June 1921): 364–92.

"Power of United States Railroad Labor Board to Enforce Awards." *Monthly Labor Review* 14, no. 6 (June 1922): 1252–55.

"The Railroad Situation — Discussion." *American Economic Review, Supplement* 11, no. 1 (March 1921): 18–21.

LABOR LEGISLATION

"The Railroad Wage Question in the United States." *Labour Gazette* 19 (September 1919): 1069–71.

"The Railroads Oppose the Labor Bill: Plan Proposed by Labor Organizations Called a Step Backward." *Railway Age* 76, no. 18 (April 5, 1924): 889–94.

"Railway Executives on Federal Ownership." *Railway Review* 65, no. 7 (August 16, 1919): 240–42.

"The Railway Problem — Discussion." *American Economic Review, Supplement* 10, no. 1 (March 1920): 186–212.

REA, SAMUEL. "Our Railroad Problem: How to Settle It Effectually in the Public Interest." *American Academy of Political and Social Science* 86, no. 175 (November 1919): 103–20.

RIPLEY, WILLIAM Z. "The Railroad Eight-Hour Law." *American Review of Reviews* 54, no. 4 (October 1916): 389–93.

SAKOLSKI, A. M. "Practical Tests of the Transportation Act." *Political Science Quarterly* 36, no. 3 (September 1921): 376–90.

RICH, EDGAR J. "The Transportation Act of 1920." *American Economic Review* 10 (September 1920): 507–27.

SEAGER, HENRY R. "Railroad Labor and the Labor Problem." *Proceedings of the Academy of Political Science* 10, no. 1 (July 1922): 15–18.

SINES, G. H. "Adjustments of Wages and Conditions of Employment under Governmental Control of Industry." *Proceedings of the Academy of Political Science* 8, no. 2 (February 1919): 229–34.

SNOW, FRANKLIN. "After Eight Years [of the Transportation Act of 1920]." *North American Review* 225, no. 842 (April 1928): 452–60.

"Supplement No. 14 of the McAdoo Award: Affecting the Classification and Pay of Federal Railroad Police in the United States." *Labor Gazette* 19 (April 1919): 475–78.

THOMAS, DAVID Y. "The Next Step in Railway Legislation." *Unpopular Review* 9, no. 17 (January 1918): 49–57.

TRUMBULL, FRANK. "The Adamson Law: The Employers' Viewpoint." *Proceedings of the Academy of Political Science* 7, no. 1 (January 1917): 179–84.

VAN HISE, CHARLES R. "The Railroad Hours of Labor Law." *Annals of the American Academy of Political and Social Science* 69, no. 158 (January 1917): 256–64.

VAN METRE, T. W. "The Railroad Predicament: How It Arose and How to Get Out of It." *Annals of the American Academy of Political and Social Science* 97, no. 186 (September 1921): 93–98.

————. "Railroad Regulation under the Transportation Act." *Proceedings of the Academy of Political Science* 10, no. 1 (July 1922): 3–12.

WARFIELD, S. DAVIES. "Railroad Necessities and the Transportation Act." *Proceedings of the Academy of Political Science* 10, no. 4 (January 1924): 751–57.

WATKINS, EDGAR. "Status of Existing Railroad Laws and Regulative Agencies under Federal Control." *Annals of the American Academy of Political and Social Science* 76, no. 165 (March 1918): 121–24.

WILLARD, DANIEL. "Railroads on a Sound Basis." *World's Work* 42, no. 2 (July 1921): 135–41.

WILLOUGHBY, W. F. "Accidents to Labor as Regulated by Law in the United States." *Bulletin of the Department of Labor* 6, no. 32 (January 1901): 1–11.

YOUNG, GARY. "The Railroad Brotherhoods and the Railway Labor Act: A Study in Progressive Political Action in the 1920's." *Industrial and Labor Relations Forum* 9, no. 3 (October 1973): 97–121.

ZIEGER, ROBERT H. "From Hostility to Moderation: Railroad Labor Policy in the 1920's." *Labor History* 9, no. 1 (Winter 1968): 23–38.

1926–46

ALDERMAN, SIDNEY S. "What the New Supreme Court Has Done to the Old Law of Negligence." *Law and Contemporary Problems* 18, no. 2 (Spring 1953): 110–59.

BERMAN, EDWARD. "The Supreme Court Interprets the Railway Labor Act." *American Economic Review, Supplement* 20, no. 4 (December 1930): 619–39.

BEYER, OTTO S., JR. "The Railway Labor Act." *Proceedings of the Academy of Political Science* 22, no. 1 (May 1946): 51–62.

"Constitutionality of Arkansas Full-crew Law Upheld." *Monthly Labor Review* 32, no. 6 (June 1931): 1353–54.

DEPARQ, WILLIAM H. "A Decade of Progress under the Federal Employers' Liability Act." *Law and Contemporary Problems* 18, no. 3 (Summer 1953): 257–80.

ELLINGTON, A. R. "The Railway Labor Act of 1926." *Journal of Political Economy* 36, no. 1 (February 1928): 53–82.

"Emergency Railroad Transportation Act, 1933." *Monthly Labor Review* 37, no. 1 (July 1933): 91.

"Federal Legislation concerning Railroad Employees." *Monthly Labor Review* 28, no. 4 (April 1929): 738–65.

"Federal Legislation concerning Railroad Employees." *Monthly Labor Review* 51, no. 6 (December 1940): 1428–36.

FISHER, CLYDE OLIN. "The New Railway Labor Act: A Comparison and an Appraisal." *American Economic Review* 17 (March 1927): 177–87.

FLETCHER, ROBERT U. "Restrictive Legislation, Rates, Wages and Taxation." *Proceedings of the Academy of Political Science* 17, no. 2 (January 1937): 189–201.

GIBSON, J. C. "The Venue Clause and Transportation Lawsuits." *Law and Contemporary Problems* 18, no. 3 (Summer 1953): 367–431.

GRIFFITH, MELVIN. "The Vindication of a National Public Policy under the Federal Employers' Liability Act." *Law and Contemporary Problems* 18, no. 2 (Spring 1953): 160–87.

HARBESON, R. W. "The Emergency Railroad Transportation Act of 1933." *Journal of Political Economy* 42, no. 1 (February 1934): 106–26.

HARRISON, GEORGE M. "Railway Labor Act." *American Federationist* 41, no. 10 (October 1934): 1053–57.

"Increased Operating Efficiency of Railroads." *Monthly Labor Review* 28, no. 2 (February 1928): 235–36.

KRAMER, ROBERT. "Foreword [to Symposium]." *Law and Contemporary Problems* 18, no. 2 (Spring 1953): 107–9.

"Labor Legislation Enacted by 73rd Congress: Railroads and Their Employees." *Monthly Labor Review* 39, no. 2 (August 1934): 352–67.

"Laws Affecting Railroad Workers." *Monthly Labor Review* 64, no. 5 (May 1947): 839–44.

LOOMIS, DANIEL P. "The Law and Railway Labor." *Railway Age* 124, no. 3 (January 17, 1948): 162–64, 173.

MCNATT, E. B. "The Amended Railway Labor Act." *Southern Economic Journal* 5, no. 2 (October 1938): 179–96.

"New Railroad Labor Law." *American Labor Legislation Review* 16, no. 2 (June 1926): 140–41.

NORTHRUP, HERBERT R. "The Railway Labor Act and Railway Labor Disputes in Wartime." *American Economic Review* 36, no. 3 (June 1946): 324–43.

"Order Enjoining Railroad Officials from Interfering with Employees in the Selection of Representatives of Their Own Choosing — Sustained." *Law and Labor* 12, no. 6 (June 1930): 130–33.

PERLEY, ALLAN H. "Emergency Railroad Transportation Act of 1933." *American Bar Association Journal* 20, no. 7 (July 1934): 444–48.

PLUMB, GLENN E. "Labor's Solution of the Railroad Problem." *Nation* 109, no. 2824 (August 16, 1919): 200–201.

"Railroad Legislation on Full Crew, Personnel and Train Lengths." *Monthly Labor Review* 50, no. 6 (June 1940): 1429–34.

"The Railroads Oppose the Labor Bill: Plan Proposed by Labor Organizations Called a Step Backward." *Railway Age* 76, no. 18 (April 5, 1924): 889–94.

"Railway Labor Act Upheld by United States Supreme Court." *Monthly Labor Review* 44, no. 5 (May 1937): 1197–201.

"Right of Railroad Employees to Collective Bargaining." *Monthly Labor Review* 29, no. 4 (October 1929): 850–52.

"Right of Railroad Employees to Collective Bargaining Upheld." *Monthly Labor Review* 26, no. 6 (June 1928): 1190–92.

ROBERTSON, D. B. "Legislation Based on Collective Bargaining." *American Federationist* 33 (March 1926): 317–23.

SNOW, FRANKLIN. "After Eight Years [of the Transportation Act of 1920]." *North American Review* 225, no. 842 (April 1928): 452–60.

TRAYLOR, ORBA F. "Railroads Must Negotiate with Labor." *Journal of Land and Public Utilities Economics* 13, no. 2 (May 1937): 216–18.

ZIEGER, ROBERT H. "From Hostility to Moderation: Railroad Labor Policy in the 1920's." *Labor History* 9, no. 1 (Winter 1968): 23–38.

1946–Present

ADDICKS, ILSE S. "New Federal Laws Affecting Labor." *Monthly Labor Review* 77, no. 10 (October 1954): 1104.

ALDERMAN, SIDNEY S. "What the New Supreme Court Has Done to the Old Law of Negligence." *Law and Contemporary Problems* 18, no. 2 (Spring 1953): 110–59.

ARPAIA, ANTHONY F. "A Matter of Necessity. Independent Tribunal to Adjudicate Labor

Disputes: Address, April 2, 1964." *Vital Speeches of the Day* 30, no. 15 (May 15, 1964): 477–80.

CURTAIN, WILLIAM J. "Transportation Strikes and the Public Interest: The Recommendations of the A.B.A.'s Special Committee." *Georgetown Law Journal* 58, no. 2 (November 1969): 243–86.

DEPARQ, WILLIAM H. "A Decade of Progress under the Federal Employers' Liability Act." *Law and Contemporary Problems* 18, no. 3 (Summer 1953): 257–80.

"End of the Line: The 'Model' Railway Labor Act Is Due for an Overhauling." *Fortune* 42, no. 8 (August 1950): 43–46.

ENNIS, JOHN M. "An Analysis of Judicial Interpretation and Application of Certain Aspects of the Federal Employers' Liability Act." *Law and Contemporary Problems* 18, no. 3 (Summer 1953): 350–66.

GIBSON, J. C. "The Venue Clause and Transportation Lawsuits." *Law and Contemporary Problems* 18, no. 3 (Summer 1953): 367–431.

GRIFFITH, MELVIN. "The Vindication of a National Public Policy under the Federal Employers' Liability Act. *Law and Contemporary Problems* 18, no. 2 (Spring 1953): 160–87.

GRUNFELD, C. "The Transport Act, 1953." *Political Quarterly* 25, no. 1 (January–March 1954): 43–54.

KRAMER, ROBERT. "Foreword [to Symposium]." *Law and Contemporary Problems* 18, no. 2 (April 1953): 107–9.

"Laws Affecting Railroad Workers." *Monthly Labor Review* 64, no. 5 (May 1947): 839–44.

LEVINSON, DAVID. "Union Shop under the Railway Labor Act." *Labor Law Journal* 6, no. 7 (July 1955): 441–52.

LIPSON, H. MICHAEL. "The Great Train Robbery: Railroad Full Crew Laws." *George Washington Law Review* 37 (October 1968): 153–67.

LOOMIS, DANIEL P. "The Law and Railway Labor." *Railway Age* 124, no. 3 (January 17, 1948): 162–64, 173.

"The 1963 Railroad Arbitration Act." *Monthly Labor Review* 86, no. 10 (October 1963): 1187–88.

"Rail Strikes: Search for End to Recurring Problems." *Congressional Quarterly Weekly Report* 29, no. 25 (June 18, 1941): 1322–27.

"Railway Labor Act: Administration Highlights, 1949–50." *Monthly Labor Review* 72, no. 4 (April 1951): 416–19.

RUSSELL, JAMES F. S. "The Railroads in the 'Conspiracy Theory' of the 14th Amendment." *Mississippi Valley Historical Review* 41, no. 4 (March 1955): 601–22.

"Summary of 1948 Amendments [to the Railroad Retirement and Railroad Unemployment Insurance Acts]." *Monthly Review of the Railroad Retirement Board* 9, no. 7 (July 1948): 134–39, 144.

WISEHARD, ARTHUR M. "Transportation Strike Control Legislation: A Congressional Challenge." *Michigan Law Review* 66, no. 8 (June 1968): 1697–722.

7. Labor Relations

1850–98

ADAMS, CHARLES F., JR. "The Prevention of Railroad Strikes — I." *Nation* 25, no. 635 (August 30, 1877): 133–34.

—————. "The Prevention of Railroad Strikes — II." *Nation* 25, no. 636 (September 6, 1877): 150–51.

—————. "Prevention of Railroad Strikes." *Scribner's Magazine* 5, no. 4 (April 1889): 424–30.

"The A.R.U." *American Monthly Review of Reviews* 10, no. 2 (August 1894): 190–91.

ATWATER, L. H. "The Great Railroad Strike." *Presbyterian Quarterly and Princeton Review* 6, no. 23 (October 1877): 719–44.

BACON, THOMAS R. "Railroad Strike in California." *Yale Review* 3, no. 2 (August 1894): 241–50.

BAKER, RAY S. "Railway Blacklisting." *Outlook* 57, no. 15 (December 11, 1897): 901–3.

BARBER, H. H. "The Railroad Disorders." *Unitarian Review and Religious Magazine* 8, no. 3 (September 1877): 311–17.

BARNARD, W. T. "Relations of Railway Managers and Employes." *Popular Science Monthly* 27, no. 5 (September 1885): 577–89; 27, no. 6 (October 1885): 768–85.

BLANK, IRA L. "Settlement of the American Railway Union Strike against the Great Northern Railway in 1894." *Industrial and Labor Relations Forum* 9, no. 3 (October 1973): 69–96.

"The Buffalo Strike." *Public Opinion* 13, no. 21 (August 27, 1892): 490–91.

CANNIFF, W. H. "The Relation of the Railroad to Its Employees." *Engineering Magazine* 8, no. 6 (March 1895): 977–84.

CARNEGIE, ANDREW. "Results of the Labor Struggle." *Forum* 1 (August 1886): 538–51.

CLARK, CHARLES WORCESTER. "Compulsory Arbitration." *Atlantic Monthly* 67, no. 399 (January 1891): 34–44.

CLARK, E. P. "Governor Altgeld and the President." *Nation* 59, no. 1515 (July 12, 1894): 22–23.

—————. "The Way the Southwestern Strike Was Ordered." *Nation* 42, no. 1090 (May 20, 1886): 418–19.

CLEVELAND, GROVER. "The American Government in the Chicago Strike of 1894." *Fortnightly Review* 82, no. 451 (July 1, 1904): 1–19.

—————. "Ex-President Cleveland on the Railroad Strike of 1894." *American Monthly Review of Reviews* 30, no. 1 (July 1904): 84–85.

—————. "The Government in the Chicago Strike of 1894." *McClure's Magazine* 23, no. 3 (July 1904): 226–40.

COOLEY, THOMAS M. "Arbitration in Labor Disputes." *Forum* 1 (June 1886): 307–13.

—————. "Labor and Capital before the Law." *North American Review* 139, no. 337 (December 1884): 503–16.

—————. "The Lessons of Recent Civil Disorders." *Forum* 18 (September 1894): 1–19.

PERIODICAL LITERATURE

CRAWFORD, T. C. "The Pullman Company and Its Striking Workmen." *Harper's Weekly* 38, no. 1961 (July 21, 1894): 686–87.

CROFFUT, W. A. "What Rights Have Laborers?" *Forum* 1 (May 1886): 294–306.

CURTIS, LEONARD E. "Labor Riots and So-Called 'Government by Injunction.'" *Engineering Magazine* 12, no. 3 (December 1896): 381–94.

DAVIS, CHARLES BELMONT. "The Great Sympathetic Strike." *Century Magazine* 47 (n.s. 25), no. 5 (March 1894): 652–56.

EGGERT, GERALD G. "A Missed Alternative: Federal Courts as Arbiters of Railway Labor Disputes, 1877–1895." *Labor History* 7, no. 3 (Fall 1966): 287–306.

EHRICH, LOUIS R. "Stock-Sharing as a Preventive of Labor Troubles." *Forum* 18 (December 1894): 433–38.

ELY, RICHARD T. "The Nature of the Railway Problem." *Harper's New Monthly Magazine* 73, no. 434 (July 1886): 250–57.

"The Federal Commission's Report upon the Chicago Strike." *Public Opinion* 17, no. 34 (November 22, 1894): 809–10.

"A First-hand Account of the Railroad Riots of July 1877." *Western Pennsylvania Historical Magazine* 57 (July 1974).

FLETCHER, HENRY J. "The Railway War." *Atlantic Monthly* 74, no. 444 (October 1894): 534–41.

FRUMERMAN, HARRY. "The Railroad Strikes of 1885–1886." *Marxist Quarterly* 1, no. 3 (October–December 1937): 394–405.

GODKIN, E. L. "Arbitration." *Nation* 44, no. 1128 (February 10, 1887): 112–13.

————. "The Late Riots." *Nation* 25, no. 631 (August 2, 1877): 68–69.

————. "The Lessons of the Strikes." *Nation* 42, no. 1088 (May 6, 1886): 376–77.

————. "The Public and the Strikers." [Telegraphers.] *Nation* 37, no. 943 (July 26, 1883): 70.

————. "Railroad Discipline." *Nation* 51, no. 1314 (September 4, 1890): 184–85.

————. "The Threatened Strike of the Telegraphers." *Nation* 37, no. 942 (July 19, 1883): 46–47.

"Governor Altgeld and the President — A Letter to the Editor." *Nation* 59, no. 1517 (July 26, 1894): 62.

"The Great Railroad Strike." *Scientific American* 71, no. 1 (July 14, 1894): 18–19.

"The Great Railroad Strike." *Scientific American* 71, no. 3 (July 21, 1894): 34–35.

GROSSCUP, PETER S. "A Notable Charge." [Indictment of the Leaders of the American Railway Union.] *Outlook* 50, no. 3 (July 21, 1894): 111.

GUTMAN, HERBERT G. "Trouble on the Railroads in 1873–1874: Prelude to the 1877 Crisis?" *Labor History* 2, no. 2 (Spring 1961): 215–35.

HADLEY, ARTHUR T. "Remedies for Railway Troubles." *Forum* 5 (June 1888): 429–35.

HARTE, WALTER BLACKBURN. "A Review of the Chicago Strike of '94." *Arena* 10, no. 58 (September 1894): 497–532.

HEYWOOD, E. H. "The Great Strike: Its Relations to Labor, Property, and Government." *Radical Review* 1, no. 2 (November 1877): 553–77.

"How Cleveland Dealt with the Chicago Strike." *Harper's Weekly* 48, no. 2482 (July 16, 1904): 1083–84.

"Judge Cooley's Address [on the Pullman Strike] before the American Bar Association." *Public Opinion* 17, no. 22 (August 30, 1894): 516.

LANE, M. A. "The [Pullman] Strike." *Harper's Weekly* 38, no. 1961 (July 21, 1894): 687, 690.

"The Latest Labor Crisis." *Yale Review* 3, no. 2 (August 1894): 113–20.

McDERMOT, GEORGE. "Ann Arbor Strike and the Law of Hiring." *Catholic World* 58, no. 5 (February 1894): 670–84.

————. "Pullman Strike Commission." *Catholic World* 60, no. 5 (February 1895): 627–35.

MACKEY, PHILIP ENGLISH. "Law and Order, 1877: Philadelphia's Response to the Railroad Riots." *Pennsylvania Magazine of History and Biography* 96 (1973): 183–202.

McMURRY, DONALD L. "The Legal Ancestry of the Pullman Strike Injunctions." *Industrial and Labor Relations Review* 14, no. 2 (January 1961): 235–56.

————. "Labor Policies of the General Managers' Association of Chicago, 1886–1894." *Journal of Economic History* 13, no. 2 (Spring 1953): 160–78.

MEANS, D. McG. "Principles Involved in the Recent Strike." *Forum* 17, no. 6 (August 1894): 633–43.

MILES, NELSON A., et al. "The Lesson of the Recent Strikes." *North American Review* 159, no. 453 (August 1894): 180–206.

"The New Issue Raised by the Recent [New York Central] Strike." *Andover Review* 14, no. 82 (October 1890): 413–17.

O'CONNELL, J. J. "The Great Strike of 1894." *United Service* 15, no. 4 (April 1896): 299–316.

OGDEN, ROLLO. "The Report on the Chicago Strike." *Nation* 59, no. 1534 (November 22, 1894): 376.

"Olney on the Rights of Labor." *Public Opinion* 17, no. 34 (November 22, 1894): 812.

PORTER, ROBERT P. "The Truth about the Strike [of 1877]." *Galaxy* 24, no. 6 (December 1877): 725–32.

"Press Comment on the Great Struggle." *Public Opinion* 17, no. 14 (July 5, 1894): 305–6.

"Press Comment on the Strike Report." *Public Opinion* 17, no. 34 (November 22, 1894): 810–12.

"The Pullman Boycott, from President Debs' Point of View." *Public Opinion* 17, no. 14 (July 5, 1894): 305.

A RED-HOT STRIKER. "So the Railway Kings Itch for an Empire, Do They?" *Radical Review* 1, no. 2 (November 1877): 523–34.

REMINGTON, FREDERICK. "Chicago under the Mob." *Harper's Weekly* 38, no. 1961 (July 21, 1894): 680–81.

————. "Chicago under the Law." *Harper's Weekly* 38, no. 1962 (July 28, 1894): 703–5.

————. "The Withdrawal of the U.S. Troops." *Harper's Weekly* 38, no. 1964 (August 11, 1894): 748–49.

RHODES, JAMES FORD. "The Railroad Riots of 1877." *Scribner's Magazine* 50, no. 1 (July 1911): 86–96.

ROBINSON, HARRY PERRY. "The Humiliating Report of the Strike Commission." *Forum* 18 (January 1895): 523–31.

SARGENT, FRANK P. "The Ann Arbor Strike." *North American Review* 156, no. 438 (May 1893): 561–66.

SCHLOSS, DAVID F. "Report of the Chicago Strike Commission." *Economic Journal* 5, no. 17 (March 1895): 83–86.

SCOTT, THOMAS A. "The Recent Strikes." *North American Review* 125, no. 258 (September 1877): 351–62.

SHERMAN, JOHN D. "Situation in Chicago." *Harper's Weekly* 38, no. 1960 (July 14, 1894): 6551.

SLANER, PHILIP A. "The Railroad Strikes of 1877." *Marxist Quarterly* 1, no. 2 (April–June 1937): 214–36.

SMITH, GOLDWIN. "The Labour War in the United States." *Contemporary Review* 30, no. 4 (September 1877): 529–41.

"The Strike Commission Taking Testimony." *Public Opinion* 17, no. 22 (August 30, 1894): 514–16.

"The Strike Commission Taking Testimony at Chicago." *Public Opinion* 17, no. 23 (September 6, 1894): 542.

SUMNER, W. G. "Industrial War." *Forum* 2 (September 1886): 1–8.

"Suppress the [Pullman] Rebellion." *Harper's Weekly* 38, no. 1960 (July 14, 1894): 650–51.

TAUSSIG, F. W. "Southwestern Strike of 1886." *Quarterly Journal of Economics* 1, no. 2 (January 1887): 184–222.

TAYLOR, FREDERIC. "Uniform Laws for Railways." *Forum* 6 (September 1888): 81–91.

TURNER, RALPH V., and WILLIAM WARREN ROGERS. "Arkansas Labor in Revolt: Little Rock and the Great Southwestern Strike." *Arkansas Historical Quarterly* 24 (1965): 29–46.

VON HOLST, H. "Are We Awakened?" *Journal of Political Economy* 2, no. 4 (September 1894): 485–516.

VOORHEES, THEODORE. "The Buffalo Strike." *North American Review* 155, no. 431 (October 1892): 407–17.

WARMAN, CY. "Relations of the Employee to the Railroad." *Engineering Magazine* 8, no. 6 (March 1895): 985–91.

WHITE, HORACE. "The Pullman Boycott." *Nation* 59, no. 1514 (July 5, 1894): 5–6.

———. "The Rioters and the Regular Army." *Nation* 25, no. 632 (August 9, 1877): 85–86.

WINSTON, A. P. "Significance of the Pullman Strike." *Journal of Political Economy* 9, no. 4 (September 1901): 540–61.

WOODWORTH, MARSHALL B. "The Railroad Strikers' Case in California." *American Law Review* 29 (July–August 1895): 512–22.

1898–1926

ADAMS, CHARLES FRANCIS, JR. "A Remedy for Strikes: Investigation and Publicity as Opposed to Compulsory Arbitration." *Cassier's Magazine* 23, no. 4 (February 1903): 558–65.

BESLER, W. G. "Relations of Railroads and Their Employees." *Proceedings of the Academy of Political Science* 8, no. 4 (January 1920): 677–89.

LABOR RELATIONS

BEYER, OTTO S., JR. "Management and Labor Cooperate on the Railroad." *Industrial Management* 73, no. 5 (May 1927): 264–70.

—————. "Union-Management Cooperation in the Railroad Industry." *Proceedings of the Academy of Political Science* 13, no. 1 (June 1928): 120–27.

BING, ALEXANDER M. "Coal and Rail Strikes." *American Labor Legislation Review* 12, no. 3 (September 1922): 150–54.

CANNIFF, W. H. "The Discipline and Control of Railway Employees." *Engineering Magazine* 20, no. 4 (January 1901): 753–60.

CHANDLER, ALBERT. "Compulsory Arbitration in Railroad Disputes." *American Monthly Review of Reviews* 55, no. 2 (February 1917): 190–92.

CUNNINGHAM, WILLIAM J. "The Locomotive Engineers' Arbitration: Its Antecedents and Its Outcomes." *Quarterly Journal of Economics* 27 (February 1913): 263–94.

—————. "Two Views of the Railroad Question: Brotherhoods and Efficiency." *Atlantic Monthly* 104, no. 3 (September 1909): 289–302.

"Decision of the Railroad Labor Board on the Living Wage." *Monthly Labor Review* 15, no. 6 (December 1922): 1287–94.

"Decision of Railroad Labor Board re Wages of Clerical and Station Employees and Others." *Monthly Labor Review* 15, no. 2 (August 1922): 346–50.

"Dissolution of the Railway Boards of Adjustment." *Monthly Labor Review* 12, no. 2 (February 1921): 363–64.

DOAK, W. N. "The Adjustment of Labor Controversies." *Proceedings of the Academy of Political Science* 8, no. 4 (January 1920): 690–95.

DUNN, SAMUEL O. "The Threatened Strike on the Railways." *North American Review* 204, no. 731 (October 1916): 575–88.

"Employees as Partners in Railroad Interests." *American Monthly Review of Reviews* 39, no. 3 (March 1909): 348–50.

FAGAN, JAMES O. "Confessions of a Railroad Signalman." (In 6 parts.) *Atlantic Monthly* 101, no. 1 (January 1908): 80–87; 101, no. 2 (February 1908): 225–32; 101, no. 4 (April 1908): 497–505; 101, no. 5 (May 1908): 684–92; 101, no. 6 (June 1908): 805–15; 102, no. 1 (July 1908): 109–20.

FISHER, CLYDE OLIN. "The Railroad Labor Board: An Appraisal." *South Atlantic Quarterly* 24, no. 1 (January 1925): 1–15.

GADSBY, MARGARET. "Strike of the Railroad Shopmen." *Monthly Labor Review* 15, no. 6 (December 1922): 1171–91.

—————. "Strike of the Railroad Shopmen." *Monthly Labor Review* 88, no. 7 (July 1965): 796.

GARRETT, GEORGE PALMER. "A Truce to Railroad-Wage Wars." *American Law Review* 57 (May–June 1923): 396–403.

"The Georgia Railroad Strike." *Outlook* 92 (June 5, 1909): 310–12.

GOMPERS, SAMUEL. "How Malignity Has Found Its Waterloo — McAdoo Disproves R.R. Managers' Falsifications." *American Federationist* 29 (March 1922): 161–76.

—————. "Miners and Railroaders: Editorial." *American Federationist* 29 (February 1922): 114–16.

————. "Transportation Act a Pandora Box: Editorial." *American Federationist* 29 (August 1922): 568–73.

HARRISON, GEORGE M. "Railroad Workers' Victory." *American Federationist* 59 (March 1952): 3–4.

————. "Transportation and Labor." *American Federationist* 53 (October 1946): 9–11.

HOFFMAN, L. E. "Federal Arbitration Legislation." *Annals of the American Academy of Political and Social Science* 69, no. 158 (January 1971): 223–28.

HOOPER, BEN W. "Work of Railroad Labor Board, April 1920, to November, 1923." *Monthly Labor Review* 18, no. 4 (April 1924): 759–62.

"Injunction against the Railroad Shopmen." *Monthly Labor Review* 15, no. 5 (October 1922): 888–90.

JEWELL, BERT M. "Recent Extension of Collective Bargaining — Cooperation — in the Railroad Industry." *American Federationist* 32 (July 1925): 525–33.

"Labor Agreements, Awards and Decisions: Railroads." *Monthly Labor Review* 14, no. 4 (April 1922): 713–34.

"Labor Results of Federalized Railroads." *Monthly Labor Review* 8, no. 3 (March 1919): 908–10.

MAGNUSSON, LEIFUR, and MARGUERITE A. GADSBY. "Federal Intervention in Railroad Disputes." *Monthly Labor Review* 11, no. 1 (July 1920): 26–43.

MATER, DAN H. "The Development and Operation of the Railroad Seniority System." *Journal of Business of the University of Chicago* 13, no. 4 (October 1940): 387–419; 14, no. 1 (January 1941): 36–67.

————. "Effects of Seniority upon the Welfare of the Employee, the Employer and Society." *Journal of Business of the University of Chicago* 14, no. 4 (October 1941): 384–418.

————. "A Statistical Study of the Effect of Seniority upon Employee Efficiency." *Journal of Business of the University of Chicago* 14, no. 2 (April 1941): 169–204.

"New Agreement for Adjustment of Railroad Labor Disputes." *Monthly Review of the U.S. Bureau of Labor Statistics* 6, no. 5 (May 1918): 1228–30.

"New System of Wage Adjustment for Railways." *Monthly Labor Review* 10, no. 5 (May 1920): 1120–23.

PLUMB, GLENN E. "Adjustment of Labor's Demands during Federal Control of Railroad Operation." *Annals of the American Academy of Political and Social Science* 76, no. 165 (March 1918): 59–69.

POWELL, FRED WILBUR. "Mediation and Arbitration of Railway Wage Controversies: A Year's Developments." *Quarterly Journal of Economics* 28 (February 1914): 360–72.

"Railroad Labor Board Decision on Railroad Shop Rules and Working Conditions." *Monthly Labor Review* 14, no. 1 (January 1922): 127–51.

"Railroad Unions Agree to Settle Wage Demand through Cummins-Esch Bill — President's Letter to Unions." *Commercial and Financial Chronicle* 110, no. 2854 (March 6, 1920): 929–32.

"Railroads — Decision of Railroad Labor Board: Classification of Employees." *Monthly Labor Review* 20, no. 2 (February 1925): 332–36.

"Railroads: Decisions of the Railroad Labor Board." *Monthly Labor Review* 16, no. 1 (January 1923): 101–6.

"Railroads — Decisions of the Railroad Labor Board on Overtime." *Monthly Labor Review* 13, no. 4 (October 1921): 840–43.

"Recent Labor Agreements and Decisions: Railroads." *Monthly Labor Review* 13, no. 1 (July 1921): 143–51.

"Recent Wage Studies and the Demands of the Locomotive Firemen." *Monthly Review of the U.S. Bureau of Labor Statistics* 6, no. 4 (April 1918): 916–20.

"Relations between Employers and Employed." *Monthly Labor Review* 12, no. 3 (March 1921): 606–9.

"Seniority and the Railway Strike: A Resume of Public and Official Opinion." *Outlook* 131 (August 16, 1922): 629–31.

SIKES, GEORGE C. "The Chicago Labor Troubles and Their Settlement." *Outlook* 71, no. 7 (June 14, 1902): 449–50.

"Status of Orders of the United States Railroad Labor Board." *Monthly Labor Review* 19, no. 1 (July 1924): 213–15.

STERNAU, H. G., comp. "The Railroad Strike Injunction." *American Labor Legislation Review* 12, no. 3 (September 1922): 157–61.

STRONG, WILLIAM J. "Blacklisting: The New Slavery." *Arena* 21, no. 3 (March 1899): 273–92.

TEAD, ORDWAY. "Railroad Labor Adjustment." *Public* 21, no. 1032 (January 11, 1918): 46–49.

"The Threatened Railroad Strike." *Monthly Labor Review* 13, no. 6 (December 1921): 1328–41.

"A Threatened Railway Strike." *Outlook* 85, no. 14 (April 6, 1907): 777–78.

TOWNSEND, R. D., and R. L. HARTT. "One Law for All: A Review of the Economic, Political, and Social Results of the Great Strikes." *Outlook* 132 (September 6, 1922): 12–16.

WARREN, BENTLEY W. "Wage Arbitration and Contracts." *AERA* [American Electric Railway Association] 5, no. 7 (February 1917): 767–75.

WESTBROOK, FRANCIS A. "Unions and Employers: The Story of a New Brand of Co-operation." *Outlook* 142 (April 14, 1926): 566–68.

"What a Digest of Several Railroad Settlement Plans Shows." *Literary Digest* 61, no. 2 (April 12, 1919): 144–47.

WINTER, LOVICK P. "The Firemen's Strike on the Georgia Railroad." *Independent* 66, no. 3158 (June 10, 1909): 1276–78.

ZIEGER, ROBERT H. "From Hostility to Moderation: Railroad Labor Policy in the 1920's." *Labor History* 9, no. 1 (Winter 1968): 23–38.

1926–46

"Activities of National Mediation Board, 1938–39." *Monthly Labor Review* 50, no. 3 (March 1940): 613–14.

"Adjustment of Disputes between Railroads and Their Employees." *Monthly Labor Review* 22, no. 6 (June 1926): 1208–17.

BEYER, OTTO S., JR. "The Machinery of Cooperation." *American Federationist* 36 (November 1929): 1311–19.

————. "Management and Labor Cooperation on the Railroads." *Industrial Management* 73, no. 5 (May 1927): 264–70.

————. "The Railway Labor Act." *Proceedings of the Academy of Political Science* 22, no. 1 (May 1946): 51–62.

CASSIDY, HARRY M. "The Chesapeake and Ohio Wage Case." *American Federationist* 35 (August 1928): 969–77.

CIMINI, MICHAEL. "Government Intervention in Railroad Disputes." *Monthly Labor Review* 94, no. 12 (December 1971): 27–34.

DANIELS, WINTHROP MOORE "The Railroad Employees' Interest in Rate Regulation." *American Federationist* 36 (March 1929): 342–46.

"Emergency Boards for Adjustment of Railroad Labor Disputes." *Monthly Labor Review* 55, no. 1 (July 1942): 92–93.

"Fact-Finding in the Railway Wages Dispute." *Commercial and Financial Chronicle* 147, no. 3826 (October 22, 1938): 2447–49.

GARRISON, LLOYD K. "Labor Relations in the Railroad Industry." *Proceedings of the Academy of Political Science* 17, no. 2 (January 1937): 163–70.

————. "The National Railroad Adjustment Board: A Unique Administrative Agency." *Yale Law Journal* 46, no. 4 (February 1937): 567–98.

"Gradual Restoration of Pay Cut Provided by Railroad Labor Agreement." *Monthly Labor Review* 38, no. 6 (June 1934): 1390–91.

HARRISON, GEORGE M. "Railroad Workers Ask for Justice." *American Federationist* 52 (December 1945): 13–14.

JEWELL, B. M. "$50,000,000 Wage Increase." *American Federationist* 36 (September 1929): 1047–50.

————. "Railroad Workers Do Their Part for Victory." *American Federationist* 52 (June 1945): 10–12.

"Judicial Review of Awards by the [National] Railroad Adjustment Board." *Yale Law Journal* 51, no. 4 (February 1942): 666–73.

KAUFMAN, JACOB J. "Grievance Procedures under the Railway Labor Act." *Southern Economic Journal* 19, no. 1 (July 1952): 66–78.

"Labor-Management Relations under the Railway Labor Act, 1934–57." *Monthly Labor Review* 81, no. 8 (August 1958): 879–81.

"Labor Relations on American Railroads, 1935–1936." *Monthly Labor Review* 44, no. 3 (March 1937): 614–16.

LOOMIS, DANIEL P. "The Law and Railway Labor." *Railway Age* 124, no. 3 (January 17, 1948): 162–64, 173.

MATER, DAN H. "The Development and Operation of the Railroad Seniority System." *Journal of Business* 13, no. 4 (October 1940): 387–419; 14, no. 1 (January 1941): 36–37.

————. "Effects of Seniority upon the Welfare of the Employee, the Employer and Society." *Journal of Business* 14, no. 4 (October 1941): 384–418.

————. "A Statistical Study of the Effect of Seniority upon Employee Efficiency." *Journal of Business* 14, no. 2 (April 1941): 169–204.

"Mileage Pay Basis Abolished on Delaware and Hudson Railroad." *Monthly Labor Review* 35, no. 5 (November 1932): 1119–21.

NEWBORN, NORTON N. "Restrictions on the Right to Strike on the Railroads: A History and Analysis." (In 2 parts.) *Labor Law Journal* 24, no. 3 (March 1973): 142–63; 24, no. 4 (April 1973): 234–50.

NORTHRUP, HERBERT R. "The Railway Labor Act and Railway Labor Disputes in Wartime." *American Economic Review* 36, no. 3 (June 1946): 324–43.

––––––––. "Unfair Labor Practice Prevention under the Railway Labor Act." *Industrial and Labor Relations Review* 3, no. 3 (April 1950): 323–40.

"Protection of Railroad Workers against Removal of Railroad Shops and Terminals." *Monthly Labor Review* 28, no. 6 (June 1929): 1191–99.

"Rail Unions Accept Wage Deduction of 10% for One Year: Savings to Roads Estimated at $210,000,000 — Roads Agree to Withdraw Proceedings for 15% Cut and Will Try to Maintain and Increase Employment." *Commercial and Financial Chronicle* 134, no. 3476 (February 6, 1932): 916–18.

"Railroad Emergency Board Recommends against Wage Reduction." *Monthly Labor Review* 47, no. 5 (November 1938): 1049–52.

"The Railway Strike." *Round Table* 14 (September 1924): 866–71.

"Recommendations of Railway Emergency Board." *Monthly Labor Review* 53, no. 6 (December 1941): 1421–25.

"Report of Emergency Board for Dispute on Denver and Rio Grande Western Railroad." *Monthly Labor Review* 38, no. 4 (April 1934): 867.

"Reports of Presidential Emergency Boards for Disputes on Railroads." *Monthly Labor Review* 37, no. 4 (October 1933): 882–85.

"Results of Arbitration Proceedings under Railroad Labor Act of 1926." *Monthly Labor Review* 25, no. 4 (October 1927): 721–25.

"Settlement of Disputes on Railroads." *Monthly Labor Review* 4, no. 3 (March 1935): 699–700.

"Settlement of Railway Disputes in 1936–1937." *Monthly Labor Review* 46, no. 3 (March 1938): 698–702.

SMITH, HOWARD R. "Capital and Labor in the Railroad Industry." *Harvard Business Review* 23, no. 2 (Winter 1945): 144–56.

"Union-Management Cooperation on the Railroads." *Monthly Labor Review* 32, no. 5 (May 1931): 1076–78.

"Wage Cut. How Capital Won $210,000,000 from Labor; A Drama in Three Acts, Featuring Daniel Willard (B&O), David Brown Robertson (Locomotive Firemen) and Mr. Elisha Lee, Who Was Heard but Not Seen; Time: The Depression; Place: Chicago." *Fortune* 5, no. 4 (April 1932): 20–25, 57–59.

WESTWOOD, H. C. "The Railroad Pension Case." *American Federationist* 42 (August 1935): 808–12.

WILLARD, DANIEL. "The New Executive Viewpoint on Labor Relations." *Industrial Management* 73, no. 5 (May 1927): 260–63.

"Work of National Mediation Board, 1942–43." *Monthly Labor Review* 58, no. 3 (March 1944): 524–25.

ZIEGER, ROBERT H. "From Hostility to Moderation: Railroad Labor Policy in the 1920's." *Labor History* 9, no. 1 (Winter 1968): 23–38.

1946–Present

AFROS, JOHN L. "Guaranteed Employment Plan of Seaboard Railroad." *Monthly Labor Review* 65, no. 2 (August 1947): 167–71.

"Arbitration Board's Award in Railroad Dispute." *Monthly Labor Review* 87, no. 1 (January 1964): 36–43.

ARPAIA, ANTHONY F. "A Matter of Necessity, Independent Tribunal to Adjudicate Labor Disputes; Address, April 2, 1964." *Vital Speeches of the Day* 30, no. 15 (May 15, 1964): 477–80.

ASSOCIATION OF AMERICAN RAILROADS. "Why Railroad Featherbeds Must Go." *Railway Digest of Developments and Comments* 14 (April 1959): 32 pp.

BACKMAN, JULES. "The Size of Crews." *Labor Law Journal* 12, no. 9 (September 1961): 805–15.

BARDEN, JOHN. "Railroad Labor Crisis." *Nation* 189, no. 7 (September 12, 1959): 128–33.

BURCK, GILBERT. "Great Featherbed Fight." *Fortune* 61 (March 1960): 151–53+.

CIMINI, MICHAEL. "Government Intervention in Railroad Disputes." *Monthly Labor Review* 94, no. 12 (December 1971): 27–34.

DUNAND, GEORGE. "Technical Progress and Job Security in the U.S. Railroads." *International Labour Review* 89, no. 5 (May 1964): 482–95.

"The F.E.C. Story: Survival without Unions?" *Railway Age* 157, no. 4 (July 27, 1964): 34–41, 54–55.

FITCH, EDWIN M. "The Government and Bargaining on the Alaska Railroad." *Monthly Labor Review* 84, no. 5 (May 1961): 459–62.

FOY, MICHAEL. "Progress on the Railroads." *American Federationist* 63 (August 1956): 12–13, 29.

GLENN, ROBERT L., and G. LLOYD WILSON. "Keeping the Peace in Railroad Transportation." *Annals of the American Academy of Political and Social Science* 248 (November 1946): 110–19.

GOMBERG, WILLIAM. "Featherbedding: An Assertion of Property Rights." *Annals of the American Academy of Political and Social Science* 333 (January 1961): 119–29.

HARRISON, GEORGE M. "Rail Labor Seeks Wage Boost." *American Federationist* 54 (September 1947): 8–9, 32.

———. "Railroad Problems Today." *American Federationist* 68 (February 1957): 4–6, 29–31.

HOROWITZ, MORRIS A. "The Diesel Firemen Issue on the Railroads." *Industrial and Labor Relations Review* 13, no. 4 (July 1960): 550–58.

———. "The Railroad's Dual System of Payment: A Make-Work Rule?" *Industrial and Labor Relations Review* 8, no. 2 (January 1955): 177–94.

"Is It Endsville for the Railroads?" *Forbes* 104, no. 8 (October 15, 1969): 30–34, 39–40.

KAUFMAN, JACOB J. "Grievance Procedures under the Railway Labor Act." *Southern Economic Journal* 19, no. 1 (July 1952): 66–78.

92

――――――. "The Railroad Labor Dispute [1959–1964]: A Marathon of Maneuvers and Improvisation." *Industrial and Labor Relations Review* 18, no. 2 (January 1965): 3–20.

――――――. "Wage Criteria in the Railroad Industry." *Industrial and Labor Relations Review* 6, no. 1 (October 1952): 119–22.

――――――. "Working Rules in the Railroad Industry." *Labor Law Journal* 5, no. 12 (December 1954): 819–27.

"Labor: The Big 'Rub.'" *Dun's Review of Modern Industry* 79, no. 6 (June 1962): 141–46.

"Labor-Management Relations under the Railway Labor Act, 1934–57." *Monthly Labor Review* 81, no. 8 (August 1958): 879–81.

"The Labor Month in Review." *Monthly Labor Review* 86, no. 8 (August 1963): iii–iv.

"The Labor Month in Review: Wage Disputes in Progress, Mid-October." *Monthly Labor Review* 78, no. 10 (October 1955): iii–iv.

LEIGHTY, GEORGE E. "Are Railroad Workers Featherbedding?" *Vital Speeches of the Day* 26, no. 6 (January 1, 1960): 175–79.

――――――. "Railroad Propaganda Ignores the Facts." *American Federationist* 66 (December 1959): 4–6, 28–30.

LEVINE, MARVIN J. "The Railroad Crew Size Controversy Revisited." *Labor Law Journal* 20, no. 6 (June 1969): 373–86.

LIPSON, H. MICHAEL. "The Great Train Robbery: Railroad Full Crew Laws." *George Washington Law Review* 37 (October 1968): 153–67.

LOOMIS, DANIEL P. "The Law and Railway Labor." *Railway Age* 124, no. 3 (January 17, 1948): 162–64, 173.

MANGUM, GARTH L. "Grievance Procedures for Railroad Operating Employees." *Industrial and Labor Relations Review* 15, no. 4 (July 1962): 474–99.

MEYERS, FREDERIC. "Criteria in the Making of Wage Decisions by 'Neutrals': Railroads as a Case Study." *Industrial and Labor Relations Review* 4, no. 3 (April 1951): 343–55.

――――――. "Organization and Collective Bargaining in the Local Mass Transportation Industry in the Southeast." *Southern Economic Journal* 15, no. 4 (April 1949): 425–40.

MURPHY, EDWARD F. "Injunctive Prevention of Strikes on Railroads and Airlines." *Labor Law Journal* 9, no. 5: 329–42.

NEWBORN, NORTON. "Restrictions on the Right to Strike on the Railroads: A History and Analysis." (In 2 parts.) *Labor Law Journal* 24, no. 3 (March 1973): 142–63; 24, no. 4 (April 1973): 234–50.

NORTHRUP, HERBERT R. "The Appropriate Bargaining Unit Question under the Railway Labor Act." *Quarterly Journal of Economics* 60 (February 1946): 250–69.

――――――. "Emergency Disputes under the Railway Labor Act." *Industrial Relations Research Association, Proceedings of the First Annual Meeting*, December 29–30, 1948: 78–97.

――――――. "Unfair Labor Practice Prevention under the Railway Labor Act." *Industrial and Labor Relations Review* 3, no. 3 (April 1950): 323–40.

NORTHRUP, HERBERT R., and MARK L. KAHN. "Railroad Grievance Machinery: A Critical Analysis — I." *Industrial and Labor Relations Review* 5, no. 3 (April 1952): 365–82.

――――――. "Railroad Grievance Machinery: A Critical Analysis — II." *Industrial and Labor Relations Review* 5, no. 6 (July 1952): 540–59.

PETTENGIL, SAMUEL. "Power versus Law: Government Failure to Uphold Railway Labor Act." *Vital Speeches of the Day* 12, no. 18 (July 1, 1946): 574–75.

"Public Loss or Private Profit; Implications of the Railway Settlement." *Round Table* 45, no. 177 (March 1955): 138–42.

"Rail Labor's Plight." *Brotherhood of Maintenance of Way Employes Journal* 62 (January 1953): 8–10.

"Rail Strikes: Search for End to Recurring Problem." *Congressional Quarterly Weekly Report* 29, no. 25 (June 18, 1941): 1322–27.

"The Railroad Commission's Recommendations." *Monthly Labor Review* 85, no. 4 (April 1962): 375–89.

"Railroad Controversy Results in 2-Day Stoppage." *Monthly Labor Review* 63, no. 1 (July 1946): 84–86.

"Railroad Employment Protective Agreement." *Monthly Labor Review* 88, no. 4 (April 1965): 416–18.

"Reduction of Backlog in Railroad Grievance Cases." *Monthly Labor Review* 70, no. 4 (April 1950): 403–4.

"Rules for the Rails." *Fortune* 65 (January 1962): 145.

"Significant Decisions in Labor Cases: On Prohibiting a Railroad from Abolishing Jobs without Consent of the Union." *Monthly Labor Review* 83, no. 6 (June 1960): 623–27.

"Significant Decisions in Labor Cases — Selective Railroad Strikes." *Monthly Labor Review* 94, no. 9 (September 1971): 62–63.

"Technological Change and the Railroads." *Railway Age* 159, no. 18 (November 8, 1965): 16–21.

TROY, LEO. "Labor Representation on American Railways." *Labor History* 2, no. 3 (Fall 1961): 295–322.

TRUMAN, HARRY S. "The Railroad Strike." *Vital Speeches of the Day* 12, no. 16 (June 1, 1946): 482–83.

"A Wage Award on the Alaska Railroad." *Monthly Labor Review* 81, no. 9 (September 1958): 965–73.

WEIDY, GARY R. "The Crew Consist Issue since 1959." *Industrial and Labor Relations Forum* 9, no. 3 (October 1973): 1–44.

"Work Rules Report: Board Asks End to Feather-bedding." *Railway Age* 152, no. 9 (March 5, 1962): 9–10, 38–39, 52–56, 58.

8. Retirement, Protective Programs

1850–98

JOHNSON, EMORY R. "Railway Departments for the Relief and Insurance of Employes." *Annals of the American Academy of Political and Social Science* 6, no. 3 (November 1895): 424–68.

"The Measure of Damages for Personal Injuries on Railways." *Merchants' Magazine and Commercial Review* 63 (November 1870): 355–60.

PITCHER, JAMES R. "Accidents and Accident Insurance." *Forum* 12 (September 1891): 131–37.

1898–1926

CLARK, LINDLEY D. "When a Railroad Employee Is Hurt: The Legal Tangle." *Journal of Political Economy* 24, no. 8 (October 1916): 805–10.

———. "Rights and Status of Employees Injured in Commerce." *Monthly Labor Review* 15, no. 2 (August 1922): 399–409.

———. "Workmen's Compensation and the Federal Congress." *Journal of Political Economy* 23, no. 8 (October 1915): 814–21.

"Extension of Civil Pensions." *Independent* 66, no. 3157 (June 3, 1909): 1252–53.

GARDNER, W. A. "Railroad Rewards and Pensions." *Independent* 53, no. 2730 (March 28, 1901): 729–30.

HENDERSON, CHARLES RICHMOND. "Insurance Plans of Railroad Corporations." *American Journal of Sociology* 13, no. 5 (March 1908): 584–616.

JOHNSON, E. R. "Brotherhood Relief and Insurance of Railway Employees." *Bulletin of the Department of Labor* 3 (July 1898): 552–96.

"Liability Law Void." *Charities and the Commons* 19 (January 18, 1908): 1402–3.

RIEBENACK, M. "Pennsylvania Railroad Pension Departments: Systems East and West of Pittsburgh and Erie, Pa.: Status to and Including the Year 1907." *Annals of the American Academy of Political and Social Science* 33, no. 2 (March 1909): 258–64.

"Rights and Status of Employees Injured in Commerce." *Monthly Labor Review* 15, no. 2 (August 1922): 399–409.

VREELAND, H. H. "Pensioning Street Railway Employees." *Outlook* 70, no. 13 (March 29, 1902): 766–67.

"When Are Railroad Employees Engaged in Interstate Commerce?" *American Law Review* 47 (September–October 1913): 771–74.

1926–46

"Agreement for Retirement Plan for Railroad Employees." *Monthly Labor Review* 44, no. 5 (May 1937): 1126–27.

"Annuity and Pension Payments under Railroad Retirement Act, 1938." *Monthly Labor Review* 48, no. 5 (May 1939): 1055–57.

BEYER, OTTO S., JR. "Cost of Occupational Accidents in the Railroad Industry." *American Labor Legislation Review* 25, no. 4 (December 1935): 174–78.

———. "Unemployment Compensation in the Transportation Industry." *Annals of the American Academy of Political and Social Science* 187 (September 1936): 95–105.

"The Board's Programs for Railroad Workers: I. Retirement and Survivor Benefits." *Monthly Review of the Railroad Retirement Board* 4, no. 11 (November 1943): 228–32.

"The Board's Programs for Railroad Workers: II. The Unemployment Insurance Benefit. *Monthly Review of the Railroad Retirement Board* 4, no. 12 (December 1943): 252–55.

"The Board's Programs for Railroad Workers: III. Placing Railroad Workers." *Monthly Review of the Railroad Retirement Board* 5, no. 1 (January–February 1944): 2–3, 16.

BROWN, PHILIP KING. "Tuberculosis Control in a Railway Health Insurance Program." *American Journal of Public Health and the Nation's Health* 25, no. 6 (June 1935): 741–48.

"The Bureau of Employment and Claims." *Monthly Review of the Railroad Retirement Board* 2, no. 7 (July 1941): 7–9, 16.

CLARK, LINDLEY D. "Workmen's Compensation and the Railroads: A Hesitating Revolution." *Journal of Political Economy* 41, no. 6 (December 1933): 806–20.

COCHRANE, C. "Railway Employees Accident Compensation." *American Labor Legislation Review* 18, no. 4 (December 1928): 341–43.

"Decision on Railroad Employees' Retirement Act of 1935." *Monthly Labor Review* 43, no. 2 (August 1936): 528–30.

"Determination of Employment Relation Practices." *Monthly Review of the Railroad Retirement Board* 2, no. 10 (October 1941): 9–14.

"Determination of Employment Relation Rules." *Monthly Review of the Railroad Retirement Board* 2, no. 9 (September 1941): 8–13, 24.

"Displacement Compensation for Railroad Workers." *Labor Information Bulletin* 3, no. 7 (July 1936): 6–7.

DOAK, W. N. "The Attitude of the Railroad Brotherhoods toward Workmen's Compensation and the Reason for Such Attitude." *Bulletin of the U.S. Bureau of Labor Statistics*, no. 564 (April 1932): 53–61.

EKERN, HERMAN L. "Railroad Pensions." *American Labor Legislation Review* 25, no. 3 (September 1934): 124–27.

"Employees' Service and Compensation for 1941." *Monthly Review of the Railroad Retirement Board* 4, no. 1 (January 1943): 4–8.

"Employment Relation Determinations and Certifications." *Monthly Review of the Railroad Retirement Board* 2, no. 12 (December 1941): 3–8, 13.

"Federal Unemployment Compensation Adopted for Railway Workers." *American Labor Legislation Review* 28, no. 3 (September 1938): 140–41.

"Field Organization of the Railroad Retirement Board." *Monthly Review of the Railroad Retirement Board* 2, no. 6 (June 1941): 5–8.

"Financing Railroad Pension Plans." *Monthly Labor Review* 31, no. 4 (October 1930): 911–14.

HARRISON, GEORGE M. "Railway Labor Favors Federal Accident Compensation Law." *American Labor Legislation Review* 24, no. 4 (December 1934): 161–63.

"How the Board Controls Its Operations: III. Administrative Controls." *Monthly Review of the Railroad Retirement Board* 6, no. 12 (December 1945): 194–96, 203.

"Labor Legislation Enacted by 73rd Congress: Railroads and Their Employees." *Monthly Labor Review* 39, no. 2 (August 1934): 352–67.

LATIMER, MURRAY W. "New Railroad Retirement Act of 1935." *American Labor Legislation Review* 25, no. 3 (September 1935): 136–38.

————. "Railroad Retirement Developments." *American Labor Legislation Review* 27, no. 1 (March 1937): 34–35.

LOREE, L. F. "Railway Employer Favors Workmen's Compensation." *American Labor Legislation Review* 23, no. 2 (June 1933): 110–11.

"The Meaning of Employment Relation." *Monthly Review of the Railroad Retirement Board* 2, no. 8 (August 1941): 5–8.

MILLER, CLARENCE A. "The Quest for a Federal Workman's Compensation Law for Railroad Employees." *Law and Contemporary Problems* 18, no. 2 (Spring 1953): 188–207.

MILLER, VERNON X. "An Interpretation of the Act of 1939 (FELA) to Save Some Remedies for Compensation Claimants." *Law and Contemporary Problems* 18, no. 2 (Spring 1953): 241–55.

MYERS, ROBERT J. "Security for Railway Workers." *American Federationist* 44 (December 1937): 1315–19.

OLIVER, E. L. "Railway Accidents and Unemployment." *American Labor Legislation Review* 26, no. 2 (June 1936): 67–71.

"Operations under Railroad Unemployment-Insurance-Act, 1939." *Monthly Labor Review* 50, no. 3 (March 1940): 640–43.

"Organized for Service: Structure of the Railroad Retirement Board." *Monthly Review of the Railroad Retirement Board* 3, no. 8 (September 1942): 207–12.

"Present Federal Agencies Dealing with the Railroads." *Congressional Digest* 18, nos. 8–9 (August–September 1939): 196–97.

"Railroad Employees Retirement Act of 1935." *Monthly Labor Review* 41, no. 4 (October 1935): 923.

"Railroad Employees' Retirement Law Declared Unconstitutional." *Monthly Labor Review* 40, no. 6 (June 1935): 1511–22.

"Railroad Retirement Act Faces Supreme Court Test." *American Labor Legislation Review* 24 (December 1934): 163–64.

"Railroad Retirement Act Held Unconstitutional by District of Columbia Supreme Court." *Monthly Labor Review* 40, no. 1 (January 1935): 76–77.

"Railroad Retirement Act of 1937." *Monthly Labor Review* 45, no. 2 (August 1937): 377–79.

"Railroad Retirement Benefits, 1941–42." *Monthly Labor Review* 55, no. 4 (October 1942): 743.

"Railroad Retirement Benefits, 1942–43." *Monthly Labor Review* 57, no. 5 (November 1943): 945–46.

"Railroad Retirement Benefits, 1943–44." *Monthly Labor Review* 60, no. 6 (June 1945): 1237–39.

"Railroad Retirement and Social Security." *Monthly Labor Review* 47, no. 4 (October 1938): 759–61.

"Railroad Unemployment-Insurance Act, 1938." *Monthly Labor Review* 47, no. 2 (August 1938): 341–44.

"Railroad Unemployment Insurance and Employment Service, 1943–44." *Social Security Bulletin* 7, no. 8 (August 1944): 31–32.

RICHBERG, DONALD R. "Advantages of a Federal Compensation Act for Railway Employees." *American Labor Legislation Review* 21, no. 4 (December 1931): 401–5.

————. "Workmen's Compensation for Railway Employees." *American Labor Legislation Review* 23, no. 1 (March 1933): 51–54.

SCHOENE, LESTER R., and FRANK WATSON. "Workmen's Compensation on Interstate Railways." *Harvard Law Review* 47, no. 3 (January 1934): 389–424.

"Twenty Years of Benefit Programs for Railroad Workers." *Monthly Labor Review* 79, no. 7 (July 1956): 815–17.

"Wages and Service of Employees in 1939." *Monthly Review of the Railroad Retirement Board* 2, no. 2 (February 1941): 5–10.

WAGNER, ROBERT F. "Federal Workmen's Compensation for Transportation Workers." *American Labor Legislation Review* 26, no. 1 (March 1936): 15–20.

"Workmen's Compensation for Railway Employees." *American Labor Legislation Review* 19, no. 4 (December 1929): 381–82.

1946–Present

AFROS, JOHN L. "Guaranteed Employment Plan of Seaboard Railroad." *Monthly Labor Review* 65, no. 2 (August 1947): 167–71.

"Benefit Exhaustions, 1948–49: Railroad Unemployment Insurance." *Monthly Labor Review* 70, no. 3 (March 1950): 299–301.

"Benefits under RUIA in 1961–62 — Part I." *Monthly Review of the Railroad Retirement Board* 24, no. 1 (January 1963): 12–14.

"Benefits under RUIA in 1961–62 — Part II." *Monthly Review of the Railroad Retirement Board* 24, no. 2 (February 1963): 3–6.

BIXBY, ALDEN F. "Statistics and Estimates for the U.S. Railroad Sickness Benefit Programme." *International Social Security Association Bulletin* 11 (June 1958): 209–19.

CARSON, DANIEL. "Sickness Benefits for Railroad Employees." *American Economic Security* 5, no. 8 (December 1948): 29–35.

DEPARQ, WILLIAM H. "A Decade of Progress under the Federal Employers' Liability Act." *Law and Contemporary Problems* 18, no. 3 (Summer 1953): 257–80.

"Development of the Railroad Retirement and Unemployment Insurance Systems, Developments through 1953." *Monthly Review of the Railroad Retirement Board* 15, no. 7 (July 1954): 123–29.

"Dual Beneficiaries under Railroad Retirement and Social Security Acts, 1962." *Monthly Review of the Railroad Retirement Board* 26, no. 3 (March 1965): 2–6, 13.

"Economic Protection for Railroad Workers." (In 8 parts.) *Monthly Review of the Railroad Retirement Board* 23, no. 12 (December 1962): 11–13; 24, no. 1 (January 1963): 6–9; 24, no. 3 (March 1963): 15–17; 24, no. 4 (April 1963): 9–11; 24, no. 5 (May 1963): 12–13; 24, no. 6 (June 1963): 11–13; 24, no. 9 (September 1963): 12–14; 24, no. 11 (November 1963): 12–14.

ELKIN, JACK M. "The 1946 Amendments to the Railroad Retirement and Railroad Unemployment Insurance Acts." *Social Security Bulletin* 9, no. 12 (December 1946): 23–33, 49–50.

"Employers and Employees Cooperating with [Railroad Retirement] Board on Setting Up Disability Standards." *Monthly Review of the Railroad Retirement Board* 7, no. 12 (December 1946): 234–36.

ENNIS, JOHN M. "An Analysis of Judicial Interpretation and Application of Certain Aspects of the Federal Employers' Liability Act." *Law and Contemporary Problems* 18, no. 3 (Summer 1953): 350–66.

"Establishing Occupational Disability Standards." *Monthly Review of the Railroad Retirement Board* 8, no. 3 (March 1947): 62–64.

RETIREMENT, PROTECTIVE PROGRAMS

GERSTLE, WALTER. "Disability, Retirement, and Mortality of American Railroaders [Address]." *Industrial Medicine and Surgery* 29 (December 1960): 570–76.

GRIFFITH, MELVIN. "The Vindication of a National Public Policy under the Federal Employers' Liability Act." *Law and Contemporary Problems* 18, no. 2 (Spring 1953): 160–87.

"Insurance Status of Railroad Employees." *Monthly Review of the Railroad Retirement Board* 10, no. 4 (April 1949): 70–76.

JAFFE, LOUIS L. "Damages for Personal Injury: The Impact of Insurance." *Law and Contemporary Problems* 18, no. 2 (Spring 1953): 219–40.

KENDRICK, B. B. "Rationalizing Social Security Protection for Railroad Workers." *American Economic Security* 4, no. 6 (October 1947): 20–26.

LAZERSON, JACOB A. "1959 Amendments to the Railroad Retirement Act." *Social Security Bulletin* 22, no. 7 (July 1959): 16–20.

"Life Insurance in Force under the RRA." *Monthly Review of the Railroad Retirement Board* 24, no. 4 (April 1963): 2–6.

LOUISELL, DAVID W., and KENNETH M. ANDERSON. "The Safety Appliance Act and the F.E.L.A.: A Plea for Clarification." *Law and Contemporary Problems* 18, no. 3 (Summer 1953): 281–95.

MATSCHECK, WALTER, and JACK M. ELKIN. "Recent Changes in the Railroad Retirement and Survivor Benefit Program." *American Economic Security* 9, no. 1 (January–February 1952): 28–36.

MILLER, CLARENCE A. "The Quest for a Federal Workmen's Compensation Law for Railroad Employees." *Law and Contemporary Problems* 18, no. 2 (Spring 1953): 188–207.

NICHOLS, ORLO. "The Railroad Retirement Amendments of 1968." *Social Security Bulletin* 31, no. 6 (June 1968): 7–13.

NIESSEN, ABRAHAM M. "Coordination between the Railroad Retirement and Social Security Systems." *Social Security Bulletin* 31, no. 9 (September 1968): 15–19.

————. "Railroad Social Insurance in America." *International Social Security Review* 23 (November 3, 1970): 425-34.

PARKER, REGINALD. "FELA or Uniform Compensation for All Workers?" *Law and Contemporary Problems* 18, no. 2 (Spring 1953): 208–18.

"Patterns of Operation . . . Board's Administrative Structure Revised." *Monthly Review of the Railroad Retirement Board* 7, no. 10 (October 1946): 182–86, 194.

"Permanent Disability Protection for Railroad Workers." *Monthly Review of the Railroad Retirement Board* 11, no. 5 (May 1950): 82–86.

POLLACK, JEROME. "The Crisis in Work Injury Compensation on and off the Railroads." *Law and Contemporary Problems* 18, no. 3 (Summer 1953): 296–319.

"Private Pension Plans for Railroad Employees, 1949." *Monthly Labor Review* 70, no. 6 (June 1950): 639–41.

"Railroad Retirement Board Operations, 1956–57." *Monthly Labor Review* 81, no. 5 (May 1958): 527–29.

"Railroad Retirement and Unemployment Insurance in 1953–54." *Monthly Labor Review* 8, no. 5 (May 1955): 560–61.

"Regulations, Rulings and Legal Opinions." *Monthly Review of the Railroad Retirement Board* 8, no. 3 (March 1947): 65.

"Retirement and Survivor Benefit Operations." *Monthly Review of the Railroad Retirement Board* 9, no. 8 (August 1948): 169–76.

REUSS, FREDERICK G. "The Amended Railroad Retirement Act and the Old-age and Survivors' Insurance System under the Social Security Act." *Social Forces* 25, no. 4 (May 1947): 446–51.

"A Review of Board Activities in 1946–47." *Monthly Review of the Railroad Retirement Board* 8, no. 8 (August 1947): 170–76.

RICHE, MARTHA F. "Railroad Unemployment Insurance." *Monthly Labor Review* 90, no. 11 (November 1967): 9–18.

"Sickness Benefits for Railroad Workers, 1947." *Monthly Labor Review* 66, no. 4 (April 1948): 402.

"Sickness and Maternity Benefits for Railroad Workers." *Monthly Labor Review* 65, no. 2 (August 1947): 194–95.

"Sickness and Unemployment Benefits for Railroad Workers." *Monthly Labor Review* 78, no. 8 (August 1955): 907–9.

"Story of the Railroad Retirement and Railroad Unemployment Acts." *Brotherhood of Locomotive Firemen and Enginemen's Magazine* 131, no. 6 (December 1951): 355–57.

"Summary of 1946 Amendments." *Monthly Review of the Railroad Retirement Board* 7, no. 9 (September 1946): 158–64.

"Summary of 1948 Amendments [to the Railroad Retirement and Railroad Unemployment Insurance Acts]." *Monthly Review of the Railroad Retirement Board* 9, no. 7 (July 1948): 134–39, 144.

"25 Years of Railroad Unemployment Insurance: Benefits and Beneficiaries, Financing of the System." *Monthly Review of the Railroad Retirement Board* 25, no. 6 (June 1964): 2–16.

"Twenty Years of Benefit Programs for Railroad Workers." *Monthly Labor Review* 79, no. 7, (July 1956): 815–17.

"Unemployment Beneficiaries in First 13 Years of Operations." *Monthly Review of the Railroad Retirement Board* 14, no. 5 (May 1953): 83–87.

"Unemployment Insurance Operations." [1946–47.] *Monthly Review of the Railroad Retirement Board* 8, no. 5 (August 1947): 183–86.

PART V

GOVERNMENT DOCUMENTS

1. Management

U.S. DEPARTMENT OF TRANSPORTATION. National Transportation Safety Board. *Good Supervisors Make Good Safety Records*. Address by John H. Reed, Chairman. Prepared for delivery at annual meeting of safety section, Association of American Railroads, Washington, D.C., June 13, 1972. Washington, D.C.: GPO, 1972. 6 pp.

U.S. RAILROAD ADMINISTRATION. Operation Division. *Efficient and Sufficient Supervision of Railroad Shops*. Bulletin 6. Paper presented before New York Railroad Club. Washington, D.C.: GPO, 1918. 8 pp.

2. Labor Force

1850–98

U.S. INDUSTRIAL COMMISSION. "Railway Labor," vol. 4, pt. 1, pp. 131–60. *Reports of the Industrial Commission, 1900–1902*. 19 vols. Washington, D.C.: GPO, 1900–1902.

————. "Railway Labor in the United States," vol. 17, pp. 709–1135. *Reports of the Industrial Commission, 1900–1902*. 19 vols. Washington, D.C.: GPO, 1900–1902.

U.S. OFFICE OF EDUCATION. "Service Report on Technical Education, with Special Reference to Baltimore and Ohio Railroad Service [Recommending Establishment of Technological School for Railroad Employees]," by W. T. Barnard. In *Art and Industry. Education in the Industrial and Fine Arts in the United States*, by Isaac E. Clarke, pt. 4, pp. 129–30, 132–47, 747–833. Washington, D.C.: GPO, 1885–98.

1898–1926

U.S. BUREAU OF EDUCATION. *Education for Efficiency in Railroad Service*. Bulletin 10. Washington, D.C.: GPO, 1909. 159 pp.

————. "Educational Training for Railroad Service," pp. 305–23. *Report of the Commissioner of Education for the Year 1900–1901*, vol. 1. Washington, D.C.: GPO, 1902.

U.S. CONGRESS. Senate. *Information Relating to Demotion of Certain Clerks in Railway Mail Service*. S. Doc. 1130, 62nd Cong., 3rd Sess. Washington, D.C.: GPO, 1913. 80 pp.

————. Senate. *Response by Post Office Department to Resolution, Information Relative to Opportunities for Promotion of Railway Mail Clerks, and Condition of Railway Mail Cars*. S. Doc. 826, 61st Cong., 3rd Sess. Washington, D.C.: GPO, 1911. 6 pp.

U.S. INDUSTRIAL COMMISSION. "Consolidation of Railroads in the United States," vol. 19, pt. 3, pp. 304–29. *Reports of the Industrial Commission, 1900–1902.* 19 vols. Washington, D.C.: GPO, 1900–1902.

————. "Railway Labor," vol. 4, pt. 1, pp. 131–60. *Reports of the Industrial Commission, 1900–1902.* 19 vols. Washington, D.C.: GPO, 1900–1902.

U.S. INTERSTATE COMMERCE COMMISSION. *Rules Governing the Classification of Steam Railway Employees and Reports of Their Service and Compensation, Effective on July 1, 1921.* Washington, D.C.: GPO, 1921. 13 pp.

————. *Rules Governing the Classification of Steam Railway Employees and Their Compensation, Effective July 1, 1915.* Washington, D.C.: GPO, 1915. 13 pp.

————. Bureau of Statistics. *Bulletin concerning Employment of Women on Large Steam Roads in 1920.* Washington, D.C.: GPO, 1921. 5 pp.

U.S. RAILROAD ADMINISTRATION. *Comparative Amounts of Railroad Labor and Pay, Dec. 1917 and Jan.–July 1919: Letter to Congress, Submitting Statements.* S. Doc. 154, 66th Cong., 1st Sess. Washington, D.C.: GPO, 1919. 184 pp.

————. Labor Division. *Number of Women Employed and Character of Their Employment, (Class 1 Roads), Eastern, Southern, and Western Territories by Roads,* prepared by Women's Service Section. Washington, D.C.: GPO, 1920. 34 pp.

U.S. RAILROAD LABOR BOARD. *Classification of Railroad Positions, Announcement of New Classification of Railroad Positions.* Chicago, 1921. 4 pp.

————. *Classification of Railroad Positions (Statement respecting the Necessity for a Classification of Railroad Positions), Sept. 22, 1920.* Chicago, 1920. 4 pp.

1926–46

U.S. BUREAU OF LABOR STATISTICS. *Labor Requirements on Railroad Electrification Program,* by Herman B. Byer. Serial No. R. 441. Washington, D.C.: GPO, 1941. 5 pp.

————. *Productivity and Unit Labor Cost in Steam Railroad Transportation, 1935–44.* Washington, D.C.: GPO, 1945. 4 pp.

————. *Wartime Labor Productivity in Railroad Transportation,* by Kenneth A. Middleton. Serial No. R. 1569. Washington, D.C.: GPO, 1943. 8 pp.

————. *Women in the Railroad Industry during and after World War I* [with bibliography], by Mary F. Jessup. Historical Study No. 70, Study of Wartime Problems, 1941–1945. Washington, D.C.: GPO, 1944. 47 pp.

U.S. COMMITTEE ON FAIR EMPLOYMENT PRACTICE (1943–46). *A Hearing to Hear Evidence on Complaints of Racial Discrimination in Employment on Certain Railroads of the United States.* Washington, D.C., 1943.

U.S. DEPARTMENT OF COMMERCE. "Railroads and Unemployment," by L. A. Downs. In *Unemployment: Industry Seeks a Solution* [series of radio addresses], pp. 30–31. Washington, D.C.: GPO, 1931.

U.S. DEPARTMENT OF LABOR. Children's Bureau. *Which Jobs for Young Workers: Advisory Standards for the Railroad Industry.* Washington, D.C.: GPO, 1944. 7 pp.

U.S. DEPARTMENT OF TREASURY. Public Health Service. *Frequency of Sickness and Nonindustrial Accidents Causing Disability Lasting 8 Calendar Days or Longer among 60,000 White Male Railroad Employees, 1930–34,* by W. M. Gafafer. Washington, D.C.: GPO, 1938. 19 pp.

U.S. INTERSTATE COMMERCE COMMISSION. *Ex parte no. 72 (sub-no. 1), In Matter of Regulations concerning Class of Employees and Subordinate Officials to Be Included within Term "Employee" under Railway Labor Act, Elevator Starters and Operators, and Information Clerks, Hudson and Manhattan Railroad Co.* Decided May 6, 1941. Opinion 23567. *ICC Reports,* vol. 245, pp. 415–28. Washington, D.C.: GPO, 1941.

————. *Ex parte no. 72 (sub-no. 1), In Matter of Regulations concerning Class of Employees and Subordinate Officials to Be Included within Term "Employee" under Railway Labor Act, News Agents, Atchison, Topeka and Santa Fe Railway Co.* Decided July 9, 1941. Opinion 23637. *ICC Reports,* vol. 246, pp. 24–26. Washington, D.C.: GPO, 1941.

————. *Ex parte no. 72 (sub-no. 1), In Matter of Regulations concerning Class of Employees and Subordinate Officials to Be Included within Term "Employee" under Railway Labor Act, Ore Dock Foremen and Laborers.* Decided October 6, 1941. Opinion 23756. *ICC Reports,* vol. 246, pp. 703–11. Washington, D.C.: GPO, 1942.

U.S. OFFICE OF DEFENSE TRANSPORTATION. *"Featherbed Rules," Railroad Manpower, and the Toledo, Peoria, and Western Railroad,* by J. B. Eastman. Interstate Commerce Building. Washington, D.C.: GPO, 1943. 11 pp.

U.S. OFFICE FOR EMERGENCY MANAGEMENT. War Manpower Commission. *Labor Market Information for U.S. Employment Service Counseling: Industry Series 40-1.* "Railroads" [with bibliography]. Washington, D.C.: GPO, 1944. 8 pp.

————. War Manpower Commission. *Postwar Apprentices of American Railroads,* by B. M. Brown. Training Bureau, Apprentice-Training Service. Washington, D.C.: GPO, 1945. 6 pp.

U.S. OFFICE OF FEDERAL COORDINATOR OF TRANSPORTATION. Section of Labor Relations. *Employment Attrition in the Railroad Industry.* Washington, D.C.: GPO, 1936. 59 pp.

U.S. RAILROAD RETIREMENT BOARD. *Compensation, Service and Age, Railroad Employees, 1939. Statistical Tables.* 6 vols. [Title varies.] Chicago, 1945–50.

1946–Present

TRANSPORTATION INVESTIGATION AND RESEARCH BOARD. *Railroad Consolidation and Employee Welfare: Letter Submitted by Mr. Stewart.* S. Doc. 77, 79th Cong., 1st Sess. Washington, D.C.: GPO, 1945. 43 pp.

U.S. BUREAU OF LABOR STATISTICS. *Employment and Changing Occupational Patterns in the Railroad Industry, 1947–60.* Bulletin 1344. Washington, D.C.: GPO, 1963. 32 pp.

————. *Employment Outlook in Railroad Occupations.* Bulletin 961. Washington, D.C.: GPO, 1949. 52 pp.

————. "Railroad Occupations," pp. 404–34. *Occupational Outlook Handbook.* Bulletin 998. Washington, D.C.: GPO, 1951.

————. *Railroad Technology and Manpower in 1970's,* by Richard Johnson. Bulletin 1717. Washington, D.C.: GPO, 1972. 90 pp.

U.S. CONGRESS. House. *Employment Outlook in Railroad Occupations* [with bibliographies], prepared by Helen Wood, Gloria Count, and Raymond D. Larson. H. Doc. 200, 81st Cong., 1st Sess. Washington, D.C.: GPO, 1949. 52 pp.

————. Joint Economic Committee. "Statement of W. P. Kennedy, President, Brotherhood of Railroad Trainmen," pp. 515–32. *New Views on Automation: Papers Sub-*

mitted to the Subcommittee on Automation and Energy Resources. Washington, D.C.: GPO, 1960.

————. Senate. Committee on Labor and Public Welfare. *Causes of Unemployment in Coal and Other Specified Industries.* S. Rept. 2042 Pursuant to S. Res. 274 with Supplemental Views of Mr. Taft, 81st Cong., 2nd Sess. Washington, D.C.: GPO, 1950. 22 pp.

————. Senate. Committee on Labor and Public Welfare. *Causes of Unemployment in the Coal and Other Specified Industries: Hearings before a Subcommittee on S. Res. 274.* 81st Cong., 2nd Sess. Washington, D.C.: GPO, 1950. 512 pp.

U.S. DEPARTMENT OF LABOR. Commissioner of Labor Statistics. *Productivity and Employment in Railroad Industry.* Address by Ewan Clague, Commissioner, before Railway Systems and Management Association, Chicago, November 28, 1962. Washington, D.C.: GPO, 1963. 14 leaves.

U.S. RAILROAD RETIREMENT BOARD. *Economic Factors Influencing Railroad Employment,* by Maurice Parmelee. Office of Director of Research. Chicago, 1946. 152 pp.

————. *Occupational Differences in Separation Rates for Railroad Workers, 1962–65,* by Jacob J. Stotland and James L. Cowen, in Actuarial Study 8 from Office of Chief, Actuary and Research. Chicago, 1968. 39 pp.

3. Working Conditions

1850-98

U.S. BUREAU OF LABOR. *Railroad Labor: Annual Report of the Commissioner of Labor, 5th, 1889.* Also issued as H. Ex. Doc. 336, 51st Cong., 1st Sess. Washington, D.C.: GPO, 1889. 888 pp.

U.S. CONGRESS. House. "Classified Statement of Earnings and Time of Railroad Employees," pp. 167–881. *Fifth Annual Report of the Commissioner of Labor.* H. Ex. Doc. 336, vol. 36, 51st Cong., 1st Sess. Washington, D.C.: GPO, 1889.

U.S. INDUSTRIAL COMMISSION. "Railway Labor," vol. 4, pt. 1, pp. 131–60. *Reports of the Industrial Commission, 1900–1902.* 19 vols. Washington, D.C.: GPO, 1900–1902.

1898-1926

BUREAU OF RAILWAY ECONOMICS. *Effect of Recent Wage Advances upon Railway Employees' Compensation during the Year Ending June 30, 1911; Variations in the Number of Railway Employees, 1909–1910–1911; Relation of the Number of Employees and Their Compensation to Traffic and Revenue, 1909–1910–1911.* Bulletin 28. Washington, D.C., 1912. 47 pp.

————. *Railway Trainmen's Earnings, 1916.* Compiled from Reports to the Interstate Commerce Commission. Bureau Consecutive 107, Miscellaneous Series 28. Washington, D.C., 1917. 18 pp.

U.S. BOARD OF RAILROAD WAGES AND WORKING CONDITIONS. *Report of Hearings at Washington, D.C., by S. E. Heberling, July 21–31, 1919.* Washington, D.C.: GPO, 1919. 64 pp.

U.S. BUREAU OF EDUCATION. "Enforced Temperance among Railway Employees," pp. 1047–49. *Report of the Commissioner of Education*, vol. 1. Washington, D.C.: GPO, 1902.

U.S. BUREAU OF LABOR STATISTICS. *Annual Earnings of Railroad Employees, 1924–33.* Serial No. R. 262. Washington, D.C.: GPO, 1935. 12 pp.

U.S. BUREAU OF STATISTICS. "Railway Employees, Total Yearly and Average Daily Compensation, Years Ended July 30, 1900–07," pp. 236–38. In *Statistical Abstract, 1908.* Washington, D.C.: GPO, 1908.

U.S. COMMISSION ON INDUSTRIAL RELATIONS (1912). "Conditions of Labor on the Pennsylvania Railroad," vol. 11, pp. 10067–449. *Reports of the Industrial Commission.* Washington, D.C.: GPO, 1916.

U.S. DEPARTMENT OF LABOR. *Accidents to Railroad Employees in New Jersey, 1888 to 1907,* by F. S. Crum. Bulletin 84, pp. 183–337. Washington, D.C.: GPO, 1909.

U.S. EIGHT-HOUR COMMISSION. *Circular to Carriers by Railway concerning Daily Record of Service and Compensation of Individual Employees.* Washington, D.C.: GPO, 1917. 4 pp.

————. *Report of the Eight-Hour Commission.* Washington, D.C.: GPO, 1918. 503 pp. See especially appendix 6, "Railway Wage Schedules and Agreements," by William Z. Ripley, and appendix 7, "Employment Conditions in Road and Yard Service," by Victor S. Clark.

U.S. INDUSTRIAL COMMISSION. "Consolidation of Railroads in the United States," vol. 19, pt. 3, pp. 304–29. *Reports of the Industrial Commission, 1900–1902.* 19 vols. Washington, D.C.: GPO, 1900–1902.

————. "Railway Labor," vol. 4, pt. 1, pp. 131–60. *Reports of the Industrial Commission, 1900–1902.* 19 vols. Washington, D.C.: GPO, 1900–1902.

U.S. INDUSTRIAL RELATIONS COMMISSION. *Conditions of Labor on Pennsylvania Railroad.* S. Doc. 415, vol. 11, pp. 10067–449. 64th Cong., 1st Sess. Washington, D.C.: GPO, 1916.

U.S. INTERSTATE COMMERCE COMMISSION. *Effect of Principle of 6-Hour Day in Employment of All Classes of Railway Employees, Letter.* H. Doc. 496, 72nd Cong., 2nd Sess. Washington, D.C.: GPO, 1932. 52 pp.

————. *Hours of Service Law and Administrative Rulings and Opinions Thereon.* Washington, D.C.: GPO, 1912. 8 pp.

————. *Hours of Service Laws, and Administrative Rulings and Opinions Thereon.* Washington, D.C.: GPO, 1916. 10 pp.

————. *Living Conditions of Railway Trainmen Who Are Compelled to Lie Over at Railroad Terminals.* S. Doc. 314, 66th Cong., 3rd Sess. Washington, D.C.: GPO, 1920. 84 pp.

————. *Rules Governing the Classification of Steam Railway Employees and Reports of Their Service and Compensation, Effective on July 1, 1921.* Washington, D.C.: GPO, 1921. 13 pp.

————. *Rules Governing the Classification of Steam Railway Employees and Their Compensation, Effective July 1, 1915.* Washington, D.C.: GPO, 1915. 13 pp.

————. *Statement of Train Wrecks and Personal Injuries to [Railroad] Employees, Showing Causes of Accidents, Hours of Duty and Hours of Rest.* S. Doc. 406, 59th Cong., 1st Sess. Washington, D.C.: GPO, 1906.

U.S. OFFICE OF FEDERAL COORDINATOR OF TRANSPORTATION. Section of Labor Relations. *Annual Earnings of Railroad Employees, 1924–1933.* Washington, D.C.: GPO, 1935. 198 pp.

U.S. PRESIDENT [Woodrow Wilson]. *Hours of Service on Railroads.* Address delivered at joint session of the two houses of Congress, August 29, 1916. H. Doc. 1340, 64th Cong., 1st Sess. Washington, D.C.: GPO, 1916. 8 pp.

U.S. RAILROAD ADMINISTRATION. *Comparative Amounts of Railroad Labor and Pay, Dec. 1917 and Jan.–July, 1919: Letter to Congress, Submitting Statements.* S. Doc. 154, 66th Cong., 1st Sess. Washington, D.C.: GPO, 1919. 184 pp.

—————. Director General of Railroads. *General Order No. 27, with Its Supplements, Addenda, Amendments and Interpretations to June 30, 1919. Wages of Railroad Employees.* Washington, D.C.: GPO, 1919. 212 pp.

U.S. RAILROAD LABOR BOARD. *Average Daily and Monthly Wage Rates of Railroad Employees on Class I Carriers.* Chicago, 1920. 12 pp.

—————. *Average Daily and Monthly Wage Rates of Railroad Employees on Class I Carriers, in Effect under Private Control (Dec. 1917); under the U. S. Railroad Administration (Jan. 1920); and under Decisions Numbers 2 and 147 of U.S. Railroad Labor Board.* Wage Series Report No. 3. Chicago, 1922. 13 pp.

—————. *Average Daily Wage Rates of Railroad Employees on Class I Carriers.* Wage Series Report No. 4. Washington, D.C.: GPO, 1924. 12 pp.

—————. *Relation between Wages and the Increased Cost of Living: An Analysis of the Effect of Increased Wages and Profits upon Commodity Prices,* by W. J. Lauck. [With tables.] Chicago, 1920. 93 pp.

U.S. RAILROAD LABOR BOARD. Statistical Bureau. *Monthly and Annual Earnings and Details of Service of Train and Engine Service Employees, Calendar Year 1923, Compiled from Reports of 15 Representative Class I Carriers.* 12 vols. Washington, D.C.: GPO, 1926. 5866 pp.

—————. Statistical Bureau. *Rates of Pay of Mechanics and Helpers in Maintenance of Equipment Department, and of Coach Cleaners, 1925, All Territories, Class I Carriers.* Washington, D.C.: GPO, 1926. 981pp.

1926–46

U.S. BUREAU OF LABOR STATISTICS. *Annual Earnings of Railroad Employees, 1924–33.* Serial No. R. 262. Washington, D.C.: GPO, 1935. 12 pp.

—————. *Changes in Railroad Wages, 1943–44,* prepared by Witt Bowden. Serial No. R. 1634. Washington, D.C.: GPO, 1944. 16 pp.

—————. *Cost of Accidents to Railroad Employees, 1932.* Serial No. R. 283. Washington, D.C.: GPO, 1935. 7 pp.

—————. *Pennsylvania Railroad Wage Data: From Report of Joint Fact Finding Committee in Wage Negotiations, 1927.* Bulletin 514. Washington, D.C.: GPO, 1930. 207 pp.

—————. *Union Wages and Hours of Street-Railway Employees, June 1, 1940,* prepared by Frank S. McElroy. Serial No. R. 1249. Washington, D.C.: GPO, 1941. 12 pp.

—————. *Wage Chronology: Railroads, Nonoperating Employees, 1920–1961,* prepared by

106

Albert A. Belman. BLS Report 208. Washington, D.C.: GPO, 1962. 21 pp. Revised in 1963 to include data for 1962.

————. Children's Bureau and Women's Bureau. *Earnings and Standard of Living of 1,000 Railway Employees during the Depression,* by Carter Goodrich. Washington, D.C.: GPO, 1934. 56 pp.

U.S. DEPARTMENT OF LABOR. Wage and Hour Division. *Wage Order, Minimum Wage Rates in Railroad Carrier Industry, in Matter of Recommendations of Industry Com-mittee No. 9 for Minimum Wage Rates in Railroad Carrier Industry, Effective March 1, 1941.* Washington, D.C.: GPO, 1941. 4 pp.

U.S. FEDERAL WAGE COMMISSION. *Argument and Brief Submitted on Behalf of Locomotive Firemen and Hostlers: Hearings in Washington, D.C., Feb. 1918.* Cleveland, 1918. 285 pp.

————. *Excessive Hours of Service Required of Railway Employees: Tables, Argument and Brief Submitted on Behalf of Locomotive Firemen and Hostlers.* Washington, D.C.: GPO, 1918. pp. 129–56.

U.S. INTERSTATE COMMERCE COMMISSION. *Hours of Service Act, as Amended, and Administrative Rulings and Opinions Thereon.* Washington, D.C.: GPO, 1926. 7 pp.

————. *Railroad Salaries, Letter of Joseph B. Eastman, Member.* S. Doc. 129, 72nd Cong., 1st Sess. Washington, D.C.: GPO, 1932. 51 pp.

————. *Railroad Salaries, Letter of Joseph B. Eastman, Member, to Clarence C. Dill.* S. Doc. 80, 73rd Cong., 1st Sess. Washington, D.C.: GPO, 1933. 27 pp.

————. Bureau of Statistics. *Collisions, Derailments, and Other Accidents Resulting in Injury to Persons, Equipment or Roadbed, Arising from the Operation of Steam Railways in Interstate Commerce, Calendar Year 1930.* Accident Bulletin 99. Washington, D.C.: GPO, 1931. 106 pp.

————. Bureau of Statistics. *Summary and Analysis of Accidents on Steam Railways in the U.S. Subject to the Interstate Commerce Act, Calendar Year 1933.* Accident Bulletin 102. Washington, D.C.: GPO, 1934. 95 pp.

U.S. OFFICE OF FEDERAL COORDINATOR OF TRANSPORTATION. Section of Labor Relations. *Annual Earnings of Railroad Employees, 1924–1933.* Washington, D.C.: GPO, 1935. 198 pp.

————. Section of Labor Relations. *The Extent of Low Wages and Long Hours in the Railroad Industry.* Washington, D.C.: GPO, 1935. 78 leaves.

————. Section of Labor Relations. *The Extent of Low Wages and Long Hours in the Railroad Industry.* Washington, D.C.: GPO, 1936. 142 pp.

————. Section of Labor Relations. *A Survey of the Rules Governing Wage Payments in Railroad Train and Engine Service.* 2 vols. Washington, D.C.: GPO, 1936. 106 pp.

————. Sections of Research and Labor Relations. *Comparative Labor Standards in Transportation.* Washington, D.C.: GPO, 1937. 147 pp.

1946–Present

BUREAU OF RAILWAY ECONOMICS. *Railroad Men and Wages,* by Joseph E. Monroe. Washington, D.C., 1947. 155 pp.

U.S. BUREAU OF LABOR STATISTICS. *Wage Chronology: Railroads, Nonoperating Employees,*

1920–1961, prepared by Albert A. Belman. BLS Report 208. Washington, D.C.: GPO, 1962. 21 pp.
Revised in 1963 to include data for 1962.

U.S. RAILROAD RETIREMENT BOARD. *Work Injuries in the Railroad Industry, 1938–40.* A report . . . to the Senate Committee on Interstate and Foreign Commerce, pursuant to S. Res. 128, 77th Congress. Chicago: The Board, 1947.

————. Division of Safety Studies. *Safety in the Railroad Industry.* Chicago, 1962.

4. Unions and Workers

U.S. BUREAU OF LABOR. *Railroad Labor: Annual Report of the Commissioner of Labor, 5th, 1889.* Also issued as H. Ex. Doc. 336, 51st Cong., 1st Sess. Washington, D.C.: GPO, 1889. 888 pp.

U.S. BUREAU OF LABOR STATISTICS. "Attitude of Railroad Brotherhoods toward Workmen's Compensation, and Reason for Such Attitude," by W. N. Doak (with discussion), pp. 53–61. *Proceedings of the Eighteenth Annual Meeting of the International Association of Industrial Accident Boards and Commissions.* Bulletin 564. Washington, D.C.: GPO, 1932.

U.S. CONGRESS. Senate. Committee on the Judiciary. *Subversive Influence in the Dining Car and Railroad Food Workers Union: Hearings before Subcommittee to Investigate the Administration of the Internal Security Act and Other Internal Security Laws.* 82nd Cong., 1st Sess. Washington, D.C.: GPO, 1951. 154 pp.

U.S. DEPARTMENT OF LABOR. *Address by Secretary of Labor James P. Mitchell before Railway Operating Brotherhoods' Spring Institute, Iowa City, Iowa.* USDL–4058. Washington, D.C.: GPO, 1960. 7 leaves.

U.S. INDUSTRIAL COMMISSION. "Consolidation of Railroads in the United States," vol. 19, pt. 3, pp. 304–29. *Reports of the Industrial Commission, 1900–1902.* 19 vols. Washington, D.C.: GPO, 1900–1902.

————. "Railway Labor," vol. 4, pt. 1, pp. 131–60. *Reports of the Industrial Commission, 1900–1902.* 19 vols. Washington, D.C.: GPO, 1900–1902.

————. "Railway Labor in the United States," vol. 17, pp. 709–1135. *Reports of the Industrial Commission, 1900–1902.* 19 vols. Washington, D.C.: GPO, 1900–1902.

U.S. PRESIDENT [Woodrow Wilson]. *Statement by President Wilson to Representatives of Railway Employees Department, American Federation of Labor (August 25, 1919), and Report of Walker D. Hines, Director General of Railroads, to the President (August 23, 1919).* [Railroad Administration.] Washington, D.C.: GPO, 1919. 8 pp.

5. Labor Legislation

1850–98

U.S. BUREAU OF LABOR. *Railroad Labor: Annual Report of the Commissioner of Labor, 5th, 1889.* Also issued as H. Ex. Doc. 336, 51st Cong., 1st Sess. Washington, D.C.: GPO, 1889. 888 pp.

U.S. CONGRESS. House. *Compilation of Laws Relating to Mediation, Conciliation, and Arbitration between Employers and Employees, Disputes between Carriers and Employers and Subordinate Officials under Labor Board, 8-hr. Laws, Employers' Liability Laws, Labor and Child Labor Laws, 1888-1967,* compiled by Gilman G. Udell, Superintendent, Document Room, House of Representatives. Washington, D.C.: GPO, 1967. 1035 pp.

————. House. *Provisions for Promoting Safety of Railroad Employees and Traveling Public, Recommended.* H. Doc. 1678, vol. 7, 52nd Cong., 1st Sess. Washington, D.C.: GPO, 1892. 8 pp.

————. House. *Report Amending and Favoring H.R. 8556, concerning [Arbitration between] Carriers Engaged in Interstate Commerce [and Their Employees].* H. Rept. 1754, vol. 2, 54th Cong., 1st Sess. Washington, D.C., 1895. 7 pp.

————. House.· *Report from Committee on Labor, Amending H.R. 268, concerning [Arbitration, etc., between] Carriers Engaged in Interstate Commerce and Their Employees.* H. Rept. 1058, 54th Cong., 1st Sess. Washington, D.C.: GPO, 1896. 3 pp.

————. Senate. *Decisions of Judge Speer, Judge Ricks and Judge Taft in Cases Involving Rights and Duties of Railroad Employees and Construction of Anti-trust and Interstate-Commerce Laws.* S. Misc. Doc. 47, 53rd Cong., Special Sess., April 15, 1893. Washington, D.C.: GPO, 1893. 35 pp.

————. Senate. *Resolution That Committee on Interstate Commerce Report as to Amendment of Interstate Commerce Law [to Protect Rights of Employees to Quit Service].* S. Misc. Doc. 35, 53rd Cong., Special Sess., April 7, 1893. Washington, D.C.: GPO, 1893. 2 pp.

————. Senate. *Resolution for Committee to Report on Legislation to Prevent Strikes on Railway Lines and on Government Ownership of Them.* S. Misc. Doc. 222, in vol. 5, 53rd Cong., 2nd Sess. Washington, D.C.: GPO, 1894. 1 p.

U.S. INDUSTRIAL COMMISSION. "Inquiry concerning Legislation Affecting Railway Labor," vol. 4, pt. 2, pp. 759-80. *Reports of the Industrial Commission, 1900-1902.* 19 vols. Washington, D.C.: GPO, 1900-1902.

1898-1926

BUREAU OF RAILWAY ECONOMICS. *The Arguments for and against Train-Crew Legislation.* Bulletin 53. Washington, D.C.: GPO, 1913. 37 pp.

KENT, OTIS B. *A Digest of Decisions (Including Dicta) under the Federal Safety Appliance and Hours of Service Acts . . . with References to or Excerpts from Additional Cases in Which the Acts Have Been Construed; Orders and Administrative Rulings of the Interstate Commerce Commission.* Washington, D.C.: GPO, 1915. 281 pp.

MICHIGAN. *Act Prohibiting the Discharging without Hearing of Railroad Employees upon Request of Special Agents or Detectives.* Public Law, Chap. 92, 1917.

NEW JERSEY. *An Act to Empower the Board of Public Utility Commissioners to Require Any Common Carrier by Railroad to Employ a Sufficient Number of Men in the Management of Any of Its Trains, and to Repeal an Act Entitled, "An Act to Promote the Safety of Travelers and Employees upon Railroads by Compelling Common Carriers by Railroads to Properly Man Their Trains."* Laws, Chap. 270, 1922.

TEXAS. *Statute of 1909. Prohibiting Any Person from Acting as a Conductor on a Railroad*

GOVERNMENT DOCUMENTS

Train without Having for 2 yrs. Prior Thereto Worked as a Brakeman or Conductor of a Freight Train. Excludes the Whole Body of the Public from the Right to Secure Employment as Conductors and Amounts, as to Persons Competent to Fill the Position but Who Have Not the Specified Qualifications, to a Denial of the Equal Protection of the Laws. Smith v. Texas, 233 U.S. 630.

U.S. CONGRESS. House. *Act to Establish 8-Hour Day for Employees of Carriers Engaged in Interstate and Foreign Commerce, and for Other Purposes.* [Approved September 3 and 5, 1916.] H.R. 17700, Public Law 252, 64th Cong., 1st Sess. Washington, D.C.: GPO, 1916. 2 pp.

—————. House. *Act to Provide for the Termination of Federal Control of Railroads and Systems of Transportation; To Provide for the Settlement of Disputes between Carriers and Their Employees; To Further Amend an Act Entitled, "An Act to Regulate Commerce" (Feb. 4, 1887), as Amended, and for Other Purposes.* H.R. 10453, Pub. no. 152, 66th Cong. Washington, D.C.: GPO, 1920. 48 pp.

—————. House. *Compilation of Laws Relating to Mediation, Conciliation, and Arbitration between Employers and Employees, Disputes between Carriers and Employers and Subordinate Officials under Labor Board, 8-hr. Laws, Employers' Liability Laws, Labor and Child Labor Laws, 1888–1967,* compiled by Gilman G. Udell, Superintendent, Document Room, House of Representatives. Washington, D.C.: GPO, 1967. 1035 pp.

—————. House. *Concurrent Resolution [62] to Correct S. 5133, to Promote Safety of Employees and Travelers upon Railroads by Limiting Hours of Service of Employees.* Statutes at Large, vol. 34, pt. 2, p. 2840, 59th Cong., 2nd Sess. Washington, D.C.: GPO, 1907.

—————. House. *Report from Committee on Labor, Amending H.R. 4372, concerning [Arbitration between] Carriers Engaged in Interstate Commerce and Their Employees.* H. Rept. 454, in vol. 2, 55th Cong., 2nd Sess., February 15, 1898. 3 pp.

—————. House. Committee on Interstate and Foreign Commerce. *Bills Affecting Interstate Commerce: Hearings on H.R. 9047, 9132, 9216, 10485, 11243, Safety on Railroads for Passengers and Employees and Hours of Service and Increase of Pay of Inspectors.* 64th Cong., 1st Sess. Washington, D.C.: GPO, 1916. 247 pp.

—————. House. Committee on Interstate and Foreign Commerce. *Eight Hour Day for Employees of Carriers of Interstate Commerce.* H. Rept. 1184 to Accompany H.R. 17700, 64th Cong., 1st Sess. Washington, D.C.: GPO, 1916. 1 p.

—————. House. Committee on Interstate and Foreign Commerce. "Hours of Service of Employees on Common Carriers," pt. 7, pp. 445–520. *Safety on Railroads: Hearings before Subcommittee on Bills Relative to Safety on Railroads.* 63rd Cong., 2nd Sess. Washington, D.C.: GPO, 1914.

—————. House. Committee on Interstate and Foreign Commerce. *Hours of Service: Hearings on H.R. 9216.* 64th Cong., 1st Sess. Washington, D.C.: GPO, 1916. 17 pp.

—————. House. Committee on Interstate and Foreign Commerce. *Hours of Service of Railroad Employees.* H. Rept. 608 to Accompany H.R. 9132, 64th Cong., 1st Sess. Washington, D.C.: GPO, 1916. 4 pp.

—————. House. Committee on Interstate and Foreign Commerce. *Hours of Service of Railroad Employees.* H. Rept. 699 to Accompany H.R. 9216, 64th Cong., 1st Sess. Washington, D.C.: GPO, 1916. 6 pp.

————. House. Committee on Interstate and Foreign Commerce. *H. Rept. 853 Favoring H.R. 25109, for Mediation, Conciliation, and Arbitration in Controversies between Employers [Engaged in Railroad and Coal Mining Business]* and Their Employees. 62nd Cong., 2nd Sess. Washington, D.C.: GPO, 1912. 3 pp.

————. House. Committee on Interstate and Foreign Commerce. *H. Rept. 1141 Favoring H.R. 26023, to Amend Act to Promote Safety of Employees and Travelers upon Railroads by Limiting Hours of Service of Employees Thereon, as Substitute for H.R. 18969 and 25040.* 62nd Cong., 2nd Sess. Washington, D.C.: GPO, 1912. 10 pp.

————. House. Committee on Interstate and Foreign Commerce. *H. Rept. 1357, Adverse to H.R. 19238, to Amend Act to Promote Safety of Employees and Travelers upon Railroads by Limiting Hours of Service of Employees Thereon So That First Proviso of Sec. 2, Relating Especially to Employment of Train Dispatchers, Shall Not Apply to Stations, Offices, and Places Where Not More than 8 Passenger Trains Pass Each Way in 24 Hours.* 60th Cong., 1st Sess. Washington, D.C.: GPO, 1908, 1 p.

————. House. Committee on Interstate and Foreign Commerce. *H. Rept. 2253 Favoring H.R. 28137 to Amend Act to Promote Safety of Employees and Travelers upon Railroads by Limiting Hours of Service of Employees [So As to Include Persons Who Signal Trains from Towers].* 60th Cong., 2nd Sess. Washington, D.C.: GPO, 1909. 1 p.

————. House. Committee on Interstate and Foreign Commerce. *Interstate Commerce on Railroads: Hearings on H.R. 19730.* 64th Cong., 2nd Sess. Washington, D.C.: GPO, 1917. 294 pp.

————. House. Committee on Interstate and Foreign Commerce. *Railroad Claims (Statute of Limitations): Hearing before a Subcommittee, on S. 571 and H.R. 3500, to Amend Section 204 of the Act Entitled, "An Act to Provide for the Termination of Federal Control of Railroads and Systems of Transportation; to Provide for the Settlement of Disputes between Carriers and Their Employees; to Further Amend an Act Entitled 'An Act to Regulate Commerce,' Approved February 4, 1887, as Amended, and for Other Purposes." Approved Feb. 28, 1920.* 71st Cong., 3rd Sess. Washington, D.C.: GPO, 1931. 21 pp.

————. House. Committee on Interstate and Foreign Commerce. *Report Amending H.R. 18671, to Promote Safety of Employees and Travelers upon Railroads by Limiting Hours of Service of Employees.* H. Rept. 4567, 59th Cong., 1st Sess. Washington, D.C.: GPO, 1906. 10 pp.

————. House. Committee on Interstate and Foreign Commerce. *Safety of Employees and Travelers upon Railroads.* H. Rept. 975 to Accompany H.R. 17893, 63rd Cong., 2nd Sess. Washington, D.C.: GPO, 1914. 1 p.

————. House. Committee on Interstate and Foreign Commerce. *Safety of Employees and Travelers on Railroads.* H. Rept. 979 to Accompany H.R. 16681, 64th Cong., 1st Sess. Washington, D.C.: GPO, 1916. 11 pp.

————. House. Committee on Interstate and Foreign Commerce. *To Limit Hours of Service of Railroad Employees: Hearings on H.R. 4438, H.R. 16676, and H.R. 18671.* 59th Cong., 1st Sess. Washington, D.C.: GPO, 1906. 156 pp.

————. House. Committee on Interstate and Foreign Commerce. *To Limit Hours of Service of Railroad Employees: Hearings on S. 5133 and H.R. 24373.* 59th Cong., 2nd Sess. Washington, D.C.: GPO, 1907. 44 pp.

————. House. Committee on Interstate and Foreign Commerce. *Views of Minority on*

S. 5133 to Promote Safety of Employees and Travelers upon Railroads by Limiting Hours of Service of Employees. H. Rept. 7641, pp. 10–12, 59th Cong., 2nd Sess. Washington, D.C.: GPO, 1907.

—————. House. Committee on the Judiciary. *Amendment of Erdman Act.* H. Rept. 30 to Accompany H.R. 6141, 63rd Cong., 1st Sess. Washington, D.C.: GPO, 1913. 2 pp.

—————. House. Committee on the Judiciary. *Amendment of Erdman Act, Mediation, Conciliation and Arbitration: Hearings on H.R. 6141 (S. 2517).* 63rd Cong., 1st Sess. Washington, D.C.: GPO, 1913. 23 pp.

—————. House. Committee on Rules. *Consideration of H. Res. 363.* H. Rept. 1183 to Accompany H. Res. 363 [for Consideration of H.R. 17700, to Establish 8-hour Day for Employees of Carriers . . .], 64th Cong., 1st Sess. Washington, D.C.: GPO, 1916. 1 p.

—————. House. Committee on Rules. *Report: To Promote Safety of Employees and Travelers on Railroads by Limiting Hours of Service as Employees.* Submitting H.R. 880 (relating to S. 5133). H. Rept. 8074, 59th Cong., 2nd Sess. Washington, D.C.: GPO, 1907. 1 p.

—————. Senate. *Act to Amend Act to Promote Safety of Employees and Travelers upon Railroads by Limiting Hours of Service of Employees Thereon.* [Approved May 4, 1916.] S. 3769, Public Law 68, 64th Cong., 1st Sess. Washington, D.C.: GPO, 1916. 1 p.

—————. Senate. *Act for Mediation, Conciliation, and Arbitration, in Controversies between [Railroad] Employers and Their Employees.* [Approved July 15, 1913.] S. 2517, 63rd Cong., 1st Sess. Washington, D.C.: GPO, 1913. 6 pp.

—————. Senate. *Compilation of Acts of Congress Affecting Railroad Employees and Orders of Interstate Commerce Commission Made in Accordance with Said Acts,* by F.G. Newlands. S. Doc. 691, 60th Cong., 2nd Sess. Washington, D.C.: GPO, 1909. 17 pp.

—————. Senate. *Compilation of Laws Relating to Number of Men Required on Railroad Trains,* by C. A. Culbertson. S. Doc. 692, 60th Cong., 2nd Sess. Washington, D.C.: GPO, 1909. 7 pp.

—————. Senate. *Erdman Act, Public Law 115, concerning [Arbitration between] Carriers Engaged in Interstate Commerce and Their Employees.* [Approved June 1, 1898.] 55th Cong., 2nd Sess. Washington, D.C.: GPO, 1916. 6 pp.

—————. Senate. *Information from Post Office Department, Pursuant to Resolution, as to Accidents Resulting from Delivering and Receiving Mail to and from Moving Trains at Catch Stations, etc.* S. Doc. 619, 60th Cong., 2nd Sess. Washington, D.C.: GPO, 1909. 2 pp.

—————. Senate. Committee on Education and Labor. *Report Amending S. 5133, to Promote Safety of Employees and Travelers upon Railroads by Limiting Hours of Service of Employees.* S. Rept. 4246, 59th Cong., 1st Sess. Washington, D.C.: GPO, 1906. 2 pp.

—————. Senate. Committee on Interstate Commerce. *Arbitration between Carriers and Employees, Boards of Adjustment.* S. Rept. 779 to Accompany S. 2646, 68th Cong., 1st Sess. Washington, D.C.: GPO, 1924. 4 pp.

—————. Senate. Committee on Interstate Commerce. *Arbitration between Carriers and Employees, Boards of Adjustment: Hearings before a Subcommittee on S. 2646.* 68th Cong., 1st Sess. Washington, D.C.: GPO, 1924. 381 pp.

—————. Senate. Committee on Interstate Commerce. *Arbitration in Controversies be-*

tween Employers and Employees: Hearings on S. 2517. S. Rept. 72, pt. 1, pp. 7–100, 63rd Cong., 1st Sess. Washington, D.C.: GPO, 1913

————. Senate. Committee on Interstate Commerce. *Government Investigation of Railway Disputes: Hearings on Tentative Bill to Amend Act Entitled "An Act Providing for Mediation, Conciliation and Arbitration in Controversies between Certain Employers and Their Employees."* [July 15, 1913.] 64th Cong., 2nd Sess. Washington, D.C.: GPO, 1917. 294 pp.

————. Senate. Committee on Interstate Commerce. *Hours of Service of Railroad Employees: Hearings before Subcommittee on H.R. 17893.* 63rd Cong., 3rd Sess. Washington, D.C.: GPO, 1915. 40 pp.

————. Senate. Committee on Interstate Commerce. *Interference with Commerce.* S. Rept. 644 to Accompany S. 4204, 66th Cong., 2nd Sess. Washington, D.C.: GPO, 1920. 12 pp.

————. Senate. Committee on Interstate Commerce. *Mediation, Conciliation and Arbitration in Controversies between Railway Employers and Their Employees.* S. Rept. 72 on S. 2517, with Hearings, 63rd Cong., 1st Sess. Washington, D.C.: GPO, 1913. 100 pp.

————. Senate. Committee on Interstate Commerce. *Prevention of Strikes: Hearings on S. 2906.* 66th Cong.. 1st Sess. Washington, D.C.: GPO, 1919. 146 pp.

————. Senate. Committee on Interstate Commerce. *Proposed Anti-strike Legislation: Hearings before Subcommittee on S. 4204 and S. 4210.* 66th Cong., 2nd Sess. Washington, D.C.: GPO, 1920. 45 pp.

————. Senate. Committee on Interstate Commerce. *The Railroad Labor Problem: Testimony by Railroad Witnesses before a Subcommittee in Opposition to S. 2646.* 68th Cong., 1st Sess. Washington, D.C.: GPO, 1924. 95 pp.

————. Senate. Committee on Interstate Commerce. *Safety of Employees and Travelers on Railroads, Railway Clearance: Hearings before Subcommittee on S. 3194.* 64th Cong., 1st Sess. Washington, D.C.: GPO, 1916. 87 pp.

————. Senate. Committee on Interstate Commerce. *Safety of Employees and Travelers on Railroads, Railway Clearance: Hearings before Subcommittee on S. 6550.* 64th Cong., 2nd Sess. Washington, D.C.: GPO, 1917. 69 pp.

————. Senate. Committee on Interstate Commerce. *To Amend Act to Promote Safety of Employees and Travelers upon Railroads: Testimony before Subcommittee on S. 3604.* S. Doc. 154, 56th Cong., 2nd Sess. Washington, D.C.: GPO, 1901. 2 pp.

————. Senate. Committee on Interstate Commerce. *To Amend Section 3 of Act to Promote Safety of Employees and Travelers upon Railroads, etc.* S. Rept. 245 to Accompany S. 3769, 64th Cong., 1st Sess. Washington, D.C.: GPO, 1916. 2 pp.

————. Senate. Committee on Interstate Commerce. *To Promote Safety of Employees and Travelers upon Railroads by Prohibiting Common Carriers Engaged in Interstate Commerce from Transporting Gunpowder: Hearings before a Subcommittee, on S. 4319.* 58th Cong., 3rd Sess. Washington, D.C.: GPO, 1904. 25 pp.

————. Senate. Committee on Post Offices and Post Roads. *Railway Mail Clerks: Hearings before Subcommittee on S. 4895 and S. 3950.* 64th Cong., 1st Sess. Washington, D.C.: GPO, 1916. 116 pp.

————. Senate. Committee on Post Offices and Post Roads. *S. Rept. 175 Favoring S.R.*

161, Calling for Information Relative to Number of Railway Mail Clerks and Other Post-Office Employees Who Have Been Demoted since Jan. 1, 1911. 62nd Cong., 2nd Sess. Washington, D.C.: GPO, 1912. 1 p.

U.S. INDUSTRIAL COMMISSION. "Inquiry concerning Legislation Affecting Railway Labor," vol. 4, pt. 2, pp. 759–80. *Reports of the Industrial Commission, 1900–1902.* 19 vols. Washington, D.C.: GPO, 1900–1902.

U.S. INTERSTATE COMMERCE COMMISSION. *Act to Regulate Commerce, as Amended, and Acts Supplementary Thereto, Commerce Court Act, Safety Appliance Acts, Act Requiring Monthly Reports of Accidents, Arbitration Act, Hours of Service Act, Boiler Inspection Act; Revised to July 1, 1911.* Washington, D.C.: GPO, 1911. 112 pp.

————. *Act to Regulate Commerce, as Amended, Including Text or Related Sections of [Other Acts]; Revised to June 1, 1918.* Washington, D.C.: GPO, 1918. 190 pp.
Includes sections on hours of service in railroad industry, railway mail service, etc.

————. *Administrative Ruling and Opinion on Act Approved Mar. 4, 1907 Entitled Act to Promote Safety of Employees and Travelers upon Railroads by Limiting Hours of Service Thereon.* Washington, D.C.: GPO, 1908. 7 pp.

————. *Erdman Act: Hearings on H.R. 22012, to Amend Erdman Act [by Extending Its Provisions to Owners of Coal Mines, Products of Which Enter into Interstate Commerce and Their Employees, and to All Classes of Railroad Employees, etc.].* Washington, D.C.: GPO, 1912. 51 pp.

————. *Full-Crew Law: Hearings on H.R. 13911.* [Statement of Isaac R. Sherwood.] Washington, D.C.: GPO, 1912. 9 pp.

————. *Hours of Service Law and Administrative Rulings and Opinions Thereon.* Washington, D.C.: GPO, 1912. 8 pp.

————. *Hours of Service Law: Hearings on H.R. 25040.* Washington, D.C.: GPO, 1912. 131 pp.

————. *Hours of Service Laws, and Administrative Rulings and Opinions Thereon.* Washington, D.C.: GPO, 1916. 10 pp.

————. *Hours of Service of Railway Employees, State Statutes and Related Court Decisions.* Washington, D.C.: GPO, 1909. 39 pp.

U.S. RAILROAD LABOR BOARD. *Transportation Act, 1920 (Public Law 152, 66th Cong., H.R. 10453): Excerpt Showing Title III — Disputes between Carriers and Their Employees and Subordinate Officials, Effective Feb. 29, 1920.* Chicago, 1920. 8 pp.

U.S. SUPREME COURT. *Arguments in the Cases Arising under the Railway Labor Act and the National Labor Relations Act.* S. Doc. 52, 75th Cong., 1st Sess. Washington, D.C.: GPO, 1937. 174 pp.

————. *Eight-Hour Workday for Railway Employees. Opinion of Supreme Court in Case of Francis M. Wilson vs. Alex. New and Henry C. Ferris, Embracing Both Concurring and Dissenting Opinions.* S. Doc. 20, 65th Cong., 1st Sess. Washington, D.C.: GPO, 1917. 30 pp.

1926–46

CALIFORNIA. Laws, Statutes, etc. *State and Federal Laws, Commission Rulings and Orders of Interest to Men in Train, Engine and Yard Service in the State of California.* San Francisco, 1928. [Updated and reissued in 1941.]

LABOR LEGISLATION

PENNSYLVANIA. Supreme Court. Proceedings on the Full Crew Bill, Middle District. *Pennsylvania Railroad Co., plaintiff and appellee v. Dennis J. Driscoll [et al]*. Appeal from the preliminary injunction awarded by the Court of Common Pleas of Dauphin County. Harrisburg, 1938.

U.S. BUREAU OF LABOR STATISTICS. *Federal Legislation concerning Railroad Employees.* Serial No. R. 1233. Washington, D.C.: GPO, 1941. 9 pp.

————. *Railroad Legislation on Full Crew, Personnel, and Train Lengths.* Serial No. R. 1131. Washington, D.C.: GPO, 1940. 6 pp.

————. *Railway Labor Act Upheld by Supreme Court.* Serial No. R. 565. Washington, D.C.: GPO, 1937. 5 pp.

U.S. CONGRESS. House. *Act to Amend Railway Labor Act Approved May 20, 1926, and to Provide for Prompt Disposition of Disputes between Carriers and Their Employees.* [Approved June 21, 1934.] H.R. 9861, Public Law 442, 73rd Cong., 2nd Sess. Washington, D.C.: GPO, 1934. 14 pp.

————. House. *Act to Authorize Acknowledgement of Oaths by Post-Office Inspectors and by Chief Clerks of Railway Mail Service.* [Approved June 15, 1934.] H.R. 6675, Public Law 355, 73rd Cong., 2nd Sess. Washington, D.C.: GPO, 1934. 1 p.

————. House. *Act to Authorize Assignment of Railway Postal Clerks and Substitute Railway Postal Clerks to Temporary Employment as Substitute Seapost Clerks.* [Approved February 14, 1929.] H.R. 58, Public Law 145, 70th Cong., 2nd Sess. Washington, D.C.: GPO, 1929. 1 p.

————. House. *Act to Levy Excise Tax upon Carriers and Certain Other Employers, and Income Tax upon Their Employees.* [Approved June 29, 1937.] H.R. 7589, Public Law 174, 75th Cong., 1st Sess. Washington, D.C.: GPO, 1937. 6 pp.

————. House. *Act to Levy Excise Tax upon Carriers and Income Tax upon Their Employees.* [Approved August 29, 1935.] H.R. 8652, Public Law 400, 74th Cong., 1st Sess. Washington, D.C.: GPO, 1935. 4 pp.

————. House. *Act to Prescribe Time Basis for Computing Pay for Overtime Work Performed by Laborers in Railway Mail Service.* [Approved October 23, 1941.] Public Law 279, 77th Cong., 1st Sess. Washington, D.C.: GPO, 1941. 1 p.

————. House. *Act to Provide Hourly Rates of Pay for Substitute Laborers in Railway Mail Service and Time Credits When Appointed as Regular Laborer.* [Approved June 14, 1934.] H.R. 7213, Public Law 349, 73rd Cong., 2nd Sess. Washington, D.C.: GPO, 1934. 1 p.

————. House. *Act to Provide for Prompt Disposition of Disputes between Carriers and Their Employees.* [Approved May 20, 1926.] H.R. 9463, Public Law 257, 69th Cong., 1st Sess. Washington, D.C.: GPO, 1926. 12 pp.

————. House. *Act Relating to Compensation of Former Employees of Railway Mail Service in Certain Positions and Reinstated Prior to Aug. 14, 1937.* [Approved August 1, 1941.] H.R. 3367, Public Law 201, 77th Cong., 1st Sess. Washington, D.C.: GPO, 1941. 1 p.

————. House. *Act to Remove Inequities in Law Governing Eligibility for Promotion to Position of Chief Clerk in Railway Mail Service.* [Approved June 5, 1934.] H.R. 7343, Public Law 289, 73rd Cong., 2nd Sess. Washington, D.C.: GPO, 1934. 1 p.

————. House. *Compilation of Laws Relating to Mediation, Conciliation, and Arbitration between Employers and Employees, Disputes between Carriers and Employers and Subordinate Officials under Labor Board, 8-hr. Laws, Employers' Liability Laws, Labor and Child Labor Laws, 1888–1967,* compiled by Gilman G. Udell, Superintendent, Document Room, House of Representatives. Washington, D.C.: GPO, 1967. 1035 pp.

————. House. *Joint Resolution to Amend Act to Levy Excise Tax upon Carriers and Income Tax upon Their Employees [so as to extend levy to June 30, 1938.]* [Approved February 27, 1937.] H.J. Res. 212, Public Res. 9, 75th Cong., 1st Sess. Washington, D.C.: GPO, 1937. 1 p.

————. House. *Joint Resolution to Authorize Interstate Commerce Commission to Make Investigation as to the Possibility of Establishing 6-Hour Day for Railway Employees.* [Approved March 15, 1932.] H.J. Res. 252, Public Res. 13, 72nd Cong., 1st Sess. Washington, D.C.: GPO, 1932. 1 p.

————. House. Committee on Interstate and Foreign Commerce. *Full Train Crews: Hearings on H.R. 11012.* 72nd Cong., 2nd Sess. Washington, D.C.: GPO, 1933. 124 pp.

————. House. Committee on Interstate and Foreign Commerce. *Railroad Labor Disputes: Hearings before the Committee on Interstate and Foreign Commerce, House of Representatives, on H.R. 7180.* 69th Cong., 1st Sess. 1926. Washington, D.C.: GPO, 1926. 397 pp.

————. House. Committee on Interstate and Foreign Commerce. *Railway Labor Act Amendments: Hearings on H.R. 7650 and to Amend Sections 1, 2, 3, 5, 6 of Railway Labor Act.* 73rd Cong., 2nd Sess. Washington, D.C.: GPO, 1934. 178 pp.

————. House. Committee on Interstate and Foreign Commerce. *Railway Labor Disputes.* H. Rept. 328 to Accompany H.R. 9463, 69th Cong., 1st Sess. Washington, D.C.: GPO, 1926. 7 pp.

————. House. Committee on Interstate and Foreign Commerce. *Railway Pay of Nonoperating Employees: Hearings on S.J. Res. 91 and H.J. Res. 187.* 78th Cong., 1st Sess. Washington, D.C.: GPO, 1944. 176 pp.

————. House. Committee on Interstate and Foreign Commerce. *Six-Hour Day for Interstate Carriers.* H. Rept. 1763 to Accompany H.R. 7430, 73rd Cong., 2nd Sess. Washington, D.C.: GPO, 1934. 3 pp.

————. House. Committee on Interstate and Foreign Commerce. *Six-Hour Day for Interstate Carriers: Hearings on H.R. 7430.* 73rd Cong., 2nd Sess. Washington, D.C.: GPO, 1934. 226 pp.

————. House. Committee on Interstate and Foreign Commerce. *Six-Hour Day for Railway Employees.* H. Rept. 274 to Accompany H.J. Res. 252, 72nd Cong., 1st Sess. Washington, D.C.: GPO, 1932. 1 p.

————. House. Committee on Interstate and Foreign Commerce. *Six-Hour Day for Train-Dispatching Offices: Hearings before a Subcommittee, May 5–June 4, 1938, on H.R. 4358, a Bill to Limit the Hours of Service of Train Dispatchers Employed by Carriers Engaged in Interstate Commerce to 6 Hours in Any 24 Hour Period, to Establish a 6-Hour Day for Such Train Dispatchers, and for Other Purposes.* 75th Cong., 3rd Sess. Washington, D.C.: GPO, 1938. 125 pp.

————. House. Committee on Interstate and Foreign Commerce. *To Amend Railway Labor Act of May 20, 1926.* H. Rept. 1944 to Accompany H.R. 9861, 73rd Cong., 2nd Sess. Washington, D.C.: GPO, 1934. 16 pp.

————. House. Committee on Post Office and Post Roads. *Basis for Computing Over-*

time Pay for Workers in Railway Mail Service. H. Rept. 336 to Accompany H.R. 2985, 77th Cong., 1st Sess. Washington, D.C.: GPO, 1941. 4 pp.

―――――. House. Committee on Post Office and Post Roads. *Basis for Computing Pay for Overtime Work by Railway Mail Laborers: Hearings on H.R. 2985.* 77th Cong., 1st Sess. Washington, D.C.: GPO, 1941. 9 pp.

―――――. House. Committee on Post Office and Post Roads. *Hours of Duty of Railway Postal Clerks: Hearings before Subcommittee on H.R. 4876.* 74th Cong.. 1st Sess. Washington, D.C.: GPO, 1935. 34 pp.

―――――. House. Committee on Post Office and Post Roads. *Laborers in Railway Mail Service: Hearings before Subcommittee on H.R. 7155.* 74th Cong., 1st Sess. Washington, D.C.: GPO, 1935. 14 pp.

―――――. House. Committee on Post Office and Post Roads. *Post Office Inspectors and Chief Clerks at Division Headquarters, Supervisory Officials of Railway Mail Service, Substitute Railway Postal Clerks: Hearings before Subcommittee on H.R. 13709, H.R. 11622, H.R. 9766.* 70th Cong., 2nd Sess. Washington, D.C.: GPO, 1929. 44 pp.

―――――. House. Committee on Post Office and Post Roads. *Railway Mail Service, Hours of Service: Hearings before Subcommittee on H.R. 4476.* 69th Cong., 1st Sess. Washington, D.C.: GPO, 1926. 98 pp.

―――――. House. Committee on Post Office and Post Roads. *Temporary Employment of Railway Postal Clerks as Substitute Sea-post Clerks.* H. Rept. 1303 to Accompany H.R. 10132, 69th Cong., 1st Sess. Washington, D.C.: GPO, 1926. 2 pp.

―――――. House. Committee on Post Office and Post Roads. *Temporary Employment of Railway Postal Clerks as Substitute Sea-post Clerks.* H. Rept. 1753 to Accompany H.R. 58, 70th Cong., 1st Sess. Washington, D.C.: GPO, 1928. 2 pp.

―――――. House. Committee on Rules. *Consideration of H.R. 9861.* H. Rept. 1987 to Accompany H. Res. 437 [to Approve Establishment of National Board of Adjustment], 73rd Cong., 2nd Sess. Washington, D.C.: GPO, 1934. 1 p.

―――――. House. Committee on Rules. *Consideration of S.J. Res. 91.* H. Rept. 1500 to Accompany H. Res. 559 [on Increases in Wages of Railroad Employees], 78th Cong., 2nd Sess. Washington, D.C.: GPO, 1944. 1 p.

―――――. House. Committee on Rules. *To Amend the Railway Labor Act Approved May 20, 1926: Hearings on H.R. 9861.* 73rd Cong., 2nd Sess. Washington, D.C.: GPO, 1934. 31 pp.

―――――. House. Committee on Ways and Means. *Carriers Taxing Act of 1937.* H. Rept. 1071 to Accompany H.R. 7589, 75th Cong., 1st Sess. Washington, D.C.: GPO, 1937. 10 pp.

―――――. House. Committee on Ways and Means. *Extension of Excise Tax upon Carriers and Income Tax upon Their Employees.* H. Rept. 219 to Accompany H.J. Res. 212, 75th Cong., 1st Sess. Washington, D.C.: GPO, 1937. 1 p.

―――――. House. Committee on Ways and Means. *Levy Excise Tax upon Carriers and Income Tax upon Their Employees.* H. Rept. 1882 to Accompany H.R. 8652, 74th Cong., 1st Sess. Washington, D.C.: GPO, 1935. 2 pp.

―――――. House. Committee on Ways and Means. *Taxation of Interstate Carriers and Employees: Hearings on H.R. 6448.* 75th Cong., 1st Sess. Washington. D.C.: GPO, 1937. 43 pp.

————. House. Committee on Ways and Means. *Taxation of Interstate Carriers, and Employees: Hearings on H.R. 8652.* 74th Cong., 1st Sess. Washington, D.C.: GPO, 1935. 105 pp.

————. Senate. Committee on Finance. *Carriers Taxing Act of 1937.* S. Rept. 818 to Accompany H.R. 7599. 75th Cong., 1st Sess. Washington, D.C.: GPO, 1937. 3 pp.

————. Senate. Committee on Finance. *Extension of Excise Tax upon Carriers and Income Tax upon Their Employees.* S. Rept. 112 to Accompany H.J. Res. 212, 75th Cong., 1st Sess. Washington, D.C.: GPO, 1937. 3 pp.

————. Senate. Committee on Finance. *Taxation of Interstate Carriers and Employees: Hearings on S. 3150.* 74th Cong., 1st Sess. Washington, D.C.: GPO, 1935. 66 pp.

————. Senate. Committee on Interstate Commerce. *Board to Settle Disputes between Carriers and Their Employees.* S. Rept. 1065, 2 pts., to Accompany S. 3266, 73rd Cong., 2nd Sess. Washington, D.C.: GPO, 1934. 5 pp.

————. Senate. Committee on Interstate Commerce. *Disposition of Disputes between Carriers and Employees.* S. Rept. 606 to Accompany H.R. 9463, 69th Cong., 1st Sess. Washington, D.C.: GPO, 1926. 7 pp.

————. Senate. Committee on Interstate Commerce. *Flagging Rules on Railroads: Hearings before Subcommittee on S. 2846.* 73rd Cong., 2nd Sess. Washington, D.C.: GPO, 1934. 126 pp.

————. Senate. Committee on Interstate Commerce. *Hours of Service for Railroad Employees.* S. Rept. 2336 to Accompany S. 1562, 74th Cong., 2nd Sess. Washington, D.C.: GPO, 1936. 2 pp.

————. Senate. Committee on Interstate Commerce. *Investigation of Six-Hour Day for Railroad Employees.* S. Rept. 398 to Accompany H. J. Res. 252, 72nd Cong., 1st Sess. Washington, D.C.: GPO, 1932. 1 p.

————. Senate. Committee on Interstate Commerce. *Railroad Wages: Hearings before a Subcommittee on S.J. Res. 91.* 78th Cong., 1st Sess. Washington, D.C.: GPO, 1943. 139 pp.

————. Senate. Committee on Interstate Commerce. *Railway Labor Act: Hearings on S. 2306.* 69th Cong., 1st Sess. Washington, D.C.: GPO, 1926. 222 pp.

————. Senate. Committee on Interstate Commerce. *Six-Hour Day for Employees of Carriers Engaged in Interstate and Foreign Commerce: Hearings on S. 2519.* 73rd Cong., 2nd Sess. Washington, D.C.: GPO, 1934. 306 pp.

————. Senate. Committee on Interstate Commerce. *To Aid in Effectuating Purposes of Railway Labor Act [Relative to Increase in Wages of Railroad Employees].* S. Rept. 563 to Accompany S.J. Res. 91, 78th Cong., 1st Sess. Washington, D.C.: GPO, 1943. 7 pp.

————. Senate. Committee on Interstate Commerce. *To Amend the Railway Labor Act: Hearings on S. 3266.* 73rd Cong., 2nd Sess. Washington, D.C.: GPO, 1934. 168 pp.

————. Senate. Committee on Interstate Commerce. *To Limit Hours of Service: Hearings before Subcommittee on S. 1562.* 74th Cong., 1st Sess. Washington, D.C.: GPO, 1935. 183 pp.

————. Senate. Committee on Interstate Commerce. *To Provide Full Crews on Trains in Interstate Commerce: Hearings before Subcommittee on S. 59.* 74th Cong., 1st Sess. Washington, D.C.: GPO, 1935. 24 pp.

————. Senate. Committee on Interstate Commerce. *To Provide for Prompt Disposition of Disputes between Carriers and Their Employees.* S. Rept. 222 to Accompany S. 2306, 69th Cong., 1st Sess. Washington, D.C.: GPO, 1926. 7 pp.

————. Senate. Committee on Post Offices and Post Roads. *Prescribing Time Basis for Computing Pay for Overtime Work by Laborers in Railway Mail Service.* S. Rept. 555 to Accompany H.R. 2985, 77th Cong., 1st Sess. Washington, D.C.: GPO, 1941. 3 pp.

————. Senate. Committee on Post Offices and Post Roads. *Relating to Compensation of Former Employees of Railway Mail Service in Certain Positions and Reinstated Prior to Aug. 14, 1937.* S. Rept. 554 to Accompany H.R. 3367, 77th Cong., 1st Sess. Washington, D.C.: GPO, 1941. 2 pp.

U.S. DEPARTMENT OF JUSTICE. Attorney General. *Collective Bargaining Agreement under Railway Labor Act.* Opinion 59, December 29, 1942. Washington, D.C.: GPO, 1942. 7 pp.

U.S. DEPARTMENT OF LABOR. *Application of State Hour Laws to Railroad Women.* Labor Information Bulletin, May 1943. Washington, D.C.: GPO, 1943. 3 pp.

U.S. INTERSTATE COMMERCE COMMISSION. *Hours of Service Act, as Amended, and Administrative Rulings and Opinions Thereon.* Washington, D.C.: GPO, 1926. 7 pp.

U.S. PRESIDENT [Franklin D. Roosevelt]. Executive Order 9172. "Establishing Panel for Creation of Emergency Boards for Adjustment of Railway Labor Disputes," pp. 3913–14. *Federal Register* 7, no. 103, May 27, 1942.

————. Executive Order 9299. "Prescribing Regulations and Procedure with Respect to Wage and Salary Adjustments for Employees Subject to Railway Labor Act," pp. 1669–70. *Federal Register* 8, no. 26, February 6, 1943.

1946–Present

U.S. CONGRESS. House. *Act to Amend Act Entitled Act to Promote Safety of Employees and Travelers upon Railroads by Limiting Hours of Service of Employees Thereon, Approved Mar. 4, 1907.* [Approved December 26, 1969.] H.R. 8449. Washington, D.C.: GPO, 1970. 3 pp.

————. House. *An Act to Amend Railway Labor Act in Order to Change Number of Carrier Representatives and Labor Organization Representatives on National Railroad Adjustment Board and for Other Purposes.* H.R. 15340, 91st Cong., 2nd Sess. Washington, D.C.: GPO, 1970. 1 p.

————. House. *Act to Amend Railway Labor Act in Order to Provide for Establishment of Special Adjustment Boards upon Request Either of Representatives of Employees or of Carriers to Resolve Disputes Otherwise Referable to National Railroad Adjustment Board, and to Make All Awards of Such Board Final.* [Approved June 20, 1966.] H.R. 706, 89th Cong., 2nd Sess. Washington, D.C.: GPO, 1966. 3 pp.

————. House. *Act to Amend Railway Labor Act to Provide That Terms of Office of Members of National Mediation Board Shall Expire on July 1.* [Approved Aug. 31, 1964.] H.R. 8344, 88th Cong., 2nd Sess. Washington, D.C.: GPO, 1964. 1 p.

————. House. *Compilation of Laws Relating to Mediation, Conciliation, and Arbitration between Employers and Employees, Disputes between Carriers and Employers and Subordinate Officials under Labor Board, 8-hr. Laws, Employers' Liability Laws, Labor and Child Labor Laws, 1888–1967,* compiled by Gilman G. Udell, Superintendent, Document Room, House of Representatives. Washington, D.C.: GPO, 1967. 1035 pp.

————. House. Committee on Interstate and Foreign Commerce. *Amend Hours of Service Act of 1907: Hearings before Subcommittee on Transportation and Aeronautics on H.R. 5196 and H.R. 8476.* 89th Cong., 2nd Sess. Washington, D.C.: GPO, 1966. 531 pp.

————. House. Committee on Interstate and Foreign Commerce. *Amending Railway Labor Act.* H. Rept. 2811 to Accompany H.R. 7789, 81st Cong., 2nd Sess. Washington, D.C.: GPO, 1950. 10 pp.

————. House. Committee on Interstate and Foreign Commerce. *Composition of First Division, National Railroad Adjustment Board: Hearings before the Subcommittee on Transportation and Aeronautics, on H.R. 15349.* 91st Cong., 2nd Sess. Washington, D.C.: GPO, 1970. 4 pp.

————. House. Committee on Interstate and Foreign Commerce. *Hours of Service Act Amendments of 1969.* H. Rept. 469 to Accompany H.R. 8449, 91st Cong., 1st Sess. Washington, D.C.: GPO, 1969. 14 pp.

————. House. Committee on Interstate and Foreign Commerce. *Hours of Service Act Amendments of 1969: Hearings on H.R. 8449, 84 and 9515.* 91st Cong., 1st Sess. Washington, D.C.: GPO, 1969. 278 pp.

————. House. Committee on Interstate and Foreign Commerce. *Railroad Safety and Hardware Materials Control: Hearings before Subcommittee on Transportation and Aeronautics on H.R. 7068 [and Similar Bills].* 91st Cong., 2nd Sess. Washington, D.C.: GPO, 1970. 285 pp.

————. House. Committee on Interstate and Foreign Commerce. *Railroad Safety: Hearings before a Subcommittee on H.R. 378, H.R. 530.* 81st Cong., 1st Sess. Washington, D.C.: GPO, 1949. 202 pp.

————. House. Committee on Interstate and Foreign Commerce. *Railway Labor Act Amendments.* H. Rept. 1114 to Accompany H.R. 706, 89th Cong., 1st Sess. Washington, D.C.: GPO, 1965. 23 pp.

————. House. Committee on Interstate and Foreign Commerce. *Railway Labor Act Amendments: Hearings on H.R. 7789.* 81st Cong., 2nd Sess. Washington, D.C.: GPO, 1950. 302 pp.

————. House. Committee on Interstate and Foreign Commerce. *Railway Labor Act Amendments Relating to NRAB: Hearings before Subcommittee on Transportation and Aeronautics, on H.R. 701, H.R. 704, and H.R. 706.* 89th Cong., 1st Sess. Washington, D.C.: GPO, 1965. 268 pp.

————. House. Committee on Interstate and Foreign Commerce. *Settlement of Labor-Management Disputes in Transportation: Hearings before Subcommittee on Transportation and Aeronautics on H.R. 3595.* 92nd Cong., 1st Sess. Washington, D.C.: GPO, 1972. 770 pp.

————. House. Committee on the Judiciary. *Certain Employees of Alaska Railroad.* H. Rept. 1860 to Accompany S. 1640, 88th Cong., 2nd Sess. Washington, D.C.: GPO, 1964. 9 pp.

————. House. Committee on the Judiciary. *Limitations of Venue in Certain Actions Brought under the Employers' Liability Act: Hearings before a Subcommittee of the*

Committee on the Judiciary, U.S. House, on S. 1567 and H.R. 1639. 80th Cong., 2nd Sess. Washington, D.C.: GPO, 1948. 299 pp.

————. House. Committee on Labor. "General Labor Conditions." *Investigation of the Causes of Labor Disputes*, pt. 2. [Testimony of A. F. Whitney.] 79th Cong., 2nd Sess. Washington, D.C.: GPO, 1946.

————. House. Committee on Rules. *Consideration of H.J. Res. 559*. H. Rept. 361 to Accompany H. Res. 511, 90th Cong., 1st Sess. Washington, D.C.: GPO, 1967. 1 p.

————. House. Committee on Rules. *Consideration of H.R. 8449 (Hours of Service Act Amendments of 1969)*. H. Rept. 483 to Accompany H. Res. 536, 91st Cong., 1st Sess. Washington, D.C.: GPO, 1969. 1 p.

————. House. Committee on Rules. *Consideration of H.R. 13300*. H. Rept. 482 to Accompany H. Res. 535, 91st Cong., 1st Sess. Washington, D.C.: GPO, 1970. 1 p.

————. Senate. *Act to Amend Railway Labor Act and to Authorize Agreements Providing for Union Membership and Agreements for Deductions from Wages of Carriers' Employees for Certain Purposes and under Certain Conditions*. [Approved January 10, 1951.] S. 3295, Public Law 914, 81st Cong., 2nd Sess. Washington, D.C.: GPO, 1951. 2 pp.

————. Senate. Committee on Commerce. *Federal Railroad Safety Act of 1968: Hearings before Subcommittee on Surface Transportation on S. 1933, S. 2915, and S. 3061*. 91st Cong., 1st Sess. Washington, D.C.: GPO, 1969. 430 pp.

————. Senate. Committee on Commerce. *Hours of Service Act Amendments of 1969*. S. Rept. 604 to Accompany H.R. 8449, 91st Cong., 1st Sess. Washington, D.C.: GPO, 1970. 15 pp.

————. Senate. Committee on Commerce. *Hours of Service of Railroad Employees: Hearings before Subcommittee on Surface Transportation, on S. 2180*. 89th Cong., 2nd Sess. Washington, D.C.: GPO, 1967. 595 pp.

————. Senate. Committee on Commerce. Subcommittee on Surface Transportation. *Hours of Service of Railroad Employees: Hearings on S. 1938*. 91st Cong., 1st Sess. Washington, D.C.: GPO, 1969. 243 pp.

————. Senate. Committee on Interstate and Foreign Commerce. *Problems of Railroads: Hearings before Subcommittee on Surface Transportation*. 85th Cong., 2nd Sess. Washington D.C.: GPO, 1958.

Part 2, testimony of motor carriers, etc., pp. 745–1337; part 3 testimony of government witnesses, etc., pp. 1337–984; part 4, testimony of railroad brotherhoods, etc., pp. 1984–2355.

————. Senate. Committee on the Judiciary. *Certain Employees of Alaska Railroad*. S. Rept. 1217 to Accompany S. 1640, 88th Cong., 2nd Sess. Washington, D.C.: GPO, 1964. 8 pp.

————. Senate. Committee on Labor and Public Welfare. *Amend the Railway Labor Act: Hearings before Subcommittee on Labor, on H.R. 706*. 89th Cong., 2nd Sess. Washington, D.C.: GPO, 1966. 317 pp.

————. Senate. Committee on Labor and Public Welfare. *Amending Railway Labor Act, as Amended, so as to Prevent Interference with Movement of Interstate Commerce*. S. Rept. 2445 [adverse] to Accompany S. 3463, 81st Cong., 2nd Sess. Washington, D.C.: GPO, 1950. 4 pp.

GOVERNMENT DOCUMENTS

————. Senate. Committee on Labor and Public Welfare. *Causes of Unemployment in Coal and Other Specified Industries.* S. Rept. 2042 Pursuant to S. Res. 274 with Supplemental Views of Mr. Taft, 81st Cong., 2nd Sess. Washington, D.C.: GPO, 1950. 22 pp.

————. Senate. Committee on Labor and Public Welfare. *Causes of Unemployment in the Coal and Other Specified Industries: Hearings before a Subcommittee on S. Res. 274.* 81st Cong., 2nd Sess. Washington, D.C.: GPO, 1950. 512 pp.

————. Senate. Committee on Labor and Public Welfare. *Railway Labor Act Amendments.* S. Rept. 1201 to Accompany H.R. 706, 89th Cong., 2nd Sess. Washington, D.C.: GPO, 1966. 14 pp.

————. Senate. Committee on Labor and Public Welfare. *Railway Labor Act Amendments.* S. Rept. 2262 on S. 3295 Together with Supplemental Views of Mr. Taft, Mr. Smith of N.J., and Mr. Donnell, 81st Cong., 2nd Sess. Washington, D.C.: GPO, 1950. 5 pp.

————. Senate. Committee on Labor and Public Welfare. *Terms of Office of Members of National Mediation Board.* S. Rept. 1387 to Accompany H.R. 8344, 88th Cong., 2nd Sess. Washington, D.C.: GPO, 1964. 6 pp.

————. Senate. Committee on Labor and Public Welfare. *To Amend the Railway Labor Act, Providing for Union Membership and Agreements for Deduction from Wages of Carrier Employees for Certain Purposes: Hearings before a Subcommittee on S. Res. 3295.* 81st Cong., 2nd Sess. Washington, D.C.: GPO, 1950. 323 pp.

————. Senate. Committee on Labor and Public Welfare. *To Prohibit Strikes and to Provide for Compulsory Arbitration in Railroad Industry: Hearings before Subcommittee on Railway Labor Act Amendments, on S. 3463.* 81st Cong., 2nd Sess. Washington, D.C.: GPO, 1950. 499 pp.

U.S. NATIONAL MEDIATION BOARD. *Railway Labor Act [as Amended 1966] Being Act to Provide for Prompt Disposition of Disputes between Carriers and Their Employees and for Other Purposes.* U.S. Code, title 45, chap. 8. Washington, D.C., 1967. 25 pp.

————. *Railway Labor Act, Being an Act to Provide for Prompt Disposition of Disputes between Carriers and Their Employees, and for Other Purposes.* U.S. Code, title 45, chap. 8. Washington, D.C., 1972. 30 pp.

U.S. SUPREME COURT. *Brotherhood of Locomotive Engineers [et al] Appellants, v. Chicago, Rock Island and Pacific Railroad Co. [et al] Appellees.* On appeal from U.S. District Court for Western District of Arkansas. Brief for the Appellants. [Arkansas full-crew law.] n.p., 1965. 74 pp.

————. *Brotherhood of Locomotive Firemen and Enginemen [et al] Appellants, v. Chicago, Rock Island, and Pacific Railroad Co. [et al] Appellees.* On appeal from U.S. District Court for Western District of Arkansas. Jurisdictional Statement. [Arkansas full-crew law.] n.p., 1968. 38 pp.

6. Labor Relations

1850–98

MISSOURI. Bureau of Labor Statistics and Inspection. *The Official History of the Great Strike of 1886 on the Southwestern Railway System.* Jefferson City: The Bureau, 1887.

NEBRASKA. State Board of Transportation. *Report to the Board upon the Matter of the Strike of the Brotherhoods of Locomotive Engineers and Firemen of the Burlington and Missouri River Railroad in Nebraska.* Lincoln, 1888. 19 pp.

PENNSYLVANIA GENERAL ASSEMBLY. Joint Committee Appointed to Investigate the Railroad Riots. *Report of the Committee Appointed to Investigate the Railroad Riots in July, 1877.* Harrisburg: Lane S. Hart, State Printer, 1878. 1000 pp.

U.S. ATTORNEY GENERAL'S COMMITTEE ON ADMINISTRATIVE PROCEDURE. *Inquiry Relating to the National Railroad Adjustment Board; Historical Background and Growth of Machinery Set Up for the Handling of Railroad Labor Disputes, 1888–1940,* compiled by Harry E. Jones, Executive Secretary, Eastern Committee for the National Railroad Adjustment Board. New York: Eastern, 1941. Two books in one vol., 427 pp. and 215 pp.

U.S. CONGRESS. House. *Appointment of Select Committee to Investigate Troubles between Railroad Companies and Their Employees in Certain States Recommended.* H. Doc. 1621, vol. 6, 49th Cong., 1st Sess. 1886. 1 p.

————. House. *Investigation of Troubles between Railroad Companies and Their Employees by the Committee on Labor, Recommended.* H. Doc. 1472, vol. 5, 49th Cong., 1st Sess. 1886. 1 p.

U.S. DEPARTMENT OF JUSTICE. *Correspondence Relating to the Action of the Government with Reference to the Interruption by Force of Interstate Commerce, the Carriage of the Mails, etc., in the Year 1894. Printed Pursuant to Concurrent Resolution of Jan. 8 and 20, 1897.* In *Appendix to the Annual Report of the Attorney General . . . 1896.* Washington, D.C.: GPO, 1896. 257 pp.

U.S. INDUSTRIAL COMMISSION. "Railway Labor," vol. 4, pt. 1, pp. 131–60. *Reports of the Industrial Commission, 1900–1902.* 19 vols. Washington, D.C.: GPO, 1900–1902.

————. "Railway Labor in the United States," vol. 17, pp. 709–1135. *Reports of the Industrial Commission, 1900–1902.* 19 vols. Washington, D.C.: GPO, 1900–1902.

U.S. STRIKE COMMISSION. *Report on the Chicago Strike of June–July 1894.* S. Ex. Doc. 7. Washington, D.C.: GPO, 1895. 681 pp.

1898–1926

BOARD OF ARBITRATION. *Controversy between the Brotherhood of Locomotive Engineers and the Eastern Railroads, 1912: Proceedings,* 263 pp.; *Report,* 123 pp. New York, 1912.

————. *Controversy between Certain Railroads and the Switchmen's Union of North America, 1916: Proceedings.* New York, 1917.

————. *Controversy between the Eastern Railroads and the Brotherhood of Locomotive Firemen and Enginemen, 1913: Proceedings.* 4 vols. New York, 1913.

————. *Controversy between the Eastern Railroads and the Order of Railway Conductors and the Brotherhood of Railroad Trainmen, 1913: Proceedings.* 3 vols. New York, 1913.

————. *Controversy between the Western Railroads and the Brotherhood of Locomotive Engineers and the Brotherhood of Locomotive Firemen and Enginemen, 1914–1915: Proceedings.* 9 vols. New York, 1915.

————. *In the Controversy between the Brotherhood of Locomotive Engineers and the Eastern Railroads: Proceedings.* [New York?], 1912. 263 pp.

————. *In the Controversy between Certain Railroads [Michigan Central, N.Y. Central and Others] and the Switchmen's Union of North America, 1916: Proceedings.* [New York?], 1917. 10 pp.

————. *In the Controversy between the Eastern Railroads and the Brotherhood of Locomotive Firemen and Engineers: Proceedings.* New York, 1913.

————. *In the Controversy between the Eastern Railroads and the Order of Railway Conductors and the Brotherhood of Railroad Trainmen: Proccedings.* New York, 1913.

————. *In the Controversy between the Western Railroads and the Brotherhood of Locomotive Engineers and Enginemen: Proceedings.* [New York?], 1915.

U.S. ATTORNEY GENERAL'S COMMITTEE ON ADMINISTRATIVE PROCEDURE. *Inquiry Relating to the National Railroad Adjustment Board; Historical Background and Growth of Machinery Set Up for the Handling of Railroad Labor Disputes, 1888–1940,* compiled by Harry E. Jones, Executive Secretary, Eastern Committee for the National Railroad Adjustment Board. New York: Eastern, 1941. Two books in one vol., 427 pp. and 215 pp.

U.S. BOARD OF MEDIATION AND CONCILIATION. *Railroad Labor Arbitrations; Report on Effects of Arbitration Proceedings upon Rates of Pay and Working Conditions of Railroad Employees,* prepared by W. Jett Lauck. S. Doc. 493, 64th Cong., 1st Sess. Washington, D.C.: GPO, 1916. 608 pp.

————. *Railway Strikes and Lockouts.* H. Doc. 2117, 64th Cong., 2nd Sess. Washington, D.C.: GPO, 1917. 367 pp.

————. *Report of Commissioner of Mediation and Conciliation on Operations of Board of Mediation and Conciliation, 1913–19.* Washington, D.C.: GPO, 1920. 109 pp.

————. *Report of the U. S. Board of Mediation and Conciliation, 1913–1917.* Washington, D.C.: GPO, 1918. 30 pp.

U.S. BUREAU OF LABOR STATISTICS. *Use of Federal Power in Settlement of Railway Labor Disputes* [with bibliography]. Bulletin 303. Washington, D.C.: GPO, 1922. 121 pp.

U.S. COMMISSION ON INDUSTRIAL RELATIONS (1912). "Harriman Railroad System Strike," vol. 10, pp. 9697–10066. *Reports.* Washington, D.C.: GPO, 1916.

————. "Pullman Employees," vol. 10, pp. 9543–695. *Reports.* Washington, D.C.: GPO, 1916.

U.S. CONGRESS. Senate. Committee on Interstate Commerce. *Threatened Strike of Railway Employees: Hearings on Bills in Connection with Legislation Relative to Threatened Strike of Railway Employees* [to be called September 4, 1916]. S. Doc. 549, 64th Cong., 1st Sess. Washington, D.C.: GPO, 1916. 171 pp.

U.S. DEPARTMENT OF JUSTICE. *Correspondence Relating to the Action of the Government with Reference to the Interruption by Force of Interstate Commerce, the Carriage of*

LABOR RELATIONS

the Mails, etc., in the Year 1922. Printed Pursuant to Concurrent Resolution of March 3, 1923, in *Appendix to the Annual Report of the Attorney General . . . 1921–22.* H. Doc. 409, pt. 2, 67th Cong., 3rd Sess. Washington, D.C.: GPO, 1924. 690 pp.

U.S. DEPARTMENT OF LABOR. *Mediation and Arbitration of Railway Labor Disputes in U.S.,* by C. P. Neill, pp. 1–63. Bulletin 98 (January 1912). Washington, D.C.: GPO, 1912.

U.S. FEDERAL WAGE COMMISSION. *Argument and Brief Submitted on Behalf of Locomotive Firemen and Hostlers: Hearings in Washington, D.C., Feb. 1918.* Cleveland, 1918. 285 pp.

————. *Excessive Hours of Service Required of Railway Employees: Tables, Argument and Brief Submitted on Behalf of Locomotive Firemen and Hostlers.* Washington, D.C.: GPO, 1918. pp. 129–56.

U.S. INDUSTRIAL COMMISSION. "Railway Labor," vol. 4, pt. 1, pp. 131–60. *Reports of the Industrial Commission, 1900–1902.* 19 vols. Washington, D.C.: GPO, 1900–1902.

U.S. INDUSTRIAL RELATIONS COMMISSION. *Harriman Railroad System Strike.* S. Doc. 415, vol. 10, pp. 9597–10066, 64th Cong., 1st Sess. Washington, D.C.: GPO, 1916. 69 pp.

U.S. PRESIDENT [Warren G. Harding]. *Strike Crisis. Address of President of U.S. Delivered before Joint Session of the Two Houses of Congress, Aug. 18, 1922.* S. Doc. 240, 67th Cong., 2nd Sess. Washington, D.C.: GPO, 1922. 10 pp.

U.S. RAILROAD ADMINISTRATION. *Agreement between Director General of Railroads in Respect of Railroads in Federal Operation and Employees Thereon, Represented by Brotherhood of Railway and Steamship Clerks, Freight Handlers, Express and Station Employees.* [Effective January 1, 1920.] Washington, D.C.: GPO, 1920. 24 pp.

————. *Agreement between Director General of Railroads in Respect of Railroads in Federal Operation and Employees Thereon Represented by United Brotherhood of Maintenance of Way Employees and Railway Shop Laborers.* [Effective December 16, 1919.] Washington, D.C.: GPO, 1919. 16 pp.

————. *Agreement between Railroad Administration and Employees Represented by Railway Employees Department of American Federation of Labor and Its Affiliated Organizations of Mechanical Section and Divisions 1–3 Thereof.* Washington, D.C.: GPO, 1919. 77 pp.

————. *Memoranda of Understandings in Connection with Memorandum of Director General, Dated Nov. 15, 1919, in Regard to Conditions under Which Time and One-half for Overtime Would Be Granted in Freight Service.* Washington, D.C.: GPO, 1920. 14 pp.

————. *Proposed Agreement to Be Submitted to Railroad Administration; Agreement between Railroad Administration and Following Organizations: 1) International Assoc. of Machinists; 2) International Brotherhood of Boilermakers, Iron Ship Builders and Helpers of America; 3) International Brotherhood of Blacksmiths and Helpers; 4) Amalgamated Sheet Metal Workers International Alliance; 5) International Brotherhood of Electrical Workers; 6) Brotherhood of Railway Carmen of America.* Washington, D.C.: GPO, 1919. 28 pp.

————. *Public Acts, Proclamations by the President Relating to the U.S. Railroad Administration and General Orders and Circulars Issued by the Director General of Railroads from Jan. 1, 1919–Feb. 29, 1920.* Supplement to Bulletin 4. Rev. ed. Washington, D.C.: GPO, 1920. 154 pp.

————. *Wage Orders, Interpretations and Supplements of U.S. Railroad Administration and U.S. Railroad Labor Board.* Cleveland: Engineers Printing, [1921 ?]. 328 pp.

U.S. RAILROAD LABOR BOARD. *Argument Supporting Request of Employees for Penalty Rates for Work (1) in Excess of Eight Hours; (2) on Sundays and Holidays; and Other Changes in Existing Agreements.* Docket No. 4040. Cleveland, May 1924. 117 pp.

————. *Brief for the Brotherhood of Railway and Steamship Clerks, Freight Handlers, Express and Station Employees: Alabama & Vicksburg Railway et al., vs. Brotherhood of Railway and Steamship Clerks et al.* Docket No. 1300. Chicago, 1922. 102 pp.

————. *Decisions with Addenda and Interpretations, 1920, with an Appendix Showing Regulations of the Board, and Court and Administrative Decisions and Regulations of the Interstate Commerce Commission in Respect to Title III of the Transportation Act, 1920.* Washington, D.C.: GPO, 1921.

————. *Decisions with Addenda and Interpretations, 1921, with an Appendix Showing Regulations of the Board, and Court and Adjustment Board Decisions and Regulations of Interstate Commerce Commission in Respect to Title III of Transportation Act, 1920. Cumulative Index-Digest.* Washington, D.C.: GPO, 1922. 1007 pp.

————. *Decisions with Addenda and Interpretations, 1922, with an Appendix Showing Resolutions and Announcements of the Railroad Labor Board.* Washington, D.C.: GPO, 1923. 1252 pp.

————. *Decisions of Railroad Labor Board, v. 5, with Addenda and Interpretations (Decisions 2069–2773), 1924, with Appendix Showing Regulations and Orders of Railroad Labor Board, Also Court Decisions in Respect to Title 3 of Transportation Act, 1920 [and with] Cumulative Index v. 1–5.* Washington, D.C., 1925. 1053 pp. & 188 pp.

————. *Railroad Earnings and Ability to Grant Punitive Overtime to Maintenance of Way Employees.* Docket No. 4040. Cleveland, June 1924. 19 pp.

————. *Railroad Labor Situation: A Brief Statement of the Railroad Labor Situation as It Existed Prior to Federal Control, during Federal Control and Subsequent to Federal Control.* Chicago, 1920. 8 pp.

————. *Report, April 15, 1920 to Dec. 31, 1925. Previous Legislation Covering Adjustment of Railway Labor Disputes.* Washington, D.C., 1926. 10 pp.

————. *Summary of the Position and Purpose of the Pennsylvania Railroad in Its Dealings with Its Employees, as Represented before the Board, July 8, 1921.* Broad St. Station, Philadelphia, 1921. 40 pp.

1926–46

NATIONAL LABOR RELATIONS BOARD. "The Railway Industry," chap. 8, pp. 115–27. *Written Trade Agreements in Collective Bargaining.* Washington, D.C.: GPO, 1940.

U.S. ATTORNEY GENERAL'S COMMITTEE ON ADMINISTRATIVE PROCEDURE. *Inquiry Relating to the National Railroad Adjustment Board; Historical Background and Growth of Machinery Set Up for the Handling of Railroad Labor Disputes, 1888–1940,* compiled by Harry E. Jones, Executive Secretary, Eastern Committee for the National Railroad Adjustment Board. New York: Eastern, 1941. Two books in one vol., 427 pp. and 215 pp.

————. *Railway Labor: The National Railroad Adjustment Board and the National*

Mediation Board. Monograph No. 17. Washington, D.C.: The Committee, 1940. 56 leaves.

U.S. CONGRESS. House. Committee on Interstate and Foreign Commerce. *Aid in Effectuating Purposes of Railway Labor Act [Relative to Settlement of Disputes between Carriers and Employees concerning Wages]*. H. Rept. 1073 Together with Minority Views to Accompany S.J. Res. 91, 78th Cong., 2nd Sess. Washington, D.C.: GPO, 1944. 7 pp.

U.S. NATIONAL MEDIATION BOARD. *Administration of the Railway Labor Act by the National Mediation Board, 1934–1957*. Washington, D.C.: GPO, 1958. 103 pp.

—————. *Administration of the Railway Labor Act by the National Mediation Board, 1934–1970*. Washington, D.C.: GPO, 1970. 203 pp.

—————. *Fifteen Years under the Railway Labor Act, Amended, and the National Mediation Board, 1934–1949*. Washington, D.C.: GPO, 1950. 92 pp.

—————. *Labor Relations in the Railroad Industry*. Washington, D.C.: GPO, 1940.

—————. *Railway Labor Act and National Mediation Board, Aug. 1940*. Washington, D.C.: GPO, 1940. 76 pp.

—————. *Twenty Years under the Railway Labor Act, Amended, and the National Mediation Board, 1934–1954*. Washington, D.C.: GPO, 1955. 109 pp.

U.S. PRESIDENT [Franklin D. Roosevelt]. Executive Order 9172. "Establishing Panel for Creation of Emergency Boards for Adjustment of Railway Labor Disputes," pp. 3913–14. *Federal Register* 7, no. 103, May 27, 1942.

U.S. RAILROAD WAGE COMMISSION. Railroad Administration. *Report to the Director General of Railroads, April 30, 1918*. Washington, D.C.: GPO, 1918. 156 pp.

1946–Present

U.S. CONGRESS. House. *Joint Resolution to Further Extend Period Provided for under Sec. 10 of Railway Labor Act Applicable in Current Dispute between Railroad Carriers Represented by National Railway Labor Conference and Certain of Their Employees*. [Approved May 2, 1967.] H. J. Res. 543. Washington, D.C.: GPO, 1967. 1 p.

—————. House. *Joint Resolution to Provide for Temporary Prohibition of Strikes or Lockouts with Respect to Current Railway Labor-Management Dispute*. H.J. Res. 1413, Public Law 541, 91st Cong., 2nd Sess. Washington, D.C.: GPO, 1971. 2 pp.

—————. House. *Legislation Relating to Railroad Strike: Message from the President Urging Enactment Relating to Nation-wide Rail Strike*. H. Doc. 268, 91st Cong., 2nd Sess. Washington, D.C.: GPO, 1970. 2 pp.

—————. House. *Nationwide Railroad Strike: Message from President of U.S. Transmitting Report on Negotiations to Ward Off Threatened Railroad Strike and Recommended Joint Resolution*. H. Doc. 104, 90th Cong., 1st Sess. Washington, D.C.: GPO, 1967. 5 pp.

—————. House. *Proposed Legislation Amending Public Law 90–10 (Rail Strike): Communication from President of U.S. Transmitting Draft*. H. Doc. 113, 90th Cong., 1st Sess. Washington, D.C.: GPO, 1967. 2 pp.

—————. House. *Rail Situation: Message from President of U.S. Transmitting Summary of Rail Situation and Proposed Resolution for Settling Dispute*. H. Doc. 118, 90th Cong., 1st Sess. Washington, D.C.: GPO, 1967. 7 pp.

————. House. *Railway Labor Dispute: Communication from President of U.S. Transmitting Report to Congress on Progress in Negotiations in Railway Labor Dispute and Recommendations for Resolution of Dispute, Pursuant to Public Law 91–541.* H. Doc. 49, 92nd Cong., 1st Sess. Washington, D.C.: GPO, 1971. 12 pp.

————. House. Committee on Education and Labor. *Investigation of Communist Influence in the Bucyrus-Erie Strike.* Washington, D.C.: GPO, 1948.

————. House. Committee on Interstate and Foreign Commerce. *Current Railway Labor-Management Dispute.* H. Rept. 182 to Accompany H.J. Res. 493, 90th Cong., 1st Sess. Washington, D.C.: GPO, 1967. 28 pp.

————. House. Committee on Interstate and Foreign Commerce. *Emergency Railroad Labor-Management Dispute, Legislation, 1970: Hearings on H.J. Res. 1413 and H.J. Res. 1414.* 91st Cong., 2nd Sess. Washington, D.C.: GPO, 1971. 100 pp.

————. House. Committee on Interstate and Foreign Commerce. *Extension of Period for Making No Change in Conditions in Current Railway Labor-Management Dispute.* H. Rept. 218 to Accompany H.J. Res. 543, 90th Cong., 1st Sess. Washington, D.C.: GPO, 1967. 10 pp.

————. House. Committee on Interstate and Foreign Commerce. *Final Settlement of Railway Labor-Management Dispute, 1970.* H. Rept. 984 Together with Minority Views to Accompany H.J. Res. 1124, 91st Cong., 2nd Sess. Washington, D.C.: GPO, 1970. 20 pp.

————. House. Committee on Interstate and Foreign Commerce. *1971 Railway Labor-Management Dispute, Signalman: Hearings on H.J. Res. 642.* 92nd Cong., 1st Sess. Washington, D.C.: GPO, 1971. 85 pp.

————. House. Committee on Interstate and Foreign Commerce. *Railroad Labor Dispute.* H. Rept. 713 to Accompany H.J. Res. 665, 88th Cong., 1st Sess. Washington, D.C.: GPO, 1963. 26 pp.

————. House. Committee on Interstate and Foreign Commerce. *Railroad Labor Dispute: Hearings on H.J. Res. 559.* 90th Cong., 1st Sess. Washington, D.C.: GPO, 1967. 497 pp.

————. House. Committee on Interstate and Foreign Commerce. *Railroad Labor-Management Dispute — 1970: Hearings on H.J. Res. 1112 and H.J. Res. 1124.* 91st Cong., 2nd Sess. Washington, D.C.: GPO, 1970. 265 pp.

————. House. Committee on Interstate and Foreign Commerce. *Railroad Work Rules Dispute: Hearings on H.J. Res. 565.* 88th Cong., 1st Sess. Washington, D.C.: GPO, 1963. 1026 pp.

————. House. Committee on Interstate and Foreign Commerce. *Railway Labor-Management Dispute, 1971.* H. Rept. 209 to Accompany H.J. Res. 642, 92nd Cong., 1st Sess. Washington, D.C.: GPO, 1971. 8 pp.

————. House. Committee on Interstate and Foreign Commerce. *Settlement of Current Railway Labor-Management Dispute.* H. Rept. 353 Together with Minority Views to Accompany H.J. Res. 559, 90th Cong., 1st Sess. Washington, D.C.: GPO, 1967. 24 pp.

————. House. Committee on Interstate and Foreign Commerce. *Temporary Prohibition of Strikes and Lockouts in Current Railway Labor-Management Dispute.* H. Rept. 1686 to Accompany H.J. Res. 1413, 91st Cong., 2nd Sess. Washington. D.C.: GPO, 1971. 14 pp.

————. House. Committee on Interstate and Foreign Commerce. *Temporary Prohibi-*

tion of Strikes and Lockouts with Respect to Current Railway Labor-Management Dispute. H. Rept. 868 to Accompany H.J. Res. 1112, 91st Cong., 2nd Sess. Washington, D.C.: GPO, 1970. 10 pp.

―――――. House. Committee on Rules. *Consideration of H.J. Res. 642.* H. Rept. 210 to Accompany H. Res. 447 [Railway Labor-Management Dispute, 1971], 92nd Cong., 1st Sess. Washington, D.C.: GPO, 1971. 1 p.

―――――. House. Committee on Rules. *Consideration of H.J. Res. 1124.* H. Rept. 985 to Accompany H. Res. 904 [Railway Labor-Management Dispute, 1970], 91st Cong., 2nd Sess. Washington, D.C.: GPO, 1970. 1 p.

―――――. House. Committee on Rules. *Consideration of H.J. Res. 1413.* H. Rept. 1687 to Accompany H. Res. 1300 [Temporary Prohibition of Strikes and Lockouts in Current Railway Labor-Management Dispute], 91st Cong., 2nd Sess. Washington, D.C.: GPO, 1971. 1 p.

―――――. Senate. *Joint Resolution to Extend Period for Making No Change of Conditions under Sec. 10 of Railway Labor Act Applicable in Current Dispute between Railroad Carriers Represented by National Railway Labor Conference and Certain of Their Employees.* [Approved April 12, 1967.] S.J. Res. 65. Washington, D.C.: GPO, 1967. 2 pp.

―――――. Senate. *Joint Resolution to Provide for Settlement of Labor Dispute between Certain Carriers by Railroad and Certain of Their Employees.* [Approved August 28, 1963.] S.J. Res. 102, 88th Cong., 1st Sess. Washington, D.C.: GPO, 1963. 3 pp.

―――――. Senate. *Joint Resolution to Provide for Settlement of Labor Dispute between Certain Carriers by Railroad and Certain of Their Employees.* [Approved July 17, 1967.] S.J. Res. 81, 90th Cong., 1st Sess. Washington, D.C.: GPO, 1967. 3 pp.

―――――. Senate. *Joint Resolution to Provide for Settlement of Labor Dispute between Certain Carriers by Railroad and Certain of Their Employees.* S.J. Res. 190, 91st Cong., 2nd Sess. Washington, D.C.: GPO, 1970. 2 pp.

―――――. Senate. *Joint Resolution to Provide for Temporary Prohibition of Strikes or Lockouts with Respect to Current Railway Labor-Management Dispute.* S.J. Res. 180, 91st Cong., 2nd Sess. Washington, D.C.: GPO, 1970. 1 p.

―――――. Senate. Committee on Commerce. *Railroad Work-Rules Dispute.* S. Rept. 459 to Accompany S.J. Res. 102, 88th Cong., 1st Sess. Washington, D.C.: GPO, 1963. 15 pp.

―――――. Senate. Committee on Commerce. *Railroad Work Rules Dispute: Hearings on the Administration of Public Law 88–108.* 89th Cong., 1st and 2nd Sess. Washington, D.C.: GPO, 1966. 2 pts., 1002 pp., and 1003–1185 pp.

―――――. Senate. Committee on Commerce. *Railroad Work Rules Dispute: Hearings on S.J. Res. 102.* 88th Cong., 1st Sess. Washington, D.C.: GPO, 1963. 740 pp.

―――――. Senate. Committee on Labor and Public Welfare. *Consideration of Legislation for Settlement of Railroad Strike.* S. Rept. 1426 to Accompany S.J. Res. 248, 91st Cong., 2nd Sess. Washington, D.C.: GPO, 1971. 14 pp.

―――――. Senate. Committee on Labor and Public Welfare. *Current Railway Labor-Management Dispute.* S. Rept. 161 to Accompany S.J. Res. 65, 90th Cong., 1st Sess. Washington, D.C.: GPO, 1967. 32 pp.

―――――. Senate. Committee on Labor and Public Welfare. *Current Railway Labor-Management Dispute.* S. Rept. 201 to Accompany S.J. Res. 79, 90th Cong., 1st Sess. Washington, D.C.: GPO, 1967. 3 pp.

————. Senate. Committee on Labor and Public Welfare. *Current Railway Labor-Management Dispute.* S. Rept. 758 to Accompany S.J. Res. 190, 91st Cong., 2nd Sess. Washington, D.C.: GPO, 1970. 19 pp.

————. Senate. Committee on Labor and Public Welfare. *Dispute between Railway Carriers and Four Operating Brotherhoods.* S. Rept. 496 Together with Minority Views, 82nd Cong., 1st Sess. Washington, D.C.: GPO, 1951. 26 pp.

————. Senate. Committee on Labor and Public Welfare. *Prohibition of Strikes or Lockouts for 37 Days with Respect to Current Railway-Management Dispute.* S. Rept. 717 to Accompany S.J. Res. 180, 91st Cong., 2nd Sess. Washington, D.C.: GPO, 1970. 9 pp.

————. Senate. Committee on Labor and Public Welfare. *Railroad Rules and Wage Disputes: Hearings before Subcommittee.* 80th Cong., 2nd Sess. Washington, D.C.: GPO, 1948. 50 pp.

————. Senate. Committee on Labor and Public Welfare. *Railroad Shopcraft Dispute: Hearings before the Subcommittee on Labor on S.J. Res. 81.* 90th Cong., 1st Sess. Washington, D.C.: GPO, 1967. 520 pp.

————. Senate. Committee on Labor and Public Welfare. *Railroad Shop Craft Dispute.* S. Rept. 292 Together with Individual Views to Accompany S.J. Res. 81, 90th Cong., 1st Sess. Washington, D.C.: GPO, 1967. 15 pp.

————. Senate. Committee on Labor and Public Welfare. *Railroad Signalmen Labor-Management Dispute, May 1971: Hearings on S.J. Res. 98.* 92nd Cong., 1st Sess. Washington, D.C.: GPO, 1971. 191 pp.

————. Senate. Committee on Labor and Public Welfare. *Railway Labor-Management Dispute, Dec. 1970: Hearings on S.J. Res. 246.* 91st Cong., 2nd Sess. Washington, D.C.: GPO, 1971. 225 pp.

————. Senate. Committee on Labor and Public Welfare. *Railway Labor-Management Negotiations: Hearings.* 90th Cong., 1st Sess. Washington, D.C.: GPO, 1967. 60 pp.

————. Senate. Committee on Labor and Public Welfare. *Railway Shopcraft Dispute, March 1970: Hearings on S.J. 178.* 91st Cong., 2nd Sess. Washington, D.C.: GPO, 1970. 132 pp.

————. Senate. Committee on Labor and Public Welfare. *Railway Shopcraft Dispute, April 1970: Hearings on S.J. 178.* 91st Cong., 2nd Sess. Washington, D.C.: GPO, 1970. 157 pp.

————. Senate. Committee on Labor and Public Welfare. Subcommittee on Labor and Labor-Management Relations. *Labor Dispute between the Railroad Carriers and Four Operating Railroad Brotherhoods: Hearings.* Washington, D.C.: GPO, 1951. 842 pp.

————. Senate. Committee on Post Office and Civil Service. *Personnel Policies of the Alaska Railroad: Hearings before Subcommittee on Civil Service on S. 2593.* 87th Cong., 2nd Sess. Washington, D.C.: GPO, 1962. 49 pp.

U.S. COURT OF APPEALS FOR THE EIGHTH CIRCUIT. No. 17,098. Civil. *Brotherhood of Locomotive Engineers, Appellant vs. Chicago and North Western Railway Co., Appellee.* Appeal from the U.S. District Court for the Southern District of Iowa. Record. St. Louis: St. Louis Law Printing, 1962. 361 pp.

U.S. DEPARTMENT OF LABOR. *Railroad Shopcraft Factfinding Study,* prepared by Labor-Management Services Administration, September 1968. Washington, D.C.: GPO, 1969. 175 pp.; appendix vol. 211 pp.

U.S. DEPARTMENT OF TRANSPORTATION. Federal Railroad Administration. *Joint Labor-Management Program to Improve Operating Practices, Work Rules and Employee Compensation Programs in Railroad Industry*, by John L. Gable. Washington, D.C.: GPO, 1969. 45 leaves.

U.S. NATIONAL MEDIATION BOARD. *Administration of the Railway Labor Act by the National Mediation Board, 1934–1957*. Washington, D.C.: GPO, 1958. 103 pp.

————. *Administration of the Railway Labor Act by the National Mediation Board, 1934–1970*. Washington, D.C.: GPO, 1970. 203 pp.

————. *Fifteen Years under the Railway Labor Act, Amended, and the National Mediation Board, 1934–1949*. Washington, D.C.: GPO, 1950. 92 pp.

————. *Twenty Years under the Railway Labor Act, Amended, and the National Mediation Board, 1934–1954*. Washington, D.C.: GPO, 1955. 109 pp.

U.S. PRESIDENT [Lyndon B. Johnson]. *Railway Labor Dispute: The President's Message to the Congress (May 4, 1967) Recommending Procedures to Complete Collective Bargaining*, pp. 103–6. In *Weekly Compilation of Presidential Documents*, vol. 5, May 8, 1967.

U.S. PRESIDENT [John F. Kennedy]. *Railroad-Labor Dispute. Message from President of U.S., July 22, 1963*. H. Doc. 142, 88th Cong., 1st Sess. Washington, D.C.: GPO, 1963. 32 pp.

U.S. PRESIDENTIAL RAILROAD COMMISSION. *Report of the Presidential Railroad Commission*. Processed. Washington, D.C.: GPO, 1962. 327 pp.

————. *Studies Relating to Railroad Operating Employees*. Washington, D.C.: GPO, 1962. 269 pp.

7. Retirement, Protective Programs

1850–98

U.S. BUREAU OF LABOR. *Railroad Labor: Annual Report of the Commissioner of Labor, 5th., 1889*. Also issued as H. Ex. Doc. 336, 51st Cong., 1st Sess. Washington, D.C.: GPO, 1889. 888 pp.

U.S. CONGRESS. House. *Compilation of Laws Relating to Mediation, Conciliation, and Arbitration between Employers and Employees, Disputes between Carriers and Employers and Subordinate Officials under Labor Board, 8-hr. Laws, Employers' Liability Laws, Labor and Child Labor Laws, 1888–1967*, compiled by Gilman G. Udell, Superintendent, Document Room, House of Representatives. Washington, D.C.: GPO, 1967. 1035 pp.

————. House. *Provision for Protection of Railroad Employees Recommended*. H. Doc. 3014, vol. 7, 51st Cong., 1st Sess. Washington, D.C.: GPO, 1890. 6 pp.

1898–1926

U.S. CONGRESS. House. *Compilation of Laws Relating to Mediation, Conciliation, and Arbitration between Employers and Employees, Disputes between Carriers and Employers and Subordinate Officials under Labor Board, 8-hr. Laws, Employers' Liability Laws,*

Labor and Child Labor Laws, 1888–1967, compiled by Gilman G. Udell, Superin-. tendent, Document Room, House of Representatives. Washington, D.C.: GPO, 1967. 1035 pp.

————. House. Committee on Judiciary. *Amendments to Federal Employers' Liability Act: Hearings on H.R. 14973.* 64th Cong., 1st Sess. Washington, D.C.: GPO, 1916. 21 pp.

————. House. Committee on Judiciary. *Liability of Common Carriers.* H. Rept. 1084 to Accompany H.R. 14973, 64th Cong., 1st Sess. Washington, D.C.: GPO, 1916. 3 pp.

————. House. Committee on Judiciary. *Liability of Common Carriers. Argument [by H. R. Fuller] on H.R. 7041.* 58th Cong., 3rd Sess. Washington, D.C.: GPO, 1904. 55 pp.

————. House. Committee on Judiciary. *Report Amending H.R. 17263, to Amend Act Relating to Liability of Common Carriers by Railroad to Their Employees in Certain Cases.* H. Rept. 513, 61st Cong., 2nd Sess. Washington, D.C.: GPO, 1910. 14 pp.

————. House. Committee on Judiciary. *Report on H.R. 239 Relating to Liability of Common Carriers to Their Employees.* H. Rept. 2335, 59th Cong., 1st Sess. Washington, D.C.: GPO, 1906. 8 pp.

————. House. Committee on Judiciary. *Workmen's Compensation: Hearings on H.R. 1 (to Change General Law for Injuries Received on Mail Routes).* 61st Cong., 2nd Sess. Washington, D.C.: GPO, 1910. 183 pp.

————. Senate. Committee on Interstate Commerce. *Liability of Employers, Relating to Liability of Common Carriers by Railroads: Hearings before Subcommittee on H.R. 239, S. 159 and S. 1657.* 59th Cong., 1st Sess. Washington, D.C.: GPO. 360 pp.

————. Senate. Committee on Interstate Commerce. *Report Amending H.R. 239, Relating to Liability of Common Carriers to Their Employees.* S. Rept. 3639, 59th Cong., 1st Sess. Washington, D.C.: GPO, 1906. 1 p.

————. Senate. Committee on Judiciary. *Report Amending H.R. 17263, to Amend Act Relating to Liability of Common Carriers by Railroad to Their Employees in Certain Cases.* S. Rept. 432, 61st Cong., 2nd Sess. Washington, D.C.: GPO, 1910. 15 pp.

————. Senate. Committee on Judiciary. *To Amend Act Relating to Liability of Common Carriers by Railroad to Their Employees in Certain Cases: Hearings before Subcommittee on H.R. 17263.* 61st Cong., 2nd Sess. Washington, D.C.: GPO, 1910. 13 pp.

U.S. INDUSTRIAL COMMISSION. "Consolidation of Railroads in the United States," vol. 19, pt. 3, pp. 304–29. *Reports of the Industrial Commission, 1900–1902.* 19 vols. Washington, D.C.: GPO, 1900–1902.

U.S. RAILROAD ADMINISTRATION. Operation Division. *Survey and Recommendations of Committee on Health and Medical Relief, Revised.* Washington, D.C.: GPO, 1920. 84 pp.

1926–46

U.S. BUREAU OF LABOR STATISTICS. "Attitude of Railroad Brotherhoods toward Workmen's Compensation, and Reason for Such Attitude," by W. N. Doak (with discussion), pp. 53–61. *Proceedings of the Eighteenth Annual Meeting of the International Association of Industrial Accident Boards and Commissions.* Bulletin 564. Washington, D.C.: GPO, 1932.

————. *Laws Relating to Interstate and Foreign Commerce, 1916–1940,* compiled by

Elmer A. Lewis, Superintendent, Document Room, House of Representatives. Washington, D.C.: GPO, 1940. 484 pp.
Includes railroad retirement acts and unemployment insurance laws.

————. *Railroad Retirement Act as Amended (1935–1942), and Railroad Unemployment Insurance Act as Amended (1938–1942),* compiled by John W. Lambert, Superintendent, Document Room, Senate. Washington, D.C.: GPO, 1945. 89 pp.

U.S. CONGRESS. House. *Act to Amend Act to Establish Retirement System for Employees of Carriers Subject to Interstate Commerce Act.* [Approved June 24, 1937.] H.R. 7519, Public Law 162, 75th Cong., 1st Sess. Washington, D.C.: GPO, 1937. 14 pp.

————. House. *Act to Amend Railroad Unemployment Insurance Act.* [Approved June 20, 1939.] H.R. 5474, Public Law 151, 76th Cong., 1st Sess. Washington, D.C.: GPO, 1939. 5 pp.

————. House. *Act to Establish Retirement System for Employees of Carriers Subject to Interstate Commerce Act.* [Approved August 29, 1935.] H.R. 8651, Public Law 399, 74th Cong., 1st Sess. Washington, D.C.: GPO, 1935. 8 pp.

————. House. *Act to Extend Crediting of Military Service under Railroad Retirement Acts.* [Approved April 8, 1942.] H.R. 6387, Public Law 520, 77th Cong., 2nd Sess. Washington, D.C.: GPO, 1942. 9 pp.

————. House. *Act to Provide Revenue, and for Other Purposes [Including Crediting Military Service for Annuity Purposes under Railroad Retirement Acts].* [Approved October 8, 1940.] H.R. 10413, Public Law 801, 76th Cong., 3rd Sess. Washington, D.C.: GPO, 1940. 50 pp.

————. House. *Act to Regulate Interstate Commerce by Establishing Unemployment Insurance System for Individuals Employed by Certain Employers Engaged in Interstate Commerce.* [Approved June 25, 1938.] H.R. 10127, Public Law 722, 75th Cong., 3rd Sess. Washington, D.C.: GPO, 1938. 22 pp.

————. House. *Compilation of Laws Relating to Mediation, Conciliation, and Arbitration between Employers and Employees, Disputes between Carriers and Employers and Subordinate Officials under Labor Board, 8-hr. Laws, Employers' Liability Laws, Labor and Child Labor Laws, 1888–1967,* compiled by Gilman G. Udell, Superintendent, Document Room, House of Representatives. Washington, D.C.: GPO, 1967. 1035 pp.

————. House. *Joint Resolution Making Appropriations, Fiscal Year 1938, for Civilian Conservation Corps, Railroad Retirement Account, and Other Activities.* [Approved July 1, 1937.] H.J. Res. 433, Public Res. 50, 75th Cong., 1st Sess. Washington, D.C.: GPO, 1937. 3 pp.

————. House. *Joint Resolution Providing for More Uniform Coverage under Railroad Retirement Acts of 1935 and 1937, Carriers Taxing Act of 1937, and Subchap. B of Chap. 9 of Internal Revenue Code.* [Approved June 11, 1940.] H.J. Res. 496, Public Res. 81, 76th Cong., 3rd Sess. Washington, D.C.: GPO, 1940. 2 pp.

————. House. Committee on Appropriations. *Appropriations, Civilian Conservation Corps, Railroad Retirement Account, etc. Fiscal Year 1938.* H. Rept. 1146 to Accompany H.J. Res. 433, 75th Cong., 1st Sess. Washington, D.C.: GPO, 1937. 3 pp.

————. House. Committee on Interstate and Foreign Commerce. *Amend Railroad Unemployment Insurance Act: Hearings on H.R. 9706, H.R. 10082 and H.R. 10085.* 76th Cong., 3rd Sess. Washington, D.C.: GPO, 1940. 197 pp.

————. House. Committee on Interstate and Foreign Commerce. *Amending Railroad Unemployment Insurance Act.* H. Rept. 686 to Accompany H.R. 5474, 76th Cong., 1st Sess. Washington, D.C.: GPO, 1939. 13 pp.

————. House. Committee on Interstate and Foreign Commerce. *Commission to Investigate Desirability of Further Retirement and Annuity Legislation Applicable to Interstate Carriers by Railroad.* H. Rept. 1505 to Accompany H.J. Res. 314, 74th Cong., 1st Sess. Washington, D.C.: GPO, 1935. 2 pp.

————. House. Committee on Interstate and Foreign Commerce. *Crediting of Military Service under Railroad Retirement Acts: Hearings on H.R. 3984.* 77th Cong., 1st Sess. Washington, D.C.: GPO, 1941. 43 pp.

————. House. Committee on Interstate and Foreign Commerce. *Establish Unemployment Insurance System for Railroad Employees.* H. Rept. 2668 to Accompany H.R. 10127, 75th Cong., 3rd Sess. Washington, D.C.: GPO, 1938. 21 pp.

————. House. Committee on Interstate and Foreign Commerce. *Extending Crediting of Military Service under Railroad Retirement Acts.* H. Rept. 1604 to Accompany H.R. 6837, 77th Cong., 2nd Sess. Washington, D.C.: GPO, 1942. 10 pp.

————. House. Committee on Interstate and Foreign Commerce. *Provide Retirement System for Railroad Employees.* H. Rept. 1988 to Accompany H.R. 9911, 73rd Cong., 2nd Sess. Washington, D.C.: GPO, 1934. 4 pp.

————. House. Committee on Interstate and Foreign Commerce. *Providing for Acquisition of Data by Railroad Retirement Board [Needed in Carrying Out Provisions of Railroad Retirement Acts].* H. Rept. 2899 to Accompany S.J. Res. 267, 76th Cong., 3rd Sess. Washington, D.C.: GPO, 1940. 3 pp.

————. House. Committee on Interstate and Foreign Commerce. *Providing for More Uniform Coverage under Railroad Retirement Acts, Carriers Taxing Act, and Internal Revenue Code.* H. Rept. 2029 to Accompany H.J. Res. 496, 76th Cong., 3rd Sess. Washington, D.C.: GPO, 1940. 2 pp.

————. House. Committee on Interstate and Foreign Commerce. *Railroad Employees Retirement System: Hearings on H.R. 9596.* 73rd Cong., 2nd Sess. Washington, D.C.: GPO, 1934. 69 pp.

————. House. Committee on Interstate and Foreign Commerce. *Railroad Employment Protection: Hearings before a Subcommittee on H.R. 11609.* 74th Cong., 2nd Sess. Washington, D.C.: GPO, 1936. 126 pp.

————. House. Committee on Interstate and Foreign Commerce. *Railroad Retirement.* H. Rept. 1069 to Accompany H.R. 7519, 75th Cong., 1st Sess. Washington, D.C.: GPO, 1937. 19 pp.

————. House. Committee on Interstate and Foreign Commerce. *Railroad Retirement: Hearings on H.R. 1362.* 79th Cong., 1st Sess. Washington, D.C.: GPO, 1945. 1254 pp.

————. House. Committee on Interstate and Foreign Commerce. *Railroad Unemployment Insurance Act Amendments.* H. Rept. 2945 to Accompany H.J. Res. 496, 76th Cong., 3rd Sess. Washington, D.C.: GPO, 1940. 13 pp.

————. House. Committee on Interstate and Foreign Commerce. *Railroad Unemployment Insurance System: Hearings before Subcommittee on H.R. 10127.* 75th Cong., 3rd Sess. Washington, D.C.: GPO, 1938. 265 pp.

————. House. Committee on Interstate and Foreign Commerce. *Retirement System for*

Employees of Carriers Subject to Interstate Commerce Act. H. Rept. 1711 to Accompany H.R. 8651, 74th Cong., 1st Sess. Washington, D.C.: GPO, 1935. 12 pp.

―――――. House. Committee on Interstate and Foreign Commerce. *Retirement System for Interstate Carriers' Employees: Hearings on H.R. 6956.* 75th Cong., 1st Sess. Washington, D.C.: GPO, 1937. 156 pp.

―――――. House. Committee on Interstate and Foreign Commerce. *Retirement System for Interstate Carriers' Employees: Hearings before Subcommittee on H.R. 8651.* 74th Cong., 1st Sess. Washington, D.C.: GPO, 1935. 138 pp.

―――――. House. Committee on Judiciary. *Amendment of Sec. 77 of Bankruptcy Act as to Preferred Claims [Relative to Claims for Personal Injuries or Death of Railroad Employees].* H. Rept. 1458 to Accompany S. 2654, 76th Cong., 1st Sess. Washington, D.C.: GPO, 1939. 2 pp.

―――――. Senate. *Act to Amend Railroad Unemployment Insurance Act, as Amended.* [Approved October 10, 1940.] S. 3920, Public Law 833, 76th Cong., 3rd Sess. Washington, D.C.: GPO, 1940. 9 pp.

―――――. Senate. *Act to Amend Subsec. (n), Sec. 77 of Bankruptcy Act, as Amended, concerning Payment of Preferred Claims [Relative to Claims for Personal Injuries or Death of Railroad Employees].* [Approved August 11, 1939.] S. 2654, Public Law 386, 76th Cong., 1st Sess. Washington, D.C.: GPO, 1939. 1 p.

―――――. Senate. *Act to Provide Retirement System for Railroad Employees, to Provide Unemployment Relief, and for Other Purposes.* [Approved June 27, 1934.] S. 3231, Public Law 485, 73rd Cong., 2nd Sess. Washington, D.C.: GPO, 1934. 7 pp.

―――――. Senate. *Joint Resolution Providing for Acquisition by Railroad Retirement Board of Data Needed in Carrying Out Provisions of Railroad Retirement Acts.* [Approved October 9, 1940.] S.J. Res. 267, Public Res. 102, 76th Cong., 3rd Sess. Washington, D.C.: GPO, 1940. 3 pp.

―――――. Senate. Committee on Interstate Commerce. *Acquisition by Railroad Retirement Board of Data.* S. Rept. 1805 to Accompany S.J. Res. 267, 76th Cong., 3rd Sess. Washington, D.C.: GPO, 1940. 4 pp.

―――――. Senate. Committee on Interstate Commerce. *Amending Railroad Unemployment Insurance Act.* S. Rept. 325 to Accompany S. 2017, 76th Cong., 1st Sess. Washington, D.C.: GPO, 1939. 6 pp.

―――――. Senate. Committee on Interstate Commerce. *Amending Railroad Unemployment Insurance Act, as Amended.* S. Rept. 1752 to Accompany S. 3920, 76th Cong., 3rd Sess. Washington, D.C.: GPO, 1940. 29 pp.

―――――. Senate. Committee on Interstate Commerce. *Amendment of Railroad Retirement Acts of 1935 and 1937, Carriers Taxing Act of 1937, and Subchap. B of Chap. 9 of Internal Revenue Code.* S. Rept. 1572 to Accompany S.J. Res. 234, 76th Cong., 3rd Sess. Washington, D.C.: GPO, 1940. 1 p.

―――――. Senate. Committee on Interstate Commerce. *Directing Railroad Retirement Board to Investigate Injuries and Diseases of Railroad Employees and Social and Economic Consequences.* S. Rept. 561 to Accompany S. Res. 128, 77th Cong., 1st Sess. Washington, D.C.: GPO, 1941. 1 p.

―――――. Senate. Committee on Interstate Commerce. *Extend Crediting of Military Service of Railroad Retirement Acts.* S. Rept. 1192 to Accompany H.R. 6387, 77th Cong., 2nd Sess. Washington, D.C.: GPO, 1942. 3 pp.

GOVERNMENT DOCUMENTS

————. Senate. Committee on Interstate Commerce. *Pensions and Retirement for Employees of Interstate Railways: Hearings before a Subcommittee on S. 3892 and S. 4646.* 72nd Cong., 2nd Sess. Washington, D.C.: GPO, 1933. 459 pp.

————. Senate. Committee on Interstate Commerce. *Railroad Retirement Bill.* S. Rept. 697 to Accompany S. 2395, 75th Cong., 1st Sess. Washington, D.C.: GPO, 1937. 20 pp.

————. Senate. Committee on Interstate Commerce. *Railroad Retirement: Hearings before a Subcommittee on S. 293.* 79th Cong., 1st Sess. Washington, D.C.: GPO, 1945. 558 pp.

————. Senate. Committee on Interstate Commerce. *Railway Retirement Act of 1935.* S. Rept. 1363 to Accompany S. 3151, 74th Cong., 1st Sess. Washington, D.C.: GPO, 1935. 4 pp.

————. Senate. Committee on Interstate Commerce. *Retirement Pension System for Railroad Employees: Hearings before Subcommittee on S. 3231.* 73rd Cong., 2nd Sess. Washington, D.C.: GPO, 1934. 185 pp.

————. Senate. Committee on Interstate Commerce. *Retirement System of Employees of Carriers: Hearings before Subcommittee on S. 3151.* 74th Cong., 1st Sess. Washington, D.C.: GPO, 1935. 236 pp.

————. Senate. Committee on Interstate Commerce. *Retirement System for Interstate Carriers' Employees: Hearings on S. 2395.* 75th Cong.. 1st Sess. Washington, D.C.: GPO, 1937. 123 pp.

————. Senate. Committee on Interstate Commerce. *Retirement System for Railroad Employees.* S. Rept. 974 to Accompany S. 3231, 73rd Cong., 2nd Sess. Washington, D.C.: GPO, 1934. 5 pp.

————. Senate. Committee on Interstate Commerce. *To Amend Paragraph 6 of Sec. 5 of Interstate Commerce Act, as Amended So as to Direct I.C.C. to Protect Railroad Employees against Uncompensated Injury Resulting from Consolidation of Carriers.* S. Rept. 632 to Accompany S. 4205, 71st Cong., 2nd Sess. Washington, D.C.: GPO, 1930. 2 pp.

————. Senate. Committee on Interstate Commerce. *To Amend the Railroad Retirement Act: Hearings before a Subcommittee on S. 306, S. 328, S. 593, S. 968, S. 969, S. 1112, S. 1724, S. 1784, S. 1828, S. 2159, S. 2443.* 76th Cong., 1st Sess. Washington, D.C.: GPO, 1939. 90 pp.

————. Senate. Committee on Interstate Commerce. *To Amend the Railroad Unemployment Insurance Act: Hearings before Subcommittee on S. 3920 and S. 3925.* 76th Cong., 3rd Sess. Washington, D.C.: GPO, 1940. 118 pp.

————. Senate. Committee on Interstate Commerce. *To Limit Hours of Service of Train Dispatchers Employed in Interstate Commerce: Hearings before Subcommittee on S. 1492.* 75th Cong., 2nd Sess. Washington, D.C.: GPO, 1938. 103 pp.

————. Senate. Committee on Interstate Commerce. *Unemployment Insurance System for Employees Engaged in Interstate Commerce: Hearings on S. 3772.* 75th Cong., 3rd Sess. Washington, D.C.: GPO, 1938. 201 pp.

————. Senate. Committee on Interstate Commerce. *Unemployment Insurance System for Railroad Employees.* S. Rept. 2164 to Accompany S. 3772, 75th Cong., 3rd Sess. Washington, D.C.: GPO, 1938. 21 pp.

————. Senate. Committee on Judiciary. *Amending Sec. 77 of Bankruptcy Act as to Preferred Claims [Relative to Claims for Personal Injuries or Death of Railroad Employ-*

ees]. S. Rept. 978 to Accompany S. 2654, 76th Cong., 1st Sess. Washington, D.C.: GPO, 1939. 1 p.

―――――. Senate. Committee on Judiciary. *Assumption of Risks of Employment [by Railroad Employees] in Actions against Common Carriers*. S. Rept. 1257 to Accompany S. 1060, 72nd Cong., 2nd Sess. Washington, D.C.: GPO, 1933. 7 pp.

U.S. COURT OF APPEALS FOR THE TENTH CIRCUIT, No. 2456, No. 2457. *Utah Copper Co. [et al], Appellants vs. Railroad Retirement Board [et al], Appellees; Nevada Consolidated Copper Corp. [et al], Appellants vs. Railroad Retirement Board [et al], Appellees. Brief of Appellees, Railway Labor Executives Association, and Brotherhood of Railroad Trainmen*. Toledo, Ohio, 1942. 43 pp.

U.S. DEPARTMENT OF LABOR. Children's Bureau. *Welfare of Children of Maintenance-of-Way Employees*, by H. R. Wright. Bureau Publication 211. Washington, D.C.: GPO, 1932. 192 pp.

U.S. INTERSTATE COMMERCE COMMISSION. *Employee Retirement and Unemployment Insurance as Affecting Railway Finances*, prepared by Edward Crane. Statement 4374. Washington, D.C.: GPO, 1943. 58 pp.

U.S. OFFICE OF FEDERAL COORDINATOR OF TRANSPORTATION. Section of Labor Relations. *Unemployment Compensation for Transportation Employees*. Washington, D.C.: GPO, 1936. 110 pp.

U.S. PRESIDENT [Franklin D. Roosevelt]. *Recommendations Incident to Preserving Insurance Protection under Social Security Act, Railroad Retirement Act, and Railroad Unemployment Insurance Act*. H. Doc. 951, 76th Cong., 3rd Sess. Washington, D.C.: GPO, 1940. 1 p.

U.S. RAILROAD RETIREMENT BOARD. *Employees' Handbook*. Chicago: The Board, 1945. 38 pp.

―――――. *Instructions to Employers and Manual of Operations for Collection of Prior Service Records, Required by Joint Resolution of Congress, Approved Oct. 9, 1940, Revised May 27, 1941*. Washington, D.C.: GPO, 1941. 39 pp.

―――――. *Law Bulletin, Issued December 1940*. Washington, D.C.: GPO, 1940. 558 pp.

―――――. *Railroad Retirement Acts with Amendments to Nov. 1940; Prior Service Records Resolution, Oct. 1940*. Washington, D.C.: GPO, 1941. 22 pp.

―――――. *The Railroad Retirement and Unemployment Insurance Systems; Twenty-five Years of Operations, 1935–60*. Chicago, 1960. 28 pp.

―――――. *Unemployment Insurance for Railroad Employees, Employees Booklet 1, November 1940*. Washington, D.C.: GPO, 1940. 22 pp.

1946–Present

U.S. COMMISSION ON RAILROAD RETIREMENT. *Interim Report as of July 15, 1971*. [For use of House Committee on Interstate and Foreign Commerce, and Senate Committee on Labor and Public Welfare, 92nd Cong., 1st Sess.] Washington, D.C.: GPO, 1971. 42 pp.

U.S. CONGRESS. House. *Act to Amend Internal Revenue Code of 1954 with Respect to Definition of Compensation for Purposes of Tax under Railroad Retirement Tax Act, and for Other Purposes*. [Approved October 22, 1968.] H.R. 7567, Public Law 90–624, 90th Cong., 2nd Sess. Washington, D.C.: GPO, 1968. 2 pp.

————. House. *Act to Amend Railroad Retirement Act, as Amended, and Railroad Unemployment Insurance Act, as Amended, and for Other Purposes.* [Approved June 23, 1948.] H.R. 6766, Public Law 744, 80th Cong., 2nd Sess. Washington, D.C.: GPO, 1948. 3 pp.

————. House. *Act to Amend Railroad Retirement Act of 1937, as Amended.* [Approved June 16, 1954.] H.R. 356, Public Law 398, 83rd Cong., 2nd Sess. Washington, D.C.: GPO, 1954. 1 p.

————. House. *Act to Amend Railroad Retirement Act of 1937, as Amended, and Railroad Unemployment Insurance Act.* [Approved August 12, 1955.] H.R. 4744, Public Law 383, 84th Cong., 1st Sess. Washington, D.C.: GPO, 1955. 1 p.

————. House. *Act to Amend Railroad Retirement Act of 1937 and Railroad Retirement Tax Act to Eliminate Certain Provisions Which Reduce Spouse's Annuities, to Provide Coverage for Tips, to Increase Base on Which Railroad Retirement Benefits and Taxes Are Computed, and to Change Railroad Retirement Tax Rates.* [Approved September 29, 1965.] H.R. 10875, 89th Cong., 1st Sess. Washington, D.C.: GPO, 1965. 5 pp.

————. House. *Act to Amend Railroad Retirement Act of 1937 and Railroad Retirement Tax Act, and for Other Purposes.* [Approved October 30, 1966.] H.R. 17285, 89th Cong., 2nd Sess. Washington, D.C.: GPO, 1967. 7 pp.

————. House. *Act to Amend Railroad Retirement Act of 1937 and Railroad Retirement Tax to Provide for Extension of Supplemental Annuities, and for Other Purposes.* [Approved March 17, 1970.] H.R. 13300, Public Law 91–215, 91st Cong., 2nd Sess. Washington, D.C.: GPO, 1970. 3 pp.

————. House. *Act to Amend Railroad Retirement Act of 1937, Railroad Retirement Tax Act, and Railroad Unemployment Insurance Act, So as to Provide Increases in Benefits, and for Other Purposes.* [Approved May 19, 1959.] H.R. 5610, Public Law 28, 86th Cong., 1st Sess. Washington, D.C.: GPO, 1959. 8 pp.

————. House. *Act to Amend Railroad Retirement Act of 1937, and Railroad Unemployment Insurance Act to Provide for Increase in Benefits, and for Other Purposes.* [Approved February 15, 1968.] H.R. 14563, Public Law 90–257, 90th Cong., 2nd Sess. Washington, D.C.: GPO, 1968. 10 pp.

————. House. *Act to Amend Railroad Retirement Act of 1937, Railroad Unemployment Insurance Act and Railroad Retirement Tax Act to Make Certain Technical Changes, to Provide for Survivor Benefits to Children Ages 18–21 Inclusive, and for Other Purposes.* [Approved October 30, 1966.] H.R. 14355, 89th Cong., 2nd Sess. Washington, D.C.: GPO, 1967. 10 pp.

————. House. *Act to Amend Railroad Retirement Act, Railroad Retirement Tax Act, and Railroad Unemployment Insurance Act.* [Approved August 31, 1954.] H.R. 7840, Public Law 746, 83rd Cong., 2nd Sess. Washington, D.C.: GPO, 1954. 6 pp.

————. House. *Act to Amend Railroad Retirement Act and Railroad Unemployment Insurance Act, and for Other Purposes.* [Approved October 30, 1951.] H.R. 3669, Public Law 234, 82nd Cong., 1st Sess. Washington, D.C.: GPO, 1951. 9 pp.

————. House. *Act to Amend Railroad Retirement Act of 1967 to Provide Temporary 15 Percentum Increase in Annuities, to Change for Temporary Period Method of Computing Interest on Investments of Railroad Retirement Accounts, and for Other*

Purposes. [Approved August 12, 1970.] H.R. 15733, 91st Cong., 2nd Sess. Washington, D.C.: GPO, 1970. 4 pp.

_____. House. *Act to Amend Railroad Retirement Acts, Railroad Unemployment Insurance Act, and Subchap. B of Chap. 9 of Internal Revenue Code.* [Approved July 31, 1946.] H.R. 1362, Public Law 572, 79th Cong., 2nd Sess. Washington, D.C.: GPO, 1946. 24 pp.

_____. House. *An Act to Extend Temporary Provision for Disregarding Income of Old-Age, Survivors and Disability Insurance and Railroad Retirement Recipients in Determining Need for Public Assistance.* 91st Cong., 2nd Sess. Washington, D.C.: GPO, 1971. 2 pp.

_____. House. *Act to Extend Time within Which Applications May Be Made to Railroad Retirement Board for Certain Refunds from Unemployment Trust Fund.* [Approved August 6, 1947.] H.R. 3632, Public Law 378, 80th Cong., 1st Sess. Washington, D.C.: GPO, 1947. 1 p.

_____. House. *Act to Provide for Refunds to Railroad Employees in Certain Cases, So as to Place the Various States on Equal Basis, under Railroad Unemployment Insurance Act, with Respect to Contributions of Employees.* [Approved August 2, 1946.] H.R. 3420, Public Law 599, 79th Cong., 2nd Sess. Washington, D.C.: GPO, 1946, 1 p.

_____. House. *Act to Provide Temporary Extended Railroad Unemployment Insurance Benefits, and for Other Purposes.* [Approved March 24, 1961.] H.R. 5075, Public Law 7, 87th Cong., 1st Sess. Washington, D.C.: GPO, 1961. 2 pp.

_____. House. *Compilation of Laws Relating to Mediation, Conciliation, and Arbitration between Employers and Employees, Disputes between Carriers and Employers and Subordinate Officials under Labor Board, 8-hr. Laws, Employers' Liability Laws, Labor and Child Labor Laws, 1888–1967,* compiled by Gilman G. Udell, Superintendent, Document Room, House of Representatives. Washington, D.C.: GPO, 1967. 1035 pp.

_____. House. *Railroad Retirement and Unemployment Insurance Act, as Amended (June 29, 1935–Oct. 30, 1966),* compiled by Gilman G. Udell, Superintendent, Document Room, House of Representatives. Washington, D.C.: GPO, 1967. 197 pp.

_____. House. *Railroad Retirement and Unemployment Insurance Act, as Amended (June 29, 1935–Jan. 11, 1971),* compiled by Gilman G. Udell, Superintendent, Document Room, House of Representatives. Washington, D.C.: GPO, 1971. 227 pp.

_____. House. *To Amend Railroad Retirement Act of 1937, Railroad Retirement Tax Act, Railroad Unemployment Insurance Act, and Temporary Extended Railroad Unemployment Insurance Benefits Act of 1961 to Increase Creditable and Taxable Compensation, and for Other Purposes.* [Approved October 5, 1963.] H.R. 8100, 88th Cong., 1st Sess. Washington, D.C.: GPO, 1963. 5 pp.

_____. House. Committee of Conference. *Railroad Retirement Act Amendments.* H. Rept. 1337 to Accompany H.R. 15733, 91st Cong., 2nd Sess. Washington, D.C.: GPO, 1970. 7 pp.

_____. House. Committee of Conference. *Railroad Retirement Amendments.* H. Rept. 1215 to Accompany H.R. 3669, 82nd Cong., 1st Sess. Washington, D.C.: GPO, 1951. 13 pp.

_____. House. Committee on Interstate and Foreign Commerce. *Amending Railroad Retirement Act of 1937, as Amended and Railroad Unemployment Insurance Act.*

H. Rept. 1046 to Accompany H.R. 4744, 84th Cong., 1st Sess. Washington, D.C.: GPO, 1955. 27 pp.

————. House. Committee on Interstate and Foreign Commerce. *Amending Railroad Retirement Act of 1937, as Amended, and Railroad Unemployment Insurance Act, as Amended.* H. Rept. 2154 to Accompany H.R. 6766, 80th Cong., 2nd Sess. Washington, D.C.: GPO, 1948. 5 pp.

————. House. Committee on Interstate and Foreign Commerce. *Amending Railroad Retirement Act of 1937 so as to Eliminate Reductions of Annuities and Pensions in Certain Cases.* H. Rept. 758 and Minority Views to Accompany H.R. 356, 83rd Cong., 1st Sess. Washington, D.C.: GPO, 1953. 2 pts., 13 pp. and 26 pp.

————. House. Committee on Interstate and Foreign Commerce. *Amending Railroad Retirement Act of 1937 to Provide Increases in Benefits.* H. Rept. 2418 to Accompany H.R. 9065, 84th Cong., 2nd Sess. Washington, D.C.: GPO, 1956. 28 pp.

————. House. Committee on Interstate and Foreign Commerce. *Amending the Railroad Retirement Act of 1937, and the Railroad Unemployment Insurance Act: Hearings on H.R. 14563.* 90th Cong., 1st Sess. Washington, D.C.: GPO, 1968. 39 pp.

————. House. Committee on Interstate and Foreign Commerce. *Amending Railroad Retirement Act of 1937, Railroad Unemployment Insurance Act, and Railroad Retirement Tax Act.* H. Rept. 2171 to Accompany H.R. 14355, 89th Cong., 2nd Sess. Washington, D.C.: GPO, 1966. 53 pp.

————. House. Committee on Interstate and Foreign Commerce. *Amending Railroad Retirement Act, Railroad Retirement Tax Act, and Railroad Unemployment Insurance Act: Hearings on H.R. 7840.* 83rd Cong., 2nd Sess. Washington, D.C.: GPO, 1954. 179 pp.

————. House. Committee on Interstate and Foreign Commerce. *Amending Railroad Retirement Act and Railroad Unemployment Insurance Act: Hearings before a Subcommittee on H.R. 4744.* 84th Cong., 1st Sess. Washington, D.C.: GPO, 1955. 71 pp.

————. House. Committee on Interstate and Foreign Commerce. *Amending Railroad Unemployment Insurance Act.* H. Rept. 735 and Minority Views to Accompany H.R. 3150, 80th Cong., 1st Sess. Washington, D.C.: GPO, 1947. 2 pts., 11 pp. and 7 pp.

————. House. Committee on Interstate and Foreign Commerce. *Amendments to Railroad Retirement Act of 1937, and Railroad Retirement Tax Act.* H. Rept. 976 to Accompany H.R. 10874, 89th Cong., 1st Sess. Washington, D.C.: GPO, 1965. 27 pp.

————. House. Committee on Interstate and Foreign Commerce. *Amendments to Railroad Retirement Act of 1937, Railroad Retirement Tax Act, and Railroad Unemployment Insurance Act.* H. Rept. 243 to Accompany H.R. 5610, 86th Cong., 1st Sess. Washington, D.C.: GPO, 1959. 123 pp.

————. House. Committee on Interstate and Foreign Commerce. *Amendments to Railroad Retirement Act of 1937, the Railroad Retirement Tax Act, and the Railroad Unemployment Insurance Act.* H. Rept. 2562 to Accompany H.R. 4353, 85th Cong., 2nd Sess. Washington, D.C.: GPO, 1958. 116 pp.

————. House. Committee on Interstate and Foreign Commerce. *Amendments to Railroad Retirement Act of 1937, Railroad Retirement Tax Act, Railroad Unemployment Insurance Act, and Temporary Extended Railroad Unemployment Insurance Benefits Act of 1961.* H. Rept. 748 to Accompany H.R. 8100, 88th Cong., 1st Sess. Washington, D.C.: GPO, 1963. 60 pp.

————. House. Committee on Interstate and Foreign Commerce. *Amendments to Railroad Retirement Act, Railroad Retirement Tax Act, and Railroad Unemployment Insurance Act.* H. Rept. 1899 to Accompany H.R. 7840, 83rd Cong., 2nd Sess. Washington, D.C.: GPO, 1954. 47 pp.

————. House. Committee on Interstate and Foreign Commerce. *Amendments to Railroad Retirement Act, Railroad Unemployment Insurance Act, and Related Provisions of Law.* H. Rept. 1989 to Accompany H.R. 1362, 79th Cong., 2nd Sess. Washington, D.C.: GPO, 1946. 77 pp.

————. House. Committee on Interstate and Foreign Commerce. *Elimination of Restriction against Payment of Social Security Benefits to Spouses of Retired Railroad Employees.* H. Rept. 1807 to Accompany H.R. 12362, 88th Cong., 2nd Sess. Washington, D.C.: GPO, 1964. 5 pp.

————. House. Committee on Interstate and Foreign Commerce. *Extending Time within Which Applications May Be Made to Railroad Retirement Board for Certain Refunds from Unemployment Trust Fund.* H. Rept. 928 to Accompany H.R. 3632, 80th Cong., 1st Sess. Washington, D.C.: GPO, 1947. 2 pp.

————. House. Committee on Interstate and Foreign Commerce. *Providing Temporary Extension of Railroad Unemployment Insurance Benefits.* H. Rept. 54 to Accompany H.R. 5075, 87th Cong., 1st Sess. Washington, D.C.: GPO, 1961. 16 pp.

————. House. Committee on Interstate and Foreign Commerce. *Railroad Retirement Act Amendments — 1965: Hearings on H.R. 10874.* 89th Cong., 1st Sess. Washington, D.C.: GPO, 1965. 52 pp.

————. House. Committee on Interstate and Foreign Commerce. *Railroad Retirement Act Amendments of 1972: Hearings on H.R. 15927 and H.R. 15922.* 92nd Cong., 2nd Sess. Washington, D.C.: GPO, 1972. 62 pp.

————. House. Committee on Interstate and Foreign Commerce. *Railroad Retirement Act (Dual Benefits): Hearings on H.R. 356.* 83rd Cong., 1st Sess. Washington, D.C.: GPO, 1953. 268 pp.

————. House. Committee on Interstate and Foreign Commerce. *Railroad Retirement Act of 1937, Annuities of Male Employees at Age 62.* H. Rept. 1067 to Accompany H.R. 8597, 87th Cong., 1st Sess. Washington, D.C.: GPO, 1961.

————. House. Committee on Interstate and Foreign Commerce. *Railroad Retirement Act (Reduced Annuities for Men at Age 62): Hearings on H.R. 8597 and H.R. 5027.* 87th Cong., 1st Sess. Washington, D.C.: GPO, 1961. 30 pp.

————. House. Committee on Interstate and Foreign Commerce. *Railroad Retirement Act, Supplemental Benefits: Hearings before the Subcommittee on Commerce and Finance, on H.R. 17285.* 89th Cong., 2nd Sess. Washington, D.C.: GPO, 1960. 38 pp.

————. House. Committee on Interstate and Foreign Commerce. *Railroad Retirement Act, Technical Amendments and Providing Benefits for Students: Hearings before the Subcommittee on Commerce and Finance, on H.R. 17285.* 89th Cong., 2nd Sess. Washington, D.C.: GPO, 1966. 53 pp.

————. House. Committee on Interstate and Foreign Commerce. *Railroad Retirement Amendments.* H. Rept. 976 to Accompany H.R. 3669, 82nd Cong., 1st Sess. Washington, D.C.: GPO, 1951. 83 pp.

————. House. Committee on Interstate and Foreign Commerce. *Railroad Retirement*

Amendments — 1951: Hearings on H.R. 3669 and H.R. 3755. 82nd Cong., 1st Sess. Washington, D.C.: GPO, 1951. 564 pp.

————. House. Committee on Interstate and Foreign Commerce. *Railroad Retirement Benefit Increase — 1971: Hearings before Subcommittee on Transportation and Aeronautics on H.R. 4172, 5453, 6177, 6444, 6516, 6525-2726, and 6775.* 92nd Cong., 1st Sess. Washington, D.C.: GPO, 1971. 91 pp.

————. House. Committee on Interstate and Foreign Commerce. *Railroad Retirement (Dual Benefits for Spouses): Hearings before Subcommittee on Commerce and Finance on H.R. 615, 1645; H.R. 1501; H.R. 3157, 6296.* 89th Cong., 1st Sess. Washington, D.C.: GPO, 1965. 34 pp.

————. House. Committee on Interstate and Foreign Commerce. *Railroad Retirement 15 Percent Benefit Increase: Hearings before Subcommittee on Transportation and Aeronautics on H.R. 15733.* 91st Cong., 2nd Sess. Washington, D.C.: GPO, 1970. 60 pp.

————. House. Committee on Interstate and Foreign Commerce. *Railroad Retirement: Hearings on H.R. 6766.* 80th Cong., 2nd Sess. Washington, D.C.: GPO, 1948. 59 pp.

————. House. Committee on Interstate and Foreign Commerce. *Railroad Retirement Legislation: Hearings.* 83rd Cong., 2nd Sess. Washington, D.C.: GPO, 1954. 172 pp.

————. House. Committee on Interstate and Foreign Commerce. *Railroad Retirement Legislation: Hearings before a Subcommittee.* 84th Cong., 2nd Sess. Washington, D.C.: GPO, 1956. 278 pp.

————. House. Committee on Interstate and Foreign Commerce. *Railroad Retirement and Railroad Unemployment Insurance Legislation: Hearings.* 85th Cong., 1st Sess. Washington, D.C.: GPO, 1957. 507 pp.

————. House. Committee on Interstate and Foreign Commerce. *Railroad Retirement and Railroad Unemployment Insurance Legislation, 1959: Hearings.* 86th Cong., 1st Sess. Washington, D.C.: GPO, 1959. 407 pp.

————. House. Committee on Interstate and Foreign Commerce. *Railroad Retirement and Railroad Unemployment Insurance Legislation (Supplementary Testimony): Hearings.* 85th Cong., 2nd Sess. Washington, D.C.: GPO, 1958. 91 pp.

————. House. Committee on Interstate and Foreign Commerce. *Railroad Retirement Supplemental Annuities, 1969: Hearings.* 91st Cong., 1st Sess. Washington, D.C.: GPO, 1969. 78 pp.

————. House. Committee on Interstate and Foreign Commerce. *Railroad Retirement and Unemployment Insurance (Creditable and Taxable Compensation): Hearings on H.R. 8100.* 88th Cong., 1st Sess. Washington, D.C.: GPO, 1963. 57 pp.

————. House. Committee on Interstate and Foreign Commerce. *Railroad Unemployment Insurance Act — 1947: Hearings before Subcommittee on H.R. 3150.* 80th Cong., 1st Sess. Washington, D.C.: GPO, 1947. 168 pp.

————. House. Committee on Interstate and Foreign Commerce. *Railroad Unemployment Insurance Act — 1952: Hearings on H.R. 6525.* 82nd Cong., 2nd Sess. Washington, D.C.: GPO, 1952. 182 pp.

————. House. Committee on Interstate and Foreign Commerce. *Railroad Unemployment Insurance Benefits.* H. Rept. 1727 to Accompany H.R. 6525, 82nd Cong., 2nd Sess. Washington, D.C.: GPO, 1952. 13 pp.

————. House. Committee on Interstate and Foreign Commerce. *Refunds to Railroad Employees of Contributions Made under Railroad Unemployment Insurance Act.* H. Rept. 2320 to Accompany H.R. 3420, 79th Cong., 2nd Sess. Washington, D.C.: GPO, 1946. 2 pp.

————. House. Committee on Interstate and Foreign Commerce. *Spouses Annuities under Railroad Retirement Act of 1937.* H. Rept. 379 to Accompany H.R. 3157, 89th Cong., 1st Sess. Washington, D.C.: GPO, 1966. 7 pp.

————. House. Committee on Interstate and Foreign Commerce. *Technical and Administrative Amendments to Railroad Retirement Act, Railroad Unemployment Insurance Act, and Social Security Act.* H. Rept. 2641 to Accompany H.R. 7166, 85th Cong., 2nd Sess. Washington, D.C.: GPO, 1958. 53 pp.

————. House. Committee on Interstate and Foreign Commerce. *Temporary Increase in Railroad Retirement Annuities.* H. Rept. 115 to Accompany H.R. 6444, 92nd Cong., 1st Sess. Washington, D.C.: GPO, 1971. 46 pp.

————. House. Committee on Judiciary. *Extending Statute of Limitations with Respect to Certain Suits.* H. Rept. 2329 to Accompany H.R. 168, 82nd Cong., 2nd Sess. Washington, D.C.: GPO, 1952. 3 pp.
Relates to claims of railway employees under Federal Employers' Liability Act.

————. House. Committee on Judiciary. *Limitation of Venue in Certain Actions Brought under the Employers' Liability Act: Hearings before Subcommittee on H.R. 1639.* 80th Cong., 1st Sess. Washington, D.C.: GPO, 1947. 170 pp.

————. House. Committee on Rules. *Consideration of H.R. 1362.* H. Rept. 2077 to Accompany H. Res. 625, 79th Cong., 2nd Sess. Washington, D.C.: GPO, 1946. 1 p.
Amends Railroad Retirement Act, Railroad Unemployment Insurance Act, etc.

————. House. Committee on Ways and Means. *Deduction for Certain Railroad Retirement Employee Taxes.* H. Rept. 2330 Including Minority Views to Accompany H.R. 5551, 85th Cong., 2nd Sess. Washington, D.C.: GPO, 1958. 11 pp.

————. House. Committee on Ways and Means. *Disregarding of O.A.S.D.I. and Railroad Retirement Income in Determining Need for Public Assistance.* H. Rept. 1716 to Accompany H.R. 19915, 91st Cong., 2nd Sess. Washington, D.C.: GPO, 1971. 3 pp.

————. House. Committee on Ways and Means. *Income Tax Exemption for Employees' Contributions to Railroad Retirement Fund: Hearings on H.R. 10578 and H.R. 11764.* 84th Cong., 2nd Sess. Washington, D.C.: GPO, 1956. 72 pp.

————. House. Committee on Ways and Means. *Railroad Unemployment Insurance: Hearings on H.R. 5711.* 80th Cong., 2nd Sess. Washington, D.C.: GPO, 1948. 73 pp.

————. House. Committee on Ways and Means. *Treatment of Certain Nonresident Aliens under Railroad Retirement Tax Act, etc.* H. Rept. 1844 to Accompany H.R. 7567, 90th Cong., 2nd Sess. Washington, D.C.: GPO, 1968. 8 pp.

————. Joint Committee on Railroad Retirement Legislation. *Railroad Retirement Legislation — 1952: Hearings Pursuant to S. Con. Res. 51.* 82nd Cong., 2nd Sess. Washington, D.C.: GPO, 1952. 194 pp.

————. Joint Committee on Railroad Retirement Legislation. *Retirement System, Report Pursuant to S. Con. Res. 51 and 56.* S. Rept. 6, 83rd Cong., 1st Sess. Washington, D.C.: GPO, 1953.

————. Senate. *Act to Amend Manpower Development and Training Act of 1962 with*

Regard to Reimbursement of Railroad Unemployment Insurance Account. [Approved October 1, 1962.] S. 3529, Public Law 729, 87th Cong., 2nd Sess. Washington, D.C.: GPO, 1962. 1 p.

————. Senate. *Act to Amend Railroad Retirement Act of 1937 to Provide Increases in Benefits, and for Other Purposes.* [Approved August 7, 1956.] S. 3616, Public Law 1013, 84th Cong., 2nd Sess. Washington, D.C.: GPO, 1956. 1 p.

————. Senate. *Act to Amend Railroad Retirement Act of 1937 to Provide Reduced Annuities to Male Employees Who Have Attained Age 62, and for Other Purposes.* [Approved September 22, 1961.] S. 2395, Public Law 285, 87th Cong., 1st Sess. Washington, D.C.: GPO, 1961. 1 p.

————. Senate. *Act to Amend Railroad Retirement Act of 1937, Railroad Unemployment Insurance Act, and Social Security Act.* [Approved September 6, 1958.] S. 2020, Public Law 927, 85th Cong., 2nd Sess. Washington, D.C.: GPO, 1958. 6 pp.

————. Senate. *Act to Amend Railroad Unemployment Insurance Act.* [Approved May 15, 1952.] S. 2639, Public Law 343, 82nd Cong., 2nd Sess. Washington, D.C.: GPO, 1952. 1 p.

————. Senate. Committee on Finance. *Treatment of Certain Nonresident Aliens under Railroad Retirement Tax Act, etc.* S. Rept. 1650 to Accompany H.R. 7567, 90th Cong., 2nd Sess. Washington, D.C.: GPO, 1968. 7 pp.

————. Senate. Committee on Interstate Commerce. *Amendments to Railroad Retirement Acts, Railroad Unemployment Insurance Act, and Related Provisions of Law.* S. Rept. 1710 and Supplemental Report to Accompany H.R. 1362, 79th Cong., 2nd Sess. Washington, D.C.: GPO, 1946. 2 pts., 8 pp. and 27 pp.

————. Senate. Committee on Interstate Commerce. *Refunds to Railroad Employees of Contributions Made under Railroad Unemployment Insurance Act.* S. Rept. 1711 to Accompany H.R. 3420, 79th Cong., 2nd Sess. Washington, D.C.: GPO, 1946. 2 pp.

————. Senate. Committee on Labor and Public Welfare. *Amending Railroad Retirement Act of 1937.* S. Rept. 1281 to Accompany S. 988. 91st Cong., 2nd Sess. Washington, D.C.: GPO, 1970. 4 pp.

————. Senate. Committee on Labor and Public Welfare. *Amending Railroad Retirement Act of 1937.* S. Rept. 2747 to Accompany S. 3616, 84th Cong., 2nd Sess. Washington, D.C.: GPO, 1956. 9 pp.

————. Senate. Committee on Labor and Public Welfare. *Amending Railroad Retirement Act of 1937, as Amended, Railroad Retirement Tax Act, and Railroad Unemployment Insurance Act.* S. Rept. 890 to Accompany S. 1347, 82nd Cong., 1st Sess. Washington, D.C.: GPO, 1951. 72 pp.

————. Senate. Committee on Labor and Public Welfare. *Amending Railroad Retirement Act of 1937, as Amended, and Railroad Unemployment Insurance Act.* S. Rept. 1040 to Accompany H.R. 4744, 84th Cong., 1st Sess. Washington, D.C.: GPO, 1955. 19 pp.

————. Senate. Committee on Labor and Public Welfare. *Amending Railroad Retirement Act of 1937, as Amended, and Railroad Unemployment Insurance Act, as Amended.* S. Rept. 1574 to Accompany S. 2782, 80th Cong., 2nd Sess. Washington, D.C.: GPO, 1948. 4 pp.

————. Senate. Committee on Labor and Public Welfare. *Amending Railroad Retirement Act of 1937, so as to Eliminate Reductions of Annuities and Pensions in Certain*

Cases. S. Rept. 1476 to Accompany S. 2178, 83rd Cong., 2nd Sess. Washington, D.C.: GPO, 1954. 5 pp.

————. Senate. Committee on Labor and Public Welfare. *Amending the Railroad Retirement Act of 1937: Hearings before the Subcommittee on Railroad Retirement of the Committee on S. 729, S. 1356, and S. 2056.* 88th Cong., 1st Sess. Washington, D.C.: GPO, 1963. 121 pp.

————. Senate. Committee on Labor and Public Welfare. *Amending the Railroad Retirement Act of 1937: Hearings before the Subcommittee on Railroad Retirement on S. 360.* 85th Cong., 1st Sess. Washington, D.C.: GPO, 1957. 640 pp.

————. Senate. Committee on Labor and Public Welfare. *Amending the Railroad Retirement Act of 1937: Hearings before Subcommittee on Railroad Retirement on S. 226 [and Others].* 86th Cong., 1st Sess. Washington, D.C.: GPO, 1959. 405 pp.

————. Senate. Committee on Labor and Public Welfare. *Amending the Railroad Retirement Act of 1937: Hearings before Subcommittee on Railroad Retirement on S. 3157.* 89th Cong., 1st Sess. Washington, D.C.: GPO, 1965. 34 pp.

————. Senate. Committee on Labor and Public Welfare. *Amending Railroad Retirement Act of 1937 to Provide Temporary 15 Percent Increase in Annuities.* S. Rept. 960 to Accompany H.R. 15733, 91st Cong., 2nd Sess. Washington, D.C.: GPO, 1970. 14 pp.

————. Senate. Committee on Labor and Public Welfare. *Amending Railroad Retirement Act of 1937 and Railroad Retirement Tax Act.* S. Rept. 645 to Accompany H.R. 3157, 89th Cong., 1st Sess. Washington, D.C.: GPO, 1965. 17 pp.

————. Senate. Committee on Labor and Public Welfare. *Amending Railroad Retirement Act of 1937 and Railroad Retirement Tax Act.* S. Rept. 650 Together with Supplemental and Minority Views to Accompany H.R. 13300, 91st Cong., 2nd Sess. Washington, D.C.: GPO, 1970. 21 pp.

————. Senate. Committee on Labor and Public Welfare. *Amending Railroad Retirement Act of 1937, Railroad Retirement Tax Act, and Railroad Unemployment Insurance Act.* S. Rept. 2365 Together with Minority and Individual Views to Accompany S. 1313, 85th Cong., 2nd Sess. Washington, D.C.: GPO, 1958. 43 pp.

————. Senate. Committee on Labor and Public Welfare. *Amending Railroad Retirement Act of 1937, Railroad Retirement Tax Act, and Railroad Unemployment Insurance Act.* S. Rept. 222 Together with Individual Views to Accompany S. 226, 86th Cong., 1st Sess. Washington, D.C.: GPO, 1959. 51 pp.

————. Senate. Committee on Labor and Public Welfare. *Amending Railroad Retirement Act of 1937, Railroad Retirement Tax Act, Railroad Unemployment Insurance Act, and Temporary Extended Railroad Unemployment Insurance Benefits Act of 1961.* S. Rept. 510 to Accompany H.R. 8100, 88th Cong., 1st Sess. Washington, D.C.: GPO, 1963. 48 pp.

————. Senate. Committee on Labor and Public Welfare. *Amending Railroad Retirement Act of 1937 and Railroad Unemployment Insurance Act.* S. Rept. 954 to Accompany S. 2839, 90th Cong., 2nd Sess. Washington, D.C.: GPO, 1968. 74 pp.

————. Senate. Committee on Labor and Public Welfare. *Amending Railroad Retirement Act of 1937, Railroad Unemployment Insurance Act and Railroad Retirement Tax Act.* S. Rept. 1719 Together with Individual Views to Accompany H.R. 14355, 89th Cong., 2nd Sess. Washington, D.C.: GPO, 1966. 53 pp.

————. Senate. Committee on Labor and Public Welfare. *Amending Railroad Retirement Act, Railroad Retirement Tax Act, and Railroad Unemployment Insurance Act: Hearings before Special Subcommittee on Railroad Retirement Legislation on S. 2930.* 83rd Cong., 2nd Sess. Washington, D.C.: GPO, 1954. 145 pp.

————. Senate. Committee on Labor and Public Welfare. *Amending Railroad Unemployment Insurance Act.* S. Rept. 1466 to Accompany S. 2639, 82nd Cong., 2nd Sess. Washington, D.C.: GPO, 1952. 16 pp.

————. Senate. Committee on Labor and Public Welfare. *Amendment of Manpower Development and Training Act of 1962 to Provide for Reimbursement of Railroad Unemployment Insurance Account.* S. Rept. 1853 to Accompany S. 3529, 87th Cong., 2nd Sess. Washington, D.C.: GPO, 1962. 8 pp.

————. Senate. Committee on Labor and Public Welfare. *Amendment to Railroad Unemployment Insurance Act — 1947: Hearings before Subcommittee on S. 670.* 80th Cong., 1st Sess. Washington, D.C.: GPO, 1947. 196 pp.

————. Senate. Committee on Labor and Public Welfare. *Amendments to Railroad Retirement Act of 1937, as Amended.* S. Rept. 837 to Accompany S. 2395, 87th Cong., 1st Sess. Washington, D.C.: GPO, 1961. 6 pp.

————. Senate. Committee on Labor and Public Welfare. *Amendments to Railroad Retirement Act, Railroad Retirement Tax Act, and Railroad Unemployment Insurance Act.* S. Rept. 2222 Together with Minority Views to Accompany H.R. 7840, 83rd Cong., 2nd Sess. Washington, D.C.: GPO, 1954. 46 pp.

————. Senate. Committee on Labor and Public Welfare. *Consideration of Legislation for Temporary Settlement of Railroad Labor Dispute.* S. Rept. 110 to Accompany S.J. Res. 100, 92nd Cong., 1st Sess. Washington, D.C.: GPO, 1971. 15 pp.

————. Senate. Committee on Labor and Public Welfare. *Extending Time within Which Applications May Be Made to Railroad Retirement Board for Certain Refunds from Unemployment Trust Fund.* H. Rept. 768 to Accompany H.R. 3632, 80th Cong., 1st Sess. Washington, D.C.: GPO, 1947. 2 pp.

————. Senate. Committee on Labor and Public Welfare. *Providing Temporary Extension of Railroad Unemployment Insurance Benefits.* S. Rept. 72 to Accompany H.R. 5075, 87th Cong., 1st Sess. Washington, D.C.: GPO, 1961. 10 pp.

————. Senate. Committee on Labor and Public Welfare. *Railroad Retirement Act (Dual Benefits): Hearings before Special Subcommittee on Railroad Retirement Legislation, on H.R. 356, S. 1355, S. 1776, S. 1911, S. 2178.* 83rd Cong., 2nd Sess. Washington, D.C.: GPO, 1954. 184 pp.

————. Senate. Committee on Labor and Public Welfare. *Railroad Retirement Act and Railroad Unemployment Insurance Act Amendments of 1968: Hearings before Subcommittee on Railroad Retirement, on S. 2839.* 90th Cong., 2nd Sess. Washington, D.C.: GPO, 1968. 66 pp.

————. Senate. Committee on Labor and Public Welfare. *Railroad Retirement Amendments of 1970: Hearings before the Subcommittee on Railroad Retirement, on H.R. 15733.* 91st Cong., 2nd Sess. Washington, D.C.: GPO, 1970. 78 pp.

————. Senate. Committee on Labor and Public Welfare. *Railroad Retirement Annuity Increase — 1971: Hearings before the Subcommittee on Railroad Retirement on S. 1304, S. 1473 and H.R. 6444.* 92nd Cong., 1st Sess. Washington, D.C.: GPO, 1971. 108 pp.

————. Senate. Committee on Labor and Public Welfare. *Railroad Retirement Benefits — 1966: Hearings before the Subcommittee on Railroad Retirement on S. 3777.* 89th Cong., 2nd Sess. Washington, D.C.: GPO, 1966. 42 pp.

————. Senate. Committee on Labor and Public Welfare. *Railroad Retirement: Hearings before the Subcommittee on Railroad Retirement on S. 1589.* 84th Cong., 1st Sess. Washington, D.C.: GPO, 1955. 49 pp.

————. Senate. Committee on Labor and Public Welfare. *Railroad Retirement: Hearings before Subcommittee on Railroad Retirement on S. 3616 and S. 3654.* 84th Cong., 2nd Sess. Washington, D.C.: GPO, 1956. 104 pp.

————. Senate. Committee on Labor and Public Welfare. *Railroad Retirement Legislation — 1951: Hearings before Subcommittee on Railroad Retirement Legislation on S. 399.* 82nd Cong., 1st Sess. Washington, D.C.: GPO, 1951. 623 pp.

————. Senate. Committee on Labor and Public Welfare. *Railroad Retirement and Railroad Unemployment Insurance Acts Amendments: Hearings before Subcommittee on S. 994, S. 2055, S. 2228, S. 2300, S. 2423, S. 2437 and S. 2438.* 80th Cong., 2nd Sess. Washington, D.C.: GPO, 1948. 197 pp.

————. Senate. Committee on Labor and Public Welfare. *Railroad Retirement Supplemental Annuities, 1969: Hearings before the Subcommittee on Railroad Retirement, on H.R. 13300 and S. 988.* 91st Cong., 1st Sess. Washington, D.C.: GPO, 1969. 259 pp.

————. Senate. Committee on Labor and Public Welfare. *Railroad Unemployment Insurance Act: Hearings on S. 2639.* 82nd Cong., 2nd Sess. Washington, D.C.: GPO, 1952. 148 pp.

————. Senate. Committee on Labor and Public Welfare. *Supplementary Pension Plans in the Railroad Industry: A Digest of Representative Plans for the Subcommittee on Railroad Retirement.* 86th Cong., 2nd Sess. Washington, D.C.: GPO, 1961. 64 pp.

————. Senate. Committee on Labor and Public Welfare. *Technical Amendments to Railroad Retirement Act of 1937 and Railroad Unemployment Insurance Act: Hearings before Subcommittee on Railroad Retirement on S. 2020.* 85th Cong., 2nd Sess. Washington, D.C.: GPO, 1958. 48 pp.

————. Senate. Committee on Labor and Public Welfare. *Temporary Increase in Railroad Retirement Annuities, 1971.* S. Rept. 206 to Accompany H.R. 6444, 92nd Cong., 1st Sess. Washington, D.C.: GPO, 1971. 25 pp.

————. Senate. Committee on Labor and Public Welfare. *To Eliminate Restrictions on Spouse's Benefits under the Railroad Retirement Act of 1937: Hearings before Subcommittee on Railroad Retirement on H.R. 1236.* 88th Cong., 2nd Sess. Washington, D.C.: GPO, 1964. 22 pp.

————. Senate. Committee on Labor and Public Welfare. *Widow's Pensions under Railroad Retirement: Hearings on S. 2838.* 90th Cong., 2nd Sess. Washington, D.C.: GPO, 1968. 41 pp.

————. Senate. Committee on Post Office and Civil Service. *R.P.O. Employees: Hearings on S. 1771.* 91st Cong., 1st Sess. Washington, D.C.: GPO, 1969. 20 pp.

————. Senate. Committee on Post Office and Civil Service. *R.P.O. Employees: Hearings before Subcommittee on Retirement on S. 2333.* 90th Cong., 1st Sess. Washington, D.C.: GPO, 1967. 44 pp.

U.S. DEPARTMENT OF LABOR. Employment Security Bureau. *Experience and Problems under*

Temporary Disability Insurance Laws, California, New Jersey, N.Y., Rhode Island, Railroads, prepared by Margaret Dahm [1955]. Washington, D.C.: GPO, 1957. 21 pp. and 13 pp.

U.S. GENERAL ACCOUNTING OFFICE. *Problem Areas in Implementing Amendatory Legislation Affecting Railroad Retirement Annuities, Report to the Congress on the Railroad Retirement Board by the Comptroller-General of the U.S.* Washington, D.C.: GPO, 1968. 33 pp.

U.S. LAWS, STATUTES, ETC. *Provisions of the Railroad Retirement Act and the Railroad Unemployment Insurance Act, as Amended through 1965.* Washington, D.C.: Railroad Retirement Board, 1966. 48 pp.

U.S. RAILROAD RETIREMENT BOARD. *Benefits for Railroad Workers and Their Families.* Chicago: The Board, 1966. 24 pp.

————. *Benefits for Railroad Workers and Their Families.* Chicago: The Board, 1968. 37 pp.

————. *Benefits for Railroad Workers and Their Families: Retirement, Disability, Survivor, Health Insurance, Unemployment, Sickness.* Chicago: The Board, 1971. 39 pp.

————. *How to Calculate Survivor Benefits under Railroad Retirement Act.* Washington, D.C.: GPO, 1947. 6 pp.

————. *How to Compute Retirement Annuities under Railroad Retirement Act.* Washington, D.C.: GPO, 1947. 6 pp.

————. *If You Work for a Railroad.* Washington, D.C.: GPO, 1947. 12 pp. Relates to unemployment, sickness, and maternity benefits.

————. *Legal Opinions; Rulings in the Administration of the Railroad Retirement Act and the Railroad Unemployment Insurance Act, 1960.* Washington, D.C.: GPO, 1962. 119 pp.

————. *Legal Opinions; Rulings in the Administration of the Railroad Retirement Act and the Railroad Unemployment Insurance Act, 1961.* Washington, D.C.: GPO, 1964. 110 pp.

————. *Occupational Differences in Separation Rates for Railroad Workers, 1962–65,* by Jacob J. Stotland and James L. Cowen, in Actuarial Study 8 from Office of Chief, Actuary and Research. Chicago, 1968. 39 pp.

————. *Present Value of Benefits Payable under the Railroad Retirement Act, 1938–59,* by A. M. Niessen. RRB Actuarial Study 3. Chicago: The Board, 1960.

————. *Provisions of New Railroad Retirement and Unemployment Insurance Laws as Amended July 31, 1946.* Processed. Washington, D.C.: GPO, 1950. 18 leaves.

————. *Provisions of Railroad Retirement and Railroad Unemployment Insurance Acts, 1949.* Processed. Washington, D.C.: GPO, 1950. 17 leaves.

————. *Questions and Answers on the Railroad Retirement Act, as Amended through 1957.* Washington, D.C.: GPO, 1958. 100 pp.

————. *Questions and Answers on the Railroad Retirement Act, as Amended through 1959.* Washington, D.C.: GPO, 1960. 103 pp.

————. *Questions and Answers on the Railroad Retirement Act, as Amended through 1963.* Washington, D.C.: GPO, 1963. 101 pp.

RETIREMENT, PROTECTIVE PROGRAMS

—————. *Railroad Retirement Act and Railroad Unemployment Insurance Act, as Amended to Oct. 1951*. Washington, D.C.: GPO, 1951. 76 pp.

—————. *Railroad Retirement Act and Railroad Unemployment Insurance Act, as Amended through Oct. 5, 1963*. Washington, D.C.: GPO, 1964. 106 pp.

—————. *Railroad Retirement Act and Railroad Unemployment Insurance Act, as Amended through Oct. 30, 1966*. Chicago, 1967. 121 pp.

—————. *Railroad Retirement Act and Railroad Unemployment Insurance Act, as Amended through Feb. 15, 1968*. Chicago, 1968. 137 pp.

—————. *The Railroad Retirement and Unemployment Insurance Systems: Twenty-five Years of Operations, 1935–60*. Chicago, 1960. 28 pp.

—————. *Your Medicare Handbook: Health Insurance for Railroad Retirement Beneficiaries Including Those Also Entitled to Social Security Benefits, Hospital Insurance, Medical Insurance*. Chicago, 1972. 31 pp.

—————. Division of Safety Studies. *Safety in the Railroad Industry*. Chicago, 1962.

—————. Office of Director of Research. *Provisions of Railroad Retirement Act and Railroad Unemployment Insurance Act as Amended through 1956*. Form RB-16 (10–57). Washington, D.C.: GPO, 1957. 29 pp.

PART VI

GOVERNMENT SERIAL PUBLICATIONS

"Employment and Earnings of Railroad Employees." Series in *Monthly Labor Review*. Title variations include "Employment and Pay-roll Totals of Railroad Employees," "Employment on Class I Steam Railroads," and others. Each article contains employment and earnings statistics for three different months — the months that precede the article by three months, four months, and one year and three months (e.g., the March 1923 article contains statistics for November 1922, December 1922, and December 1921). The series run from vol. 16, no. 3 (March 1923) through vol. 42, no. 3 (March 1936).

U.S. BOARD OF MEDIATION. *Annual Report of the United States Board of Mediation*. Washington, D.C.: GPO, 1927–34.

Continued by the *Annual Report* of the National Mediation Board beginning 1935.

————. *Decisions of Train Service Board of Adjustment, Western Region*. [Chicago ?], 1921–[32?].

From 1921–32, 4,538 decisions published in 9 volumes. In doubt as to whether publication ceased in 1932. Lengths of decisions vary, usually 1 to 3 pages.

U.S. BOARD OF MEDIATION AND CONCILIATION. *Report, 1913–1917*. Washington, D.C.: GPO, 1918. 30 pp.

A single report covering all the years from 1913 to 1917 and should technically be considered a monograph. Of the 71 cases brought before the board, 58 were settled.

U.S. BUREAU OF LABOR STATISTICS. "Employment Outlook in Railroad Occupations." In *Occupational Outlook Handbook*. Washington, D.C.: GPO, 1949–

Title varies. Earlier editions irregular; now biennial. Information from some editions reprinted in *Occupational Outlook Report Series*.

U.S. DEPARTMENT OF TRANSPORTATION. *Intra-departmental Safety Seminar, Proceedings*. Washington, D.C.: GPO, 1969.

Apparently an annual seminar which began in 1968 and continues to be held every year.

————. *Report*. Washington, D.C.: GPO, [1967 ?] – .

Annual report since 1967.

————. *Report of the Secretary of Transportation on Hazardous Materials Control*. Washington, D.C.: GPO, 1970.

Annual since 1970.

————. Railroad Safety Bureau. *Accident Bulletin*. Washington, D.C.: GPO.

Apparently an annual bulletin beginning at least as early as 1968 and continuing to the present.

————. Railroad Safety Bureau. *Rail-highway Grade-crossing Accidents*. Washington, D.C.: GPO, 1969.

Apparently issued annually for years since 1967.

U.S. EMERGENCY BOARD. *Report to the President*. Washington, D.C.: GPO, 1936– .

There were 185 such reports as of July 2, 1974. Length varies from a few pages to almost one hundred. Contain history of the dispute, issues involved, and recommendations.

————. *Transcript of Proceedings*.

A voluminous record of each case handled by an emergency board, frequently including carrier and employee exhibits. Began publication with Emergency Board No. 1 in 1936 and continues. The most recent proceedings published are those of Emergency Board No. 185 issued June 2, 1974. Place of publication varies, generally New York or Washington.

U.S. FEDERAL RAILROAD ADMINISTRATION. *Summary of Accidents Reported by All Line-haul and Switching and Terminal Railroad Companies*. Washington, D.C.: GPO, [1925 ?]– .

Apparently an annual publication beginning in 1925 covering the preceding year. Issued by various agencies; title varies. Also, monthly reports and quarterly summaries beginning [1931 ?].

————. Bureau of Railroad Safety. *Accident Bulletin; Summary and Analysis of Accidents on Railroads in the United States*. Washington, D.C.: GPO, 1901.

Issued quarterly from July 1901 through December 1921, and annually since 1922. Title varies slightly.

U.S. INTERSTATE COMMERCE COMMISSION. Bureau of Accounts. *Operating Revenues and Operating Expenses of Class I Railroads in the United States*. Washington, D.C.: GPO, 1920–1970.

Published annually from 1920 through 1970. Publication ceased in 1971. Title varies slightly.

————. Bureau of Safety. *A Statistical Analysis of Carriers' Monthly Hours of Service Reports Covering All Railroads Which Reported during the Year Ending June 30th . . . Instances in Which Employees Were on Duty for Periods Other Than Those Provided by the Federal Hours of Service Act, Together with a Comparative Summary* [covering the preceding four years]. Washington, D.C.: GPO, 1918–1952/53.

Annual except for 1932 and 1933. Apparently ceased publication after 1952/53. Title varies slightly.

————. Bureau of Transport Economics and Statistics. *Bulletin of Revenues and Expenses of Steam Railroads in the U.S.* Washington, D.C.: GPO, 1909–14.

Nos. 1–69 published from March 31, 1909, through August 1914.

————. Bureau of Transport Economics and Statistics. *Wage Statistics of Class I Railroads in the United States*. Washington, D.C.: GPO, 1921– .

Published monthly. A half-year summary was issued for the six months ending December 1921. Yearly summaries issued beginning with 1922. Title varies slightly but has been titled as above since 1965.

U.S. NATIONAL MEDIATION BOARD. *Annual Report of the National Mediation Board Including the Report of the National Railroad Adjustment Board*. Washington, D.C.: GPO, 1935– .

Reports vary in length, usually 50 to 100 pages, and generally include statistical tables.

————. *Determination of Craft or Class of the National Mediation Board.* Washington, D.C.: GPO, 1948– .

Four volumes of determinations published to date: vol. 1 (538 pp.) includes all determinations made from July 6, 1934, through June 30, 1948; vol. 2 (244 pp.), July 1, 1948, through June 30, 1953; vol. 3 (233 pp.), July 1, 1953, through June 30, 1961; vol. 4 (312 pp.), July 1, 1961, through June 30, 1968. Vol. 5 is in process of publication.

————. *Interpretations Issued by the Board Pursuant to Section 5, Second of the Railway Labor Act, July 1, 1934–June 30, 1961.* Washington, D.C.: GPO, 1961. 170 pp.

These are interpretations by the NMB of mediation agreements already reached by the parties in NMB proceedings. Only one volume published to date.

————. *Transcript of Proceedings of the Arbitration Board.*

Began with Arbitration Board No. 1, December 4, 1935. Most recent is Arbitration Board No. 347, appointed December 11, 1974. As of this writing, boards 341, 343, 346, and 347 have not issued their awards. As a general rule, the proceedings of these boards are not publicly distributed; complete sets, however, are on file with the National Mediation Board and the Interstate Commerce Commission.

U.S. NATIONAL RAILROAD ADJUSTMENT BOARD. *Awards of the First Division.* 1936– .

Awards are generally fewer than 20 pages and include statement of the claim, carrier and employee positions, the board's findings, and the award itself. The 21,875 awards made as of April 6, 1972, are published in 167 volumes. An index digest volume published in 1939 covers awards 1–3800. Published in Chicago, various printers.

————. *Awards of the Second Division.* 1937– .

Length and content generally same as First Division awards. The 6,151 awards made as of June 15, 1971, are published in 64 volumes. Each volume has an index, but no digest, of the awards. Published in Chicago, various printers.

————. *Awards of the Third Division.* 1936– .

Length and content generally same as First Division awards. The 18,855 awards made as of November 30, 1971, are published in 188 volumes. An index digest volume was published in 1942 for awards 1–1500. Published in Chicago, various printers.

————. *Awards of the Fourth Division.* 1940– .

There were 21 volumes and 2,318 awards as of June 18, 1968. First volume, published in 1940, contains awards made from March 29, 1935, through July 25, 1940. Each volume contains an index digest of its awards. Published in La Grange (Ill.) and Chicago, various printers.

U.S. RAILROAD ADMINISTRATION. *Report of Director General of Railroads.* Washington, D.C.: GPO, 1918–[1937?].

Issued in serial set annually; some separately printed.

————. Director General of Railroads. *Decisions of Railway Board of Adjustment No. 1.* [Chicago?], 1925.

Three such boards were promulgated by the United States Railroad Administration during World War I when the railroads were placed under federal control. Board No. 1 had jurisdiction over disputes affecting train, engine, and yard-service employees; Board No. 2 over disputes affecting shop-craft employees; and Board No. 3 over disputes affecting telegraphers, switchmen, clerical and station forces, and maintenance of way employees. Board No. 1 expired February 15, 1921, and Boards 2 and 3 January

10, 1921. All decisions were compiled and published in 1925. Board No. 1 rendered 2,995 decisions and these are published in vol. 1, parts 1 and 2. Each decision is about 1 page in length.

―――――. Director General of Railroads. *Decisions of Railway Board of Adjustment No. 2.* [Chicago?], 1925.
Published in volume 2 of the series and includes 2,290 decisions.

―――――. Director General of Railroads. *Decisions of Railway Board of Adjustment No. 3.* [Chicago?], 1925.
Published in volume 3 of the series and includes 1,156 decisions.

U.S. RAILROAD LABOR BOARD. *Decisions of the United States Railroad Labor Board with Addenda and Interpretations, 1920–26.* Washington, D.C.: GPO, 1920–26.
Seven volumes. Title varies slightly. An index digest of decisions 1–949 inclusive published in 1922. A cumulative index to all decisions rendered up to January 1, 1925, included as a supplement to vol. 5.

―――――. *Report of the United States Railroad Labor Board, April 15, 1920, to December 31, 1925.* [Washington, D.C. ?, 1926].
Apparently only one report ever made by the Board and it should therefore technically be considered a monograph.

―――――. *Wage Series.* Chicago, 1920 [–26 ?].
Report no. 1 issued in 1920. No record of additional numbers.

U.S. RAILROAD RETIREMENT BOARD. *Actuarial Study.* Chicago: The Board, 1956– .
Eleven studies published as of September 1974. Topics vary, e.g., "Life Insurance in Force," "Occupational Differences in Separation Rates for Railroad Workers, 1954–56," "Present Value of Benefits," etc. Length generally 15 to 45 pages.

―――――. *Annual Report.* Washington, D.C.: GPO, 1937– .
Fiscal year report first published in 1937 for the 1935/36 fiscal year. An extensive report varying in length from 64 to 302 pages to date and sometimes including a statistical supplement.

―――――. *The Railroad Retirement and Unemployment Insurance Systems* [prepared for the informational conferences]. [Chicago].
Irregular since 1957/58 conference.

―――――. *Service and Taxable Compensation of Railroad Employees: Statistical Tables.* Chicago.
Tabulations prepared annually by the board since 1937 and published for all years except 1938. Title varies somewhat but since 1961 it has been titled as above.

―――――. Office of Director of Research. *Monthly Benefit Statistics: Railroad Retirement and Unemployment Insurance Programs.* May 1968– .
Monthly publication.

―――――. Office of Director of Research and Office of Chief Actuary. *Actuarial Valuation of the Assets and Liabilities under the Railroad Retirement Acts.* Chicago: The Board, 1938– .
Issued approximately every three years. Length varies from 64 to 177 pages.